NECROECONOMICS

NECROECONOMICS

✦

THE POLITICAL ECONOMY OF POST-COMMUNIST CAPITALISM

(Lessons from Georgia)

Vladimer Papava

iUniverse, Inc.

New York Lincoln Shanghai

NECROECONOMICS
THE POLITICAL ECONOMY OF POST-COMMUNIST CAPITALISM

iUniverse books may be ordered through booksellers or by contacting:

iUniverse
2021 Pine Lake Road, Suite 100
Lincoln, NE 68512
www.iuniverse.com
1-800-Authors (1-800-288-4677)

ISBN-13: 978-0-595-34915-9 (pbk)
ISBN-13: 978-0-595-67168-7 (cloth)
ISBN-13: 978-0-595-79630-4 (ebk)
ISBN-10: 0-595-34915-3 (pbk)
ISBN-10: 0-595-67168-3 (cloth)
ISBN-10: 0-595-79630-3 (ebk)

Printed in the United States of America

I have maintained from first to last that

the laws of economics are the laws of life.

Philip H. Wicksteed

(1844–1927; English economist)

Contents

Introduction

Winston Churchill often said, "Democracy is the worst form of government except all those other forms that have been tried from time to time." Indeed, the same could be said about a market system: it is the worst device to reap benefits, except all the others that have been covered thus far (von Weizsäcker, Lovins, Lovins, 1997, Ch. 4). For many centuries, the market has proved that it has numerous advantages over other economic systems (Samuelson, 2002). No wonder, therefore, that regional transitions to market economies over the last decade have been among the most ubiquitous and remarkable processes in the social and economic sphere.

A lot of research has been devoted to the study of transitions to market economies (e.g., Fischer, Sahay, 2000; Havrylyshyn, Nsouli (eds.), 2001; UNICEF, 2001). However, despite the multitude of academic and analytical works, a good deal of problems are still under debate, and numerous theoretical and/or practical issues still remain to be resolved. Most of these unresolved problems are not specific to one country or one example, but instead are present in many different cases, and the development of universal approaches to these problems would obviously be quite useful.

At the same time, it should be emphasized that such universal approaches to economic policies have very often been applied without (or almost without) taking account of the specific national context of the problem. This is one of the key reasons—though not the only one—that sound theoretical approaches sometimes have little success in actual implementation. There is little doubt today that, while designing and implementing an economic policy, any government must take into proper consideration specific conditions existing in its country.

United States President Harry Truman is said to have stated that he was looking for a "one-handed" economist, because every time he asked his economists for advice on economic matters they would frame their answer by saying: "On the one hand...On the other hand..." (Mankiw, 1998, p. 29).

A true economist, however, cannot be "one-handed" (i.e., while applying universally proven approaches to the process of post-Communist transformation, one has to attach due importance to the specific national context as well).

The problem of transitions to market economies has been the topic of studies both numerous and interesting. Georgian economists have also shown a great deal of interest in the theoretical and applied aspects of economic transformations (e.g., Akhvlediani, 2001; Akubardia, 2000; Beridze, 1996a, 1996b, 2000; Gogishvili, Gogodze, Tsakadze, 1996; Gotsiridze, Kandelaki, 2001; Gurgenidze, Lobzhanidze, Onoprishvili, 1994; Lapachi, 2001). In addition, international researchers have paid attention to transformations taking place in the Georgian economy (e.g., Becker, 1998; Chand, Verhoeven, Korzyk, Vroman, 1997; Cukrowski, 2000; Cukrowski, Kavelashvili, 2001; Ibadoglu, 2002; MacPhee, 2001; Wang, 1998; Wellisz, 1996).

The purpose of this monograph is to give political-economic insight into and theoretical understanding of the transitions of post-Communist economies into capitalist ones and, based on such theoretical and practical analysis, to scrutinize ongoing transformations in Georgia.

To the extent that economic policy during post-Communist transformations depends almost entirely on political developments, I believe that the reader will understand why this work refers to the study of post-Communist economic transformations as "the Political Economy of Post-Communist Capitalism."

The term *post-Communist capitalism* belongs to the author of this book (Papava, 2002b). It refers to a society that cannot be squeezed into the classic understanding of the word *capitalism* (Gwynne, Klak, Shaw, 2003) or any other theoretically generalized model of capitalism (e.g., Brown, 1995, pp. 15–177). The key reason for this phenomenon is what can be termed the *necroeconomy* (see Ch. 3, 3.2). It is precisely because of the necroeconomy that neither the economic system of post-Communist capitalism nor any permutation of it can be explained simply in the context of classic theories of capitalism. This is why the author has undertaken a monographic study of the political economy of post-Communist capitalism.

This monograph outlines the Marxist points of view of Soviet Communism and provides a systematic review of economic theories of post-Communist transformations, institutional grounds for such transformations, and the role of individuals in this process. This monograph also reveals necroeconomy as an exclusive product of post-Communist capitalism and scrutinizes the problems of market equality, the privatization of government-owned capital, state economic activities, mechanisms of the "shadow economy," corruption, tax policy, and tax federalism in post-Communist systems.

With respect to each of the aforementioned issues, the author provides numerous examples from the experiences of the country of Georgia (Gachechiladze,

1995), which was among the first republics of the Former Soviet Union (FSU) to declare independence, doing so on April 9, 1991 (Metreveli, 1995). In the Georgian context, obtaining political independence was by no means equal to the establishment of economic independence (to say nothing of military independence, energy independence, etc.). The country came to deal simultaneously with two immensely difficult tasks—building new governmental institutions and making the transition to a market economy. It is noteworthy that a similarly daunting task was set before many countries that are now in the process of post-Communist transformations. In the chapters specifically devoted to Georgia, the author analyzes the outcomes of economic reforms in Georgia, the role of the International Monetary Fund (IMF) in these reforms, and the economic situation before and after the Rose Revolution.

1

Soviet Communism or State Monopolistic Feudalism: Marxist Points of View

We are a poor country and we opted for socialist policies, but to build a socialist society you have to have a developed society.

Julius Nyerere

(1922–1999; Tanzanian statesman, President of Tanganyika, 1962–1964 and of Tanzania, 1964–1985)

Fortunately today, almost no one in post-Communist countries considers seriously whether there is an alternative to a market system; one will not hear any more useless debates about unrevealed possibilities and untapped resources of socialism; nobody is against private property. Despite the so-called well-being in the formation of public opinion, it is very hard to break down the stereotype of our way of thinking that has been formed over decades; this often prevents the implementation of economic reforms.

In order to overcome these difficulties one must gain a better understanding of the Soviet economic system. It is particularly interesting to make an analysis of this system from the Marxist point of view.

There are different estimations of the Soviet Communist economic system in special economic literature (e.g., Hayek, 1988; Kornai, 1992; von Mises, 1981; Olson, 2000; Schumpeter, 1943; Stiglitz, 1996). The wide discrepancy between Marxist and non-Marxist points of view has created some barriers in understanding the same problems. Therefore it is very important to emphasize the essence of the Soviet communist system according to the general ideology of Marxism-Leninism, and separately.

In Russia there are many publications in which scientists try to evaluate the social and economic nature of the society created in the USSR and other East European countries. Some of the following definitions of this society can be taken as accepted: "administrative-command socialism," "totalitarian socialism," "state-bureaucratic socialism," "barrack-like socialism," and so forth. As a rule, there are definitions used for severe criticism of the structure of the FSU; however, the authors using these definitions have no doubt that socialism was built, although it was extremely distorted.

In the West the term *Soviet Communism* is used to refer to the social system of the FSU. There is no doubt that a thorough study of the essence of the economic system will result in correspondingly summarized estimations. The necessity for such estimations arises from the need to find out whether the definitions of the Soviet system listed heretofore answer classical Marxist-Leninist questions of an ideological character.

In particular, one frequently faces the following questions: Is socialism really able to defeat capitalism in economic competition? Is it possible to achieve higher labor productivity in the socialist system in comparison with the capitalist one? The steps of logical consideration are very simple: If socialism (or even communism) was built in the FSU, then why were all the problems predicted by Marxism-Leninism not solved in the USSR?

As a matter of fact, according to most parameters of development, the USSR was among the most undeveloped countries of the world; all this was explained by wars, devastations, reconstructions, droughts, et cetera. However, this can be considered a lame excuse because natural calamities also occur in the most developed of countries. This gives rise to the essential questions of whether the classics of Marxism-Leninism were right in determining the historical place of capitalism and to what extent they considered the advantages of socialism over capitalism.

Returning to the aforementioned definitions of the system in the FSU, it should be kept in mind that they emphasize the excessive centralization of the public management system and the dominating role of a one-party bureaucracy that took over the entire state. In order to explain why socialism (communism) could not manage, even in a single country, to realize its advantages over capitalism (theoretically predicted by Marx and Lenin), it is not enough just to display the aforementioned negative aspects of the socialist structure. To clarify, all the evaluations of the Soviet economic system that have been here summarized must be clearly defined. It is even more important to derive these evaluations from the theoretical basis of Marxism-Leninism itself. While considering the Soviet economic system, one must select its basic, common features:

1. From the very beginning of the formation of Soviet power the land and all other principal means of production were claimed as state property. The cooperative-collective form of property was regarded as secondary for a long period of time and was subordinate to the government. There was no voluntary cooperation in the FSU and there was no difference between collective farms (*kolkhoz*) and state farms (*sovkhoz*). The mass transformation of collective farms into state farms at the end of the 1950s and the beginning of the 1960s, which meant the nationalization of cooperative-collective property, was considered a progressive step in the socialization of production in building up communism. Practically, all means of production were concentrated in the hands of the government and all spheres of the economy were placed under state control. This left no opportunity for private initiative or individual choice. (It should be noted that absolute state ownership of all means of production seems to be the primary, determining feature over the others discussed later.);

2. When state ownership is predominant, the market is not necessary at all. Hence, from the very beginning, the country is developing on the basis of some kind of natural economy, which means that the relations between economic units are based on state-regulated barter exchange. The well-known political and ideological confrontation of the FSU with the rest of the world made impossible any kind of significant foreign economic relations; thus, the national economy had to satisfy all its needs by its own means. The natural character of the economy was aggravated by at least two factors. First, the USSR appeared to be a unitary state and not a federal one. In fact, the Soviet Republics (to say nothing of other administrative-territorial units) were practically deprived of all their economic rights, and as a result the economic relations between republics based on the principle of equivalent exchange became unnecessary. Second, as a result of the disregard of the market the majority of the planned indices were not expressed in monetary terms, but in physical measures. At the same time, supplying the enterprises with the means of production was possible only on the basis of so-called state funding. After World War II, when the formation of the world socialist system (uniting countries with a naturalized national

economy) was recognized, the natural character of the economy of the FSU had slightly weakened, but economic relations within the framework of the system were mainly formed not by economic but by political means. This, in turn, expanded the bounds of the natural economy over the whole world socialist system;

3. The monopolistic position of state ownership of the means of production, as well as the absence of competition, led to the inferiority of the means of production in the FSU compared to those standard in developed countries. Not taking into consideration the development of the cosmic defense industry (stimulated by political rather than economic factors), it may be concluded that the technique and technology of production in the FSU were primitive in comparison to such developed countries as the US, Japan, Germany, UK, and France, for example;

4. Using political power, by means of centralized management of the economy, the state made workers personally dependent, which was expressed in noneconomic compulsion to work. According to Marx, this resulted in special forms of exploitation of man by man.

According to Marxism-Leninism, the main evil of private property is that it inevitably gives rise to exploitation. Proceeding from the above it was concluded that with the elimination of private property and affirmation of its antithesis—state ownership—the exploitation would be abolished. Indeed, with the introduction of private property the institution of hiring was described by Marxists as an open, direct form of exploitation. According to Marx, a worker had to give a capitalist a part of his labor results. But in reality state ownership was still unable to abolish Marx's concept of exploitation completely. Hidden and indirect forms of what Marx saw as exploitation appeared.

It is recognized nowadays that state ownership—being fundamental during the whole period of the FSU—has created real possibilities for state officers to use the opportunity of official status to gain unearned income. It was considered that they "steal from the state"; on the surface it looks just like that, as the means of production are state property. In reality, they steal not from the state but, according to the notion of political economy, they again practice latent exploitation of workers according to Marxism. A definite part of unearned income, mainly in its natural form, is misappropriated by some groups of people, who are not directly involved in government management but have access to goods.

Not all unearned income was recognized as illegal. A part of it, especially unearned income in its natural form (high quality consumer goods, vouchers to fashionable sanatoriums, etc.) was officially allotted to definite posts.

According to Marxism-Leninism, the economy, having four main features (concentration of land and main means of production in the hands of one owner, natural economy, routine (primitive) technique and technology, noneconomic compulsion to labor, exploitation of "man by man" according to Marx and natural forms of appropriation), can be described as *feudal.* In the FSU, the state, which monopolized property in land and other means of production, takes the part of a feudal lord. Hence, the FSU economic system is a type of *state monopolistic feudalism* (Papava, 1995b).

It is not denied that the discussion in terms of means of production is not so effective. Foreseeing possible reproaches by opponents in so-called excessive sketchiness, it must be noted that the concept of "administrative-command" or "government-bureaucratic" socialism suffers from more sketchiness. The Marxist theory, that capitalism is inevitably followed by socialism and that there is no way back, is also schematized.

Such a definition of the problem gives us the opportunity to answer the aforementioned question. A feudal economy, as is proved by history, has no advantages over a capitalist one, and thus the FSU, together with other countries with the same economic system, could not win in economic competition with capitalist countries. Archaic systems and economic incentives of a feudal type prevent the introduction of anything new or progressive. The main principle of the given economy is based on a vast mechanism of noneconomic management, and the main type of public reproduction is extensive.

In a feudal economy it is not the economy that must work for people but people that must work for the economy. It is precisely this feudal disposition of the economy that predetermined the extent to which the FSU lagged behind the developed countries in many areas. The economic system of state monopolistic feudalism has all the components of a classical feudal economy: the special position of a landowner; the institution of stewards; and lack of rights of working people, stipulated by Marx's postulation of man's exploitation by man.

The economic system of the state monopolistic feudalism, because of its extreme concentration of property and centralization of power, forms a complicated and ramified system of modern stewards. The absence of civil rights in concert with personal dependence on the "state-feudal-lord" can turn into mass repression of both individuals and whole nations in the name of achievement of the highest objectives. The fate of the people is determined by the authority of the state-feudal-lord.

To give a complete description of the economic system under consideration I will touch on the problem of social guarantees that this system can ensure. The guarantees were based on the values of equality and passive-executive subordination.

A free education system and medical aid were considered the main social achievements of the FSU. Well-developed capitalist countries can use these social blessings as well, and they devote twice as much of their national income to this end. The economic system of state monopolistic feudalism cannot provide this high level of economic development. Particularly, before the disintegration of the USSR, it was officially stated that more than forty million Soviet citizens lived in poverty. To appreciate the feudal character of the economic system of the FSU, it is necessary to review the attitude toward the shadow economy in the FSU according to the correlation of the economic systems of both feudalism and capitalism.

In the shadow economy of the FSU one can single out two, often interlaced spheres: *shadow enterprise,* which includes the illegal production and sale of goods and services, and *shadow parasitism,* including speculation and other activities, such as blackmail, extortion, corruption, and so forth. Proceeding from the Marxist-Leninist outlook, I would assert that one must admit the progressive nature of shadow enterprise as an embryo of the capitalist management of production in the midst of a feudal economy. The illegality of shadow enterprise and the constant persecution by the "state-feudal-lord" forced the practitioners of the shadow economy to pay protection money unofficially. Such parasitic inclinations of the "state-feudal-lord" gradually turned into the core of shadow parasitism. Thus, the latter gets considerable support from the economic system of state monopolistic feudalism.

The concept of shadow enterprise coincides in time with the creation of an economic system of state monopolistic feudalism (i.e., with the period of "war communism"). During the New Economic Policy (NEP) it was legalized, but by the end of the 1920s and the beginning of the 1930s, shadow enterprise "went underground." Since early 1985, when Perestroika started, the organization of the economic sphere was (both ideologically and politically) aimed at the legalization and development of shadow enterprise. This was expressed first of all in the attempt to legalize all forms of economic methods of management, stimulating individual labor activities and a cooperative movement. However, many types of shadow parasitism were also legalized.

Legalized shadow parasitism placed obstacles in the way of economic methods of management, stimulation of individual labor activities, and the cooperative movement and discredited them in the eyes of the public. The spectrum of legalized shadow parasitism was very wide. It began with small speculation and included efforts by the state to levy taxes on legalized shadow enterprise.

The collapse of Soviet communism and the transition to a market economy should be considered as positive even from the point of view of Marxism-Leninism, because a capitalist system was substituted for the feudal economic system (Papava, 1990). Economic reforms carried out in the countries formed after the disintegration of the USSR have the characteristic features of the economic system of Soviet communism (e.g., Ericson, 2000).

2

Theory of Post-Communist Economic Transformation

Read no history: nothing but biography,
for that is life without theory.

Benjamin Disraeli, Lord Beaconsfield
(1804–1881; British statesman and novelist; Prime Minister, 1868, 1874–1880)

2.1. READINESS OF ECONOMIC THEORY

Professor Igor Birman, the famous Russian economist who emigrated from the USSR many years ago, once noted that capitalism had been developing for many centuries and this process had never depended on educated or uneducated economists, their advice, and recipes (Birman, 1996, p. 521). Although this assertion is not unquestionable at all, in principle it alludes to that historical phase in the development of economic science when it (science) was nothing but a mere reflection of economic praxis.

Economic science has a long history, but it was not always prepared to give timely and correct answers to all topical questions that practice would raise. Nevertheless, as a rule, economic science would manage to catch up in a few years, thereby stimulating a search for new solutions to practical issues of economic growth. The rise and development of Keynesianism is one of the most remarkable examples in support of this assumption. Despite this, leading economists in the West tend to exaggerate the issue of the crisis of economic thought that, in their opinion, resides in its incapacity to suggest right solutions to the problems and predict the future of capitalist economy (Heilbroner, Milberg, 1996).

The collapse of the Communist regimes in East Europe, and the Soviet Union and an almost-concurrent disintegration of the latter resulting in the emergence of fifteen newly independent states gave rise to substantially new problems, no solution to which could be confined to any of those classical schemes that were elaborated by economic science during the whole period of its existence (Nove, 1993).

The transformation of Communist-style governmental institutions into market-based ones by itself is a very difficult task (Nunberg, 1999). In the countries that emerged as a result of the disintegration of the former federal states (such as the FSU, Yugoslavia, and Czechoslovakia) and that are not successors of the latter, the process of transition from the Communist-oriented economic system to a market economy is further aggravated by a need to lay economic and not merely economic foundations for one's own statehood (Balcerowicz, 1995, p. 146; Milanovic, 1998, p. 3; Papava, 1996a, p. 252). In this context, the challenge that the former German Democratic Republic had to deal with looks far easier, as the transition to market economics in that country was preceded by the unification of the two German states (e.g., Derlien, 1999).

This process belongs to a group of the most significant events of the end of the twentieth century (Stiglitz, 1992, p. 137), and could be regarded as a global process of transition to a market economy (Berend, 1994) whose impact on the development of economic thought could be compared with such events as the Great Depression of the 1930s (Avtonomov, 1996, p. 11) or the reconstruction of Europe after the end of World War II. As John Kenneth Galbraith has pointed out, the process is on a par with both world wars as one of the three greatest historical events of the twentieth century (Inozemtsev, 1998, p. 7). It is not by accident that in referring to the process of post-Communist transformation some economists have used the word *refolution,* which is formed by the combination of the words *reform* and *revolution* (Goldstone, 2001, p. 117).

In a number of works (e.g., Andor, Summers, 1998; Kuzin (ed.), 1994), the problems of transition to a market economy are considered in light of and by analogy to the so-called economic miracle approach (Petrakov, 1998, p. 190). (In the Georgian context, see Petukhov, 1999). The practice of evaluating successful applications of market mechanisms by using language like "economic miracle" gained in popularity, especially with respect to the countries of East Asia (WB, 1993). However, the financial crisis near the end of the twentieth century that had shaken those economies up drastically reduced reasons that could justify the use of the word *miracle* in an economic discourse (Claessens, Glaessner, 1997; Weder, 2001).

That modern economic theory is still unable to give exhaustive and theoretically justified answers to many important questions relating to the transition to market economy has been recognized by many leading economists of our time (e.g., Becker, Becker, 1997, p. 259; Stiglitz, 1996, p. 3). It may be stated without reservation that there is no economic theory of transition at all (Bertenev, 1996, p. 301; Papava, 2000b; 2005). Igor Birman, in his traditionally radical and therefore debatable style, has asserted that economic theory reaffirmed its "convincing impotence" in dealing with the problems of transition to a market economy (Birman, 1996, p. 521).

It must be emphasized that, from the standpoint of Western economists, even the problems of centrally planned development, not to mention those of transition to market, have always been considered a temporary deviation from the generally accepted capitalist norm. For this reason, thinking of transitory problems is to them nothing but a waste of time (Aukutsionek, 1996, p. 11). Nevertheless, the world's many well-known economists believe that, since the early 1990s, transition to market economy has become a key subject of economic research (Galbraith, 1992, p. 46), encouraging economists to review the problems of economic theory itself in light of post-Socialist development (Buchanan, 1992).

The first comprehensive textbooks of transition to market have already been published. Their authors come from both economies in transition and developed Western nations (e.g., Abalkin (ed.), 1997; Buzgalin, 1994; Geiger, 1992; Papava, 2002b).

2.2. THE TRANSFORMATION TERMINOLOGY

Before continuing the discussion, it would be advisable to touch on some terminological issues. Specifically, when referring to the post-Communist economies it is common to use expressions like "economy in transition" or "transitional economy," which are very vague, as it is not clear what kind of "transition" one is talking about. Although in the modern world it is transition to a market economy that usually takes place, this process is not a homogeneous one. Economists have set apart two types of transitional economy—the traditional and the new. Whereas the former is typical of Equatorial Africa and South Asia, the latter is more widespread in East Europe, the FSU, some Latin American countries, and China (Geiger, 1992, Ch. 1). It must also be noted that according to generally accepted definition "economies in transition" include just the countries of East Europe, former Soviet republics, China, and Mongolia, although there are multiple countries across the globe (up to thirty in Africa alone) that are at the stage of transition from central planning to free market (Yarbrough, Yarbrough, 1997, p. 469).

The world history of the twentieth century knows such occurrences as the transition from capitalism to socialism (Bukharin, 1990, pp. 81–207) and then to communism (Kanth, 1997, pp. 211–225; Kornai, 1992, pp. 26–30; O'Brien, 1989, pp. 6–13, 23–28); transition from capitalism to postindustrial, post-economic society (Bell, 1973; Inozemtsev, 1995, 1998); transition from modern capitalism to socialism (Brown, 1995, pp. 334–356; Buzgalin, 1994, pp. 23–32); transition from Stalinism to the socialist market economy (Nolan, 1995); and transition to drastic growth of production in the United States (Feldstein (ed.), 1980). As Peter Drucker points out, contemporary humanity is in the process of transition to a global economic system (Inozemtsev, 1998, p. 6) and is on the verge of the formation of post-Communist society (Drucker, 1993). According to John Kenneth Galbraith, ongoing transition leads to an "affluent society" (Galbraith, 1988, pp. 209–216).

In the 1990s, with the upcoming third millennium of the Common Era, the issues of cyberspace, cybereconomy, and the sovereign individual in them were raised (Davidson, Ress-Mogg, 1998, pp. 11–39). It must be noted that practically all serious economic developments observed in different regions of the planet could be reviewed in the context of the world's universal economic transition (Hinshaw (ed.), 1996).

Belarus is the most apparent example of reversion from market to a central planning economy (Antachak, Guzhinski, Kozarzhevski, 2001).

Leszek Balcerowicz suggested the following classification of historical "transitions" (Balcerowicz, 1995, p. 145):

1. Classical transition that implies the process of expanding democracy in leading capitalist nations from 1860–1920;

2. Neoclassical transition, which was reflected in democratic developments after World War II (in West Germany, Italy, and Japan in the 1940s; in Spain and Portugal in the 1970s; in some Latin American countries in the 1970s and 1980s; and in South Korea and Taiwan in the 1980s);

3. Market-oriented reforms in non-Communist countries (in West Germany and some other Western nations after World War II; in South Korea and Taiwan in the early 1960s; in Chile in the 1970s; in Turkey and Mexico in the 1980s; and in Argentina in the 1990s);

4. Asian scenario of post-Communist transition (China in the late 1970s and Vietnam in the late 1980s).

From the standpoint of the "welfare state," the whole world could be regarded as one that undergoes the process of transition in that direction (Esping-Andersen (ed.), 1997).

In the light of developments that have resulted in the shaping up of a "New World Order" the meaning of the term *transition* has expanded to connote a set of strategies that enables a society to define and achieve the given order with minimal losses (Calkins, Vezina, 1996, p. 311).

It is useless to look for a general definition of the terms "economy in transition" and "transitional economy," as it can give us nothing, neither a theoretical nor (more especially) a practical sense of what I am trying to describe here.

A good example of the general approach to the process of transition, in general, and "transitional period," in particular, consists in the definition of it as "a period of time during which a certain historical choice has to be made" (Rakitskaya, 1996, p. 87). It must be noted, however, that (as the author of this definition remarks) no "transitional period" could be in place if the choice is self-evident (Rakitskaya, 1996, p. 87).

According to one of the many ambiguous definitions of transitional economy, it is a status between any two psychologically and theoretically opposite regulatory approaches, which are separated from each other by systematic or shocking conversion and which, in turn, differ from each other by powerfulness and duration (Kuznetsov, 1994, pp. 5–6). Another definition of transitional period or transitional economy says that it embraces both transitions to a certain normal and balanced developmental status and a switch from one sustainable and balanced mode to another (Basilia, Silagadze, Chikvaidze, 2001, p. 93).

Another general approach consists in reconsidering the process of transition in the light of the "catastrophe theory." Specifically, such processes, in a sense, are typical of a transition from one social/economic organizational scheme to another, which can be referred to as a system transformation and, in a broader sense, any kind of system modification (Shurgalina, 1997, pp. 66–67).

One more example of the general approach to the process of transition is based on "institutional analysis of the evolution of transition to development" applied in different countries (Intriligator, Braguinsky, Bowen II, Tullock, Root, 1999).

It is obvious, therefore, that no generally accepted definition of transitional period has been developed yet (Berezin, 1999, p. 253; Papava, 2000b, 2005).

Based on all the approaches just described, one can conclude that whenever discussion is specifically about the transition of post-Communist economies to a market system (which, in fact, is nothing but post-Communist transition to capitalist economy) or "to something approaching a market economy" (Galbraith, 1996, p. 101), it has to be placed on record, as this kind of transition has no analogy in history (Campbell, 1991, p. 227).

To exhaust the subject of terminology, it must also be noted that out of these two terms—"post-Socialist" and "post-Communist"—I would recommend giving priority to the latter as it denotes developmental orientation of relevant nations before their transition to a market economy (Men'shikov, 1996, pp. 17–22). It is also important to note that debates over the definition of the word *socialism* could not be considered concluded (Balcerowicz, 1995, pp. 19–27), as scholars tend to distinguish between Marxist, Soviet, Chinese, Yugoslavian, and African models of socialism (Brown, 1995, pp. 181–286); furthermore, there have been suggestions to set apart so-called Afro-Asian Socialism (Nafziger, 1997, p. 541); if you add to this "Fascist" (von Mises, 1947) (especially as there is the substantial difference between post-Fascist and post-Communist models of transition to market economy (Olson, 1995, pp. 53–54)), "Islamic" (Ignatenko, 1988, pp. 130–132) and "Swedish" socialisms, the inherent vagueness of the term *post-Socialist* becomes more than apparent. Besides, according to some scholars, the system that was established in the FSU was by no means socialist, but rather "pseudo-socialist" (Mikulskiy, 1999, p. 8) or "quasi-socialist" (Simonia, 1999, p. 14), not to mention estimations like "state monopolistic feudalism" (Papava, 1995b).

Sociologists have repeatedly noted that, whenever the nature of a certain society is not completely discerned, to avoid confusions, they tend to add to it the prefix *post-* (as in the terms *post-industrial, post-economic, post-Socialist, post-Soviet,* etc.). In this connection, outstanding are the works by Leszek Balcerowicz, who prefers to replace the ambiguous terms like *post-Communist* and *post-Socialist* with the more understandable "capitalist" (Papava, 2002a, p. 5).

Like socialism, by its nature capitalism is not homogenous (Gwynne, Klak, Shaw, 2003). That model of capitalism that is shaping up after the downfall of the Communist regimes is significantly different from its American, European, or Japanese counterparts. This allows the introduction of the term *post-Communist capitalism* (Papava, 2002b).

2.3. TWO PATHS OF POST-COMMUNIST TRANSFORMATION

The practical uselessness of many classical theoretical schemes of transition to market economy resulted in the fact that in many countries this extremely sophisticated process was initiated and conducted in a wrong way.

Among the first consultants that arrived from the West to provide advisory services to the reformers in the post-Communist states, apart from the representatives of the IMF and World Bank were, as a rule, independent experts, not to mention occasional trippers and charlatans. At best, they were armed with some knowledge of economic theory and/or some experience in successful reforms implemented in Latin America, Asia, and Africa (Adams, Brock, 1993, p. XIII). Igor Birman, in his traditionally sardonic style, remarks that the reason for the mass departure of economists from the West was that nobody listened to them in their own homelands (Birman, 1996, p. 522). In general, their advice was limited to general statements of the advantages of and the need for fast transition to a market economy (Stiglitz, 1996, p. 3).

Today, owing to quite inclusive empirical data, it has become possible to develop original scientific works about post-Communist transformation containing quite serious theoretical generalizations. Based on this, both practicing reformers and economic theorists are divided into two major groups: the first one consists of the supporters of "shock" in economic reforms; the other one is composed of "gradualists." Each group has been established as one of the two key trends of the post-Communist transformation (e.g., Bogomolov, 1998, pp. 49–52; Bożyk, 1999; Hoen, 1999).

Apart from this generally accepted classification, it might be interesting to represent the post-Communist transformation of economy as three different strategies, namely *Gradualism* (implemented in Hungary), *Shock Therapy* (which has its origins in Poland and Czechoslovakia), and the *Third Road* (the cradle of which is considered to be found in the Balkans); the last consists of so-called Gradual Gradualism, which means that transition to market economy is a very long process, the privatization program is limited to small enterprises, and private ownership is allowed only in trade, services, and tourism (Berend, 1995, pp. 133–137). The Third Road might be of special interest only to those who are concerned about the idiosyncrasies of gradualism (specifically, the extreme forms of it). In this connection, it is important to note that it is very often the speed of reforms rather than core values and theoretical beliefs that lie at the heart of disagreements between economists (Birman, 1996, p. 521).

The Shock Therapy (which is basically used by the Russian economists), or "Big Bang" (e.g., Kowalik, 1994, p. 116), or "Bitter Pill" (Adams, Brock, 1993, p. XIII) is a strategy that consists in the maximization of radical transformations in the shortest possible period of time. The key elements of the strategy of Shock Therapy include liquidation (or at least minimization) of budget deficit and pursuit of tight monetary policy under the conditions of fixed money supply or fixed exchange rate. The Shock Therapy doctrine stems from the orthodox macroeconomic stabilization scenario (e.g., Kiseliova, 1996, p. 113), which stipulates that budget deficit should be liquidated (or at least minimized) and a tight monetary policy, coupled with a fixed money supply or fixed exchange rate, should be established within a limited period of time. At the same time, success depends a good deal on political stability (Johem, 1999). It is also important to note that the orthodox scenario of Shock Therapy is identical to so-called Washington Consensus, which in turn forms the basis of the IMF approach to transformational developments (Stiglitz, 1998).

If tight budgetary and monetary policies are pursued under the conditions of regulated prices and incomes, then there is a macroeconomic stabilization scenario in place, which is referred to as heterodox or non-orthodox scenario (Kiseliova, 1996, p. 113). Such an approach, as a rule, is applied in those countries where stabilization programs have not produced any positive results and to win people's support, as a temporary measure (and only as such), along with orthodox ones, the governments resort to regulated prices and incomes (Rostovskiy, 1997, pp. 102–103).

The method of Shock Therapy was first applied in West Germany after the end of World War II. It started its "new life" in post-Communist Poland (Aleksashenko, 1990; Balcerowicz, 1994; 1995, pp. 273–369; Blanchard, Dornbush, Krugman, Layaed, Summers, 1994, pp. 17–22; Johnson, Kowalska, 1994; Narinskiy, 1990; Pankow, 1993; Sachs, 1993; Schaffer, 1992; Wellisz, 1997). Later, different variants on the same method were applied with a different level of success in many other post-Communist countries (Alekseev, Volkov et al., 1995, p. 465), including some former Soviet republics (Stroev, Bliakhman, Krotov, 1999, pp. 285–352).

The gradualists—who support the idea of gradual, step-by-step reforms (WB, 1996, pp. 11–16)—have built their criticism of the Shock Therapy method on highlighting inconsistencies and contradictions between different aspects of this strategy that may become evident during accelerated implementation of reforms (Krogel, Mazner, Grabcher, 1992).

Traditional debates between the advocates of Shock Therapy and the gradualists often resemble a "Theater of the Absurd" (Adams, Brock, 1993, p. XV). An illustrative example of this is a quasi-scientific comparison, based on a very superficial resemblance, according to which the Shock Therapy supporters are seemingly the followers of Marx(?!), whereas the gradualists are also seemingly the continuators of the German Historical School (Avtonomov, 1997, pp. 6–7).

The main mistake of gradualists, in my opinion, consists in their overlooking some very practical and important conditions that could be elevated to the level of *necessary conditions to gradual reform*.

In particular, the success of gradual reforms depends on certain *political guarantees,* which should, firstly, ensure positive evaluation of reforms by the people and, secondly, enable the government to keep control of the national economy in their hands. As the experience of post-Communist reforms has demonstrated, in many countries (and, first of all, in the USSR at the time of Perestroika) this essential condition was not (or more precisely, could not be) met (WB, 1996, pp. 11–16).

Of no less importance is the second condition, which requires *strong financial support* of reforms and without which the success of post-Communist transformations is inconceivable. If a nation cannot afford such support, it should request assistance from international financial institutions and the G-7 nations. These latter, due to an established practice, ask the IMF for their opinion. The IMF, in turn, backs the Washington Consensus, which is the same thing as Shock Therapy. This means that the gradualist approach, if applied, will require a government to have huge reserves of its own financial resources, all other things being equal.

China, the country that has preserved the Communist regime, albeit in its "softer" form, represents a classical example of gradual reforms (Boone, Gomulka, Layard (eds.), 1998, pp. 153–181; Cheung, 1998; Nafziger, 1997, pp. 597–607). It is noteworthy that the retention of a leading role by the Communist Party was a stability factor of market (or quasi-market) reforms not only in China, but also in Vietnam (Dang, 1999; Kolodko, 2000, 73–78). Furthermore, under such circumstances, more or less a long period of time has to pass before the government embarks on reforms (Diykanbayeva, 2001, p. 6).

However, the chances of replicating the Chinese experience in other countries are very small, as there are no guarantees that the essential conditions precedent to success of gradual implementation of market reforms will be in place. Specifically, inability to meet the first condition precedent to the practical implementation of the gradualist approach, as well as a number of other historical/political factors, prevented the governments of the FSU and most of the post-Soviet countries from even considering the issue of transplanting the Chinese experience into their national contexts (Mau, 1999, pp. 6–9; Yevstigneeva, Yevstigneev, 1999, p. 10). There are some prominent economists in the world (not to mention ordinary ones) who like to entertain themselves with reflections on utopian models like this. For example, Joseph Stiglitz, winner of the 2001 Nobel Prize in Economics, the former Senior Vice President and the Chief Economist of the World Bank remarks that the Chinese model seemingly could have been adopted by Russia and other former Soviet republics (Stiglitz, 1999a, pp. 1–3, 25). Unfortunately, this authoritative economist shows complete disregard for the history of formation of the USSR as an imperial power, as well as all those political developments and armed conflicts that resulted from the collapse of the empire.

Another reason why the Chinese model was essentially infeasible on Soviet soil was that, by the time of Mikhail Gorbachev's coming to power, the authority of the Communist Party Leader, due to consistent—if unconscious—"attempts" by Nikita Khrushchev and Leonid Brezhnev, had been significantly weakened and gradually divided between different levels of the Communist Party's and the Soviet government's hierarchically bureaucratic machine. In China, however, even though Deng Xiaoping renounced extreme dogmas of Maoism, he never relinquished those powers that had been established in the Chinese system of governance since the Cultural Revolution. Furthermore, while the regime of Perestroika initiated by Gorbachev was preceded by the period of so-called inertial immobility, Deng embarked on reforms on the "remains" of the Cultural Revolution (Åslund, 1995, Ch. 1). In other words, theoretically—from the political standpoint—the best possible (while practically the only possible) chance to implement Chinese reforms in the FSU was at the hands of the Soviet leadership at the time of Stalin's death.

The "mystery" of success of the Chinese reforms could be explained by: first, high percentage of domestic investments in gross domestic product (GDP); second, consistency of government decisions with respect to gradual implementation of market mechanisms (in terms of establishing "free economic zones"); third, mass employment of the managers of Chinese descent trained in different developed countries by Chinese companies; and fourth, a relatively low percentage (only eighteen percent) of employment in large government-owned enterprises (Thurow, 1996, pp. 53–58).

The above explanation of the success of the Chinese reforms sheds more light on those objective preconditions that are necessary for the implementation of gradual reforms and that are missing in many other post-Communist countries. All this allows us to conclude that the success of the gradualist approach in China depended a lot on peculiarities of national context, which, by itself, can by no means demonstrate any advantages of such an approach (Bogomolov, 1998, p. 50). Furthermore, it is important to note that drawn-out reforms resulted in the loosening of fiscal/budgetary control in China, which in turn did much harm to the national economy (Tanzi (ed.), 1994, Ch. 13).

Uzbekistan represents another remarkable example of the gradualist approach to market-oriented reforms (Khikmetov (ed.), 2001). However, unlike China, the Communist regime did not survive in that country. It was replaced with a system of governance that was no less authoritarian and which has never renounced quasi-democratic Communist approaches. For example, only two political parties—both loyal to the president of Uzbekistan—were allowed to take part in the parliamentary elections in 1994; during the recent "successful" referendum a huge majority of people "voted" for the delay of a presidential election (Apostolou, 1997, p. 101). Among the key achievements of the Uzbek model of gradual reforms are the oft-mentioned slowest fall of GDP rate among all post-Soviet countries (eighteen percent in 1990–1995), preservation of industrial output at almost the same level (Zhukov, 1997, p. 48), and the intervention of significant foreign investment (Safaev, 1997, p. 100). It must be emphasized, however, that Uzbekistan is very rich in strategic resources, such as gold, oil, cotton, and wheat, which is a key factor in the country's economic growth and makes the "triumph" of the Uzbek model of reforms much less impressive (Kasenov, 1998, pp. 37–40; Rumer, 2000, pp. 36–47; Trushin Esh., 1998; Trushin Esk., 1998; Zhukov, 2000, pp. 160–169). Noteworthy in this context is the assumption that, as a rule, any deviation from common sense in any country's economic policy must be explained by national peculiarities, the content of which might often not be explained at all (Segvari, 1999, pp. 49–50).

As a general rule, no economy that is undergoing the process of post-Communist transformation can avoid a drastic decline in production as a whole, and in industrial output in particular, as well as the fall of labor efficiency, investment, and real incomes (Nove, 1993, p. 22, 1995, pp. 227–230). It is also important to note that—at the initial stage of post-Communist transformation—there is a high correlation between the reduction in the size of government and the fall of production capacity (Kolodko, 2000, pp. 252–256). To be more specific, the decrease in output most often takes place in those companies that were established before the start of post-Communist transformations (Konings, Walsh, 1998). Accordingly, the tendency to decline originates in the Communist regime itself (Åslund, 2001). It is also believed that successful post-Communist reforms may result in a shift from the fall of production to its growth (Winkler (mod.), 1992), which means that the production curve is U-shaped (Blanchard, 1997, pp. 1–20). In this regard, it must be emphasized that there is no agreement between the economists on the reasons for such a shift to economic growth (Tanzi, 1997, pp. 315–316). In conclusion, I would like to agree with John Kenneth Galbraith, who remarks that economic growth is always accompanied by destructive tendencies resulting from the growth itself, for which reason recession or depression becomes inevitable (Inozemtsev, 1998, p. 14).

The experience of fast economic reforms implemented in different countries demonstrates that the deterioration of living conditions of a vast majority of people is a universal phenomenon that is caused by the fall of production, an increases in prices, and decreases in real incomes (Standing, 1997, pp. 230–234). This phenomenon is often referred to as "Transformational Fall" (Kornai, 1993), "Transformational Crisis" (Nikipelov, 1996, pp. 189–190; Ol'sevich, 1997a, pp. 255–277; Zukowski, 1996), "post-Communist Great Depression" (Milanovic, 1998, pp. 23–30), and "Trap of Reforms" (Klaus, 1997, p. 184), the cause of which lies not in the essence of Shock Therapy, but rather in its negation (Mau, 1999, p. 11), delays in implementing reforms (Åslund, 2002), and of course, in the collapse of the old system (Sachs, 1994, Ch. 4), as those countries that opted for the "shocking" reforms were first to enter the phase of economic growth (de Melo, Denizer, Gelb, 1997; Gaidar, 1997, p. 11).

It is noteworthy that the said "Transformational Crisis" often casts doubt on the reformers' ability to maintain political stability, for which reason initiators of the "shocking" reforms, as a rule, have to resign from their positions (classical examples include Balcerowicz in Poland and Gaidar in Russia in the early 1990s) (Crawford, 1995, p. 11).

The practice has shown that the Shock Therapy produces the best results in such countries where the status of the economy before the reforms (or before the "shock") was so bad that the people were ready to tolerate whatever was deemed necessary to overcome the existing situation (Geiger, 1992, Ch. 13). In that case, negative effects of the shock are disregarded, whereas positive ones are so apparent that the initiators of the Shock Therapy can feel secure from any political threat.

Thus, the success of the Shock Therapy rests on the paradox entailed by the phrase "the worse, the better." If there is a big question mark over the country's future and its ability to survive, there must be no doubt whether the Shock Therapy method is really needed, as under such circumstances the country has no choice and positive results are almost guaranteed. Such a situation might be classified as "Minimal Shock with Maximum Therapy" or "Soft Big Bang" (Papava, 2002b, pp. 54–55).

There is a universally accepted assumption that the developed nations ought to support the post-Communist countries in order to provide them with some relief from the pains from which they suffer in the course of post-Communist transformation. In the meantime, such relief may become a key obstacle to reforms, as it may reduce the ability to appreciate the need for and inevitability of them and may further tempt governments into postponing the implementation of radical ones (Becker, Becker, 1997, pp. 261–262). Jeffrey Sachs believes that to avoid such negative effects, financial aid to the reformist governments should be closely associated with the fulfillment of certain strict conditions and the biggest portion of such aid should be used for the alleviation of hard economic conditions of the population. However attractive this suggestion may be, its rightness is still questionable (Hinshaw (ed.), 1996, pp. 128–130).

A post-Communist country's choice of economic policy model depends on whether decision makers, as well as their supporters and opponents, have (e.g., Abalkin, 1996) or have not (e.g., Illarionov, 1996) taken into account the necessary conditions of gradual reforming described earlier.

In this connection, it must also be noted that the opponents' criticism of Shock Therapy is based, on the one hand, on their assumption that the monetarist scheme this approach rests on is useless in terms of dealing with the problems of post-Communist transformation (e.g., Abalkin, 1996; Fedorenko, 2001, pp. 412–413). Additionally, on the other hand, it is based on their claim that it has nothing to do with true monetarism and that instead it proposes "false monetarism" (Ol'sevich, 1997b). More precisely, it is not pure monetarism that is being dealt with in this particular case, but rather its combination with neoclassical theory, where the latter makes a conceptual basis and the former provides guidelines for actions (Men'shikov, 1996, pp. 106–107). They also claim that the Shock Therapy method is good for "treating" the market, but is no good for creating it (Petrakov, 1998, pp. 194–195; Men'shikov, 1996, pp. 113–115).

To the extent that the monetarist approach to post-Communist reforms is broadly applied by the IMF (Allen, 1992) and the World Bank in their financial/economic programs, the opponents of Shock Therapy mechanically criticize those programs, too (e.g., Abalkin, 2001, pp. 46–50). It is interesting, however, that a history of such criticism dates from to the "pre-post-Communist" or the "pre-shock" period (Nafziger, 1997, pp. 566–574).

Everyone make mistakes, and so does the IMF (e.g., De Gregorio, Eichengreen, Ito, Wyplosz, 1999; Eichengreen, 2000; Gomulka, 1995; Papava 2003a; Stiglitz, 2002; Tirole, 2002; Vreeland, 2003). Its recommendations sometimes are good and sometimes are bad (Hinshaw (ed.), 1996, p. 134), but its goals are always acceptable to almost all. For example, many people among the Russian scientific and political circles generally agree to the assumption that the IMF goals are not in conflict with Russia's interests in the country's economic security, whereas from the standpoint of some peculiarities typical of the national context the IMF's recommendations do pose a threat to the country's economic security (Veduta, 1998, pp. 328, 362).

In this connection, especially interesting is the disagreement that occurred between the World Bank and the IMF at the end of the twentieth century. Specifically, the former refused to accept the conceptual approaches of the latter, called for the IMF to revise its traditional policies and proposed an essentially new approach that consisted in the elimination of the elements of Shock Therapy in the institutional reforms policy (Stiglitz, 1998, 1999; WB, 1999).

There are two schemes of market reforms: the "Top-Down"—market design as formal (McMillan, 2002, p. 11)—and the "Bottom-Up"—market design as informal (McMillan, 2002, p. 11). The first scheme consists of the mandatory privatization of government-owned enterprises, whereas the other one requires that the structure of the economy be modified by establishing new companies and encouraging the development of already existing private firms (Brezinski, Frirsh, 1996, p. 297); these measures, under the conditions of appropriate macroeconomic policy—namely, as a temporary measure, imposing a "light" tax burden on businesses—must ensure transition from the Communist-style economy to market. It must be emphasized that the president of the World Bank has recently developed a new "Comprehensive Development Framework" (Wolfenson, 1999) according to which a priority should be given to the "Bottom-Up" option (Stiglitz, 1999a, p. 25). It is desirable that this approach be taken as a basis for the national strategic development programs of each post-Communist state (e.g., Koichuev, 2001, pp. 163–194).

It is important to note that very often the evolutionary approach (Nelson, Winter, 1982) to post-Communist development (see Ch. 3, 3.3) is equated with gradualism (Lavigne, 1995, p. 250). In doing so, they fail to notice the fact that neither the Shock Therapy method can be confined to one single action in the course of post-Communist transformation. This can be explained in a simple way if the fact that transition to market economy requires implementation of a set of the following six steps is taken into account (Lipton, Sachs, 1990):

1. Macroeconomic stabilization;

2. Liberalization of prices;

3. Liberalization of foreign trade and ensuring convertibility of national currency in accordance with current transactions;

4. Company reform, first of all, through privatization;

5. Establishing a social security system;

6. Developing an institutional and legal infrastructure of market economy (and a market-based financial system in it).

This set of six steps could be presented in a different arrangement; for example, macroeconomic stabilization may be split into monetary and fiscal elements, whereas the company reform and the institutional structure development may be combined to form one group (Wolf, 1994, pp. 170–176).

Out of the above six steps, only the first three can be taken in a quick manner—quickness, on the one hand, is a key condition of Shock Therapy and, on the other hand, constitutes an essence of "Washington Consensus" (Stiglitz, 1998)—whereas the implementation of the rest will require a much longer period of time in any setting. This is so in light of the fact that establishing institutional and legal infrastructure, because of particularly complicated nature of the task (Boettke, 1998), is likely to take many decades (WB, 1996, pp. 11–12). It is exactly this assertion to which once very tense debates between the Shock Therapy advocates and the gradualists owe their more recently softer dialogue (Popov, 2000, p. 4).

It must be emphasized that although the Shock Therapy method is really ineffective for developing market institutions, the acceptance—at least, theoretically—of the assumption that post-Communist reforms should have started with institutional changes only (Kolodko, 1999; Stiglitz, 1999a) and that liberalization (e.g., McKinnon, 1993) and stabilization programs should have been embarked on only after the accomplishment of this task would amount to the refusal to establish all those market signals that are necessary to foster the development of private sector in a long-term perspective, as well as the conservation of a major part of Communist-style mechanisms of economic regulation. In other words, one who accepts the idea that post-Communist transformations must start with merely institutional reforms is bound to cause severe delays in the process of establishing market economy and democratic system of economic regulation.

To the extent that post-Communist transformation is, by nature, a long process, there emerge questions:

- Which way should the reform go after the end of Shock Therapy?

- What steps should be taken to follow up and build on the achievements of Shock Therapy?

On the one hand, one possible answer to these questions rests on a "Social Promotion" method of economic reforms that require the creation of certain conditions that, by encouraging the formation of a strong class of businesspeople, will speed up the process of social stratification; on the other hand, to ensure support for reforms on the part of low-income groups and improve their hard living conditions, a consistent and beneficiary-oriented social assistance policy should be developed and implemented (Papava, 1996a, pp. 260–267; 1996b; 1999, pp. 281–291). A combination of well-known mechanisms of promoting supply and demand, namely the so-called Laffer/Keynesian Synthesis, is proposed as a theoretical base of the "Social Promotion" method (Papava, 1996a, pp. 263–264, 266–267; 1999, pp. 287–291).

Another method of economic reforms, which can be used after the end of Shock Therapy, is "Institutional Chemotherapy" (Naím, 1995, pp. 31–33).

In conclusion, it must be noted that to date there is no special economic theory of post-Communist transformation. It is just in the process of developing (Kazmer, Konrad, 2004; Papava, 2000b, 2005). Nevertheless, some well-known economic theories and combinations of certain elements of the latter could be used more or less successfully to produce a complete analysis of the collapse of the Communist economic system (e.g., Rosser, Rosser, 1997) and to develop effective economic policy mechanisms applicable to the period of post-Communist transformations (e.g., Sušjan, Lah, 1997).

3

Why Necroeconomics?

The dead shall live, the living die…

John Dryden
(1631–1700; English poet, critic, and playwright)

3.1. SUBJECT MATTER OF ECONOMICS

It can be readily stated that economy as such has been subject to in-depth studies and economic theory has been developed quite well. Modern realities, however, especially post-Communist transformation processes, have revealed a bunch of as yet unsolvable problems. The goal herein is to distinguish and focus on one segment of the post-Communist economy that not only has never been scrutinized by economic theory but also has never been noticed by economists as a distinct phenomenon. To get an insight into the problem it would be helpful to give a brief overview of economic theory and its main components.

Human existence without consumption cannot be imagined. What is necessary for satisfying one's needs can seldom be found in nature in a "natural state." It is for this reason that one has to take resources (which, in turn, are limited in terms of both quantity and accessibility) and utilize them for the production of goods necessary for human consumption. This, in turn, cannot work out well if both resources and produced goods are not distributed. That is exactly what is called economy. Consequently, economy is communities utilizing scarce resources for the production of goods to be consumed and distributing those resources and goods for the said purpose. Economics is a social science, the subject matter of which is economy.

Depending on who—individuals and private companies or the government—makes the final decisions on the matters of production and consumption, market and command economies may be distinguished. However, in the modern world, as such, neither of the two exists any longer; because in reality decisions on the matters are made by individuals and entities as well as the government—each of which makes such decisions within the bounds of their respective competence. All that exists is the mixed economy.

There is a special approach that has been quite extensively applied by researchers in studying economy as such. It is called a hierarchical approach. It has been traditionally accepted to represent national economy as a two-level (consisting of lower and upper levels) arrangement.

At the lower level, the subject of studies is the behavior of individual economic agents—namely households and companies—in the course of decision making, as well as their impact on each other during market relationships. This lower level of economy is known as a microeconomy and the field of research that takes this as its subject matter is called microeconomics.

At the upper level, focus is placed on the behavior of a national economy as an entire organism (which is reflected in economic growth, inflation, employment, external trade, etc.). This level, in turn, is called a macroeconomy, and the attendant field of research is called macroeconomics.

Whenever economy is viewed from the global standpoint, one has to distinguish another level known as megaeconomy. Accordingly, megaeconomics is the field of research that deals with international integrative processes, dynamics of the world economy, and so forth.

In addition to these three classical levels of economy, which are known to every average economist, researchers have to set apart one more sphere of economic life that should be subject to a separate scrutiny. It is called *shadow economy*, a phenomenon that is present in all three aforementioned levels of economy.

By its nature, shadow economy amounts to economic activities of households and private companies that are beyond the government's reach and control. That is why shadow economy is primarily linked with microeconomy. However, because the said uncontrolled and unregistered economic activities make a part of the entire national economy, outcomes of the shadow economy may have their direct influence over macroeconomic indices and may produce a wide range of depressing effects, such as drop of fiscal revenues, circulation of unaccounted monetary resources, decrease in export-import figures, et cetera. Due to the enlargement of the scale of shadow economy, it has turned into an international phenomenon: the practice of "black" money made in one country getting "washed" in another is widespread in the modern world. This fact eventually needs to be subjected to thorough scrutiny by megaeconomists.

Out of the aforementioned branches of economic theory, microeconomics and macroeconomics are the ones that have been most fully developed. Megaeconomics is a relatively new field. As per shadow economy and its exposure at the above three levels, it is one of the most topical and, so far, least studied problems facing the modern world.

3.2. FROM "MISDEVELOPED" ECONOMY TO NECROECONOMY

Post-Communist economy, among others, consists of such a sphere that up to now has never been subject to special consideration of the economic theory, as never before has it been recognized as a distinct area of economy. To identify that sphere, it would be necessary to call to mind what kind of material and technical base, command economy rested on.

Generally speaking, command economy never recognized any form of competition, either domestically or internationally. Instead, command economies were united in an integrated economic area (the best example of that was the former Mutual Aid Economic Council, which together with the USSR had united such command economies as Bulgaria, Poland, Romania, Hungary, Czechoslovakia, East Germany, Cuba, North Vietnam and Mongolia over the four decades of its existence), within which any exchange operation used to be regulated by a central coordinating body. As per economic cooperation with market economies, up to a certain period, such a cooperation was totally impossible (in particular, before World War II the USSR had pursued an "Iron Curtain" policy in relation to the West), whereas later on it became possible, though confined to strict limits.

Under the rule of command economy, only a single form of competition was permitted, even though this permission was limited to the USSR, for example, the competition with the West in the field of military production, which encouraged the USSR to develop the production of nuclear and conventional weapons, explore space, and so on.

The denial of competition forced command economies to reject the only effective stimulus of economic development. As a result, farms and factories produced low quality goods whose prices were artificially reduced at the expense of government's subsidies paid out of the budgetary funds. Proceeds from the sales of alcoholic beverages were the main source of the Soviet national budget. The only way of getting foreign currency resources was the sale of minerals (primarily oil) on international markets.

As a result of analysis and generalization of essential features of the Polish command economy, Adam Lipowski concludes that under the circumstances in which the world is divided into "developed" and "developing" countries, command economies cannot be attributed to either group. To characterize such economies, he coined the term *misdeveloped* and set out a number of features characteristic of misdeveloped economies (Lipowski, 1998, p. 9):

- Excessively high share of industry in GDP at the expense of domestic and foreign trade and financial and insurance services;

- Excessively high share of manufacturing of production inputs, at the expense of the production of the means of consumption;

- Insufficient share of internationally competitive goods in industrial production;

- Large scope of low-quality unwanted production imposed upon buyers;

- Excessive share of obsolete goods in industrial production at the expense of new and up-to-date products.

The collapse of the Communist regime and the breakdown of command economy "stripped off" the post-Communist economies *vis-à-vis* the international market. It turned out that—with rare exceptions (partially hydroelectric power, mining, and primary processing of extracted raw materials)—all goods produced in these countries were incompatible with international standards and could not compete with the Western products due to low quality and/or high prices. There is no market for such goods and there is no hope that such markets can ever exist. I believe that the economy of that type can only be referred to as "dead" economy, or "necroeconomy" (in the old Greek language *nekros* meant "dead"), and the theory studying this type of economy—necroeconomics (Papava, 2001a, 2001c, 2002c). It should be noted that a "Necroeconomy" would be similar to the Gaddy-Ickes "Virtual Economy" (Gaddy, Ickes, 1998, 2002; Woodruff, 1999a, 1999b, pp. 174–175), although the term *virtual economy* has a much broader sense (e.g., Carrier, Miller (eds.), 1998; Potemkin, 2000).

Lipowski labeled the aforementioned process of "stripping" of command economy as "divestment" (Drucker, 1986; Taylor, 1988). By this, he meant the process in the course of which a "misdeveloped" economy divests itself of all the above "pathologies" (Lipowski, 1998, pp. 31–32). I believe that necroeconomy is an ultimate result of that process.

Naturally, even if a certain section of economy is "dead," the other sections may be "alive." For this reason, this section may be referred to as "vital" economy, or vitaeconomy (in Latin *vita* means "life"), while the corresponding theory is economics.

The very first question that may arise in this regard is what the resemblances and differences are between necroeconomy and vitaeconomy.

In necroeconomy, as in vitaeconomy, production of goods, in principle, is possible. In other words, supply is existent. However, unlike the goods produced in vitaeconomy, those produced in necroeconomy (because of their poor quality and/or expense) cannot cause any demand. Consequently, in necroeconomy no act of purchase and sale may be committed and no balanced prices can exist.

The next question is no less important: if a certain segment of economy is dead, or, in other words, if it can not be revived, one should seemingly not face any problem at all, because a dead segment should not have any influence on a more-or-less healthy segment and, therefore, could be easily neglected.

Under the conditions of market economy that is exactly how it works: noncompetitive businesses usually "pass away" without doing any harm to the rest of the economy. Perhaps this is exactly why economic theory, which in principle has always been concerned solely with the problems of market economy, has never paid any attention to necroeconomy: as there was no real threat from the side of necroeconomy, there was no reason for regarding it as a subject matter of economic research either.

The situation is essentially different in the post-Communist economies, which are presently undergoing the process of transition. The significant part of the material and technical base of command economies now have turned into a foundation on which necroeconomy rests. This process was most dramatically reflected in the industrial sector.

3.3. THE REPRODUCTIVE BASE OF NECROECONOMY

To explain mutual impact of necroeconomy and vitaeconomy on each other, it would be helpful to break the entire organism of post-Communist economy into the following groups:

- Necroeconomy existing in the public sector;
- Vitaeconomy existing in the public sector;

- Privatized necroeconomy;

- Privatized vitaeconomy;

- Private sector based on new investments-vitaeconomy.

The first group, as a rule, consists of large and medium enterprises which, because of their importance, are assessed as strategic objects, although their products are completely noncompetitive, which makes all these objects dead under the conditions of free market.

Energy sector (especially electric power generation, oil and gas extraction/supply), transport, and communications comprise a vitaeconomic segment of the public sector. If the privatization of any companies of these sectors takes place, then such companies may move to the fourth group referred to as "privatized vitaeconomy." This group also consists of some medium and, more often, small industrial companies.

The third group consists of the former first-group enterprises after their privatization. The change of ownership itself cannot result in the revival of frozen production, because what is dead cannot be recovered—whoever the owner of the dead may be, the government or a private company. It is for this very reason that the process of privatization is often discredited, as it (privatization), especially in its initial phases, in isolation from any investments, has often been assigned the function of reviver of the "frozen" production, without considering the question. This production is either dead or alive.

The fifth and the last group integrate the healthiest segment of the post-Communist economy: a new private sector based on new investments and principles of market economy. Despite this, one has to take into account the fact that this group also faces certain problems that need proper contemplation. In particular, I am referring to some foreign investments through which the post-Communist nations, instead of the newest technologies, are swamped by outdated and old-fashioned (more precisely, morally depreciated, as compared to international standards) tools and equipment, which, I think, could be readily labeled as "secondhand investments." Obviously, goods manufactured with such technologies can only be acceptable within the boundaries of emerging markets and just for a certain period of time (i.e., until the internationally competitive products invade such markets).

Another question that needs to be answered is what is the reason for such a constancy of necroeconomy in the post-Communist countries. I believe that the evolutionary theory of economic change (Nelson and Winter, 1982) is the one that could be applied to that issue in the most effective manner. The main tool of the theory consists in a concept of "routine," by which the company's customary rules and methods of behavior, which regulate the reproduction of the company's activities, is meant (Murrell, 1992).

It is precisely "routine," which has been deeply rooted in the command economy over many decades, which is the main factor that forces "dead" enterprises to work in a no-longer-existing regime of command economy. As a result, warehouses of those enterprises are flooded by poor quality goods, and debts to the national budget, social schemes, energy sector and other enterprises, incurred because of inability to market such goods, are growing every day. This is exactly how an unfathomable net of mutual outstanding liabilities is formed (e.g., Åslund, 1995, Ch. pp. 6).

It has been a long tradition of any command economy that whenever any enterprise would have accumulated (sometimes on purpose) a bunch of debts, its leadership would request the governmental agencies (Communist Party management organs, the Planning Committee, the Ministry of Finance, etc.) to write them down and, as a rule, such requests would easily be satisfied. Thus, to the extent that any debts could have been written down, the accumulation of debts, as such, had never been considered a "dangerous" practice. The "routine" of debt accumulation/down-writing is so deeply rooted in the command economic system that it can periodically reveal itself in the process of transformations as well, although it may be disguised by things like "tax amnesty," which sometimes can be backed even by some new politicians pretending to be genuine reformers.

3.4. *HOMO TRANSFORMATICUS* AND *POST-DELTSY*

In fact, the human factor plays a decisive role in any economic process. The routine that reproduces necroeconomy depends, *inter alia,* on the behavior of a human that undergoes the transformation from *homo sovieticus* (one who is totally oppressed by and totally depends on the state), formed under the conditions of command economy, into *homo economicus* (one whose motivation is based either on getting maximum benefit in one's household, or maximum profit in one's company), a type of human being that is characteristic to market economy.

To do justice, one has to note that, according to a very remarkable belief, one of the characteristic features of the Russian economic school is the recognition of the primacy of social approaches over individuals' behavior and motivation, as a result of which the Russian worldview rebuffs the idea of *homo economicus.*

According to the same belief, Vladimir Lenin just reproduced in his doctrine the traditions of the Russian economic thought (Abalkin, 2000, p. 15). If one agrees with this, then one will have to recognize that *homo sovieticus* is nothing but a product of the Russian idea of how the world is organized.

That type of man—one that is in the middle of post-Communist transformation—may be referred to as *homo transformaticus.* This is a kind of human that is not yet entirely liberated from the fear of the state and due to a traditional way of life still depends on the state, but in his behavior one can detect the awakening of personal interests and motivation (Papava 1996a, 1999).

In entrepreneurship *homo transformaticus* assumes a special shape whose roots can be found in command economy.

Even command economy could not succeed in rooting out market economy (more precisely, individual elements of it) in its entirety. The latter was so much suppressed by the state that it could survive only under the protection of shadow economy (Shokhin, 1989, pp. 57–83). As a matter of fact, no single director of command-economy-controlled enterprises (with rare exceptions) could avoid the breach of Communist rules in managing his enterprise, which breach sometimes consisted in applying the elements of market economy, and for that reason, their activities could only be assessed as "shadow" economic activities. Despite this, directors of command-economy-controlled enterprises failed to transform themselves into market-type entrepreneurs. In principle, success was totally impossible, as they had to confine themselves to the limits of command economy.

Perhaps it is for this reason that market-oriented behavior of enterprise directors was labeled as *deletsship* rather than entrepreneurship and they were known as *deltsy* rather than entrepreneurs. The Russian word *delets* (pl. *deltsy*) stems from the word *delo,* which should be translated as *business.* To that extent, a word-by-word translation of *delets* must be *businessman.* However, such a translation would be incorrect, as an English businessman denotes a person who is engaged in lawful activities, while Russian *delets* is a derogatory word used in reference to anyone who makes illegal, illegitimate, or even shameful deals. As long as the phenomenon that is described by the word *delets* is essentially of Soviet origin, there is no reason to translate it into English.

After the collapse of command economy many *deltsy* managed to retain their positions. Furthermore, after the privatization of their enterprises they took advantage of the rights of employees and became the owners of those enterprises (Åslund, 1996). Some of them have hired managers, but all of them have tried (especially at the initial stage of the post-privatization period) to apply their *delets*-type mentality in the course of company management.

Just like *homo transformaticus* is not yet *homo economicus,* former *deltsy* have not transformed into entrepreneurs yet. Thus, in the realm of entrepreneurship, *homo tranformaticus* assumes a title of "*post-delets*" (Papava and Khaduri, 1997, pp. 28–29).

It is exactly *post-deltsy* who are at the back of public- or private-sector-based necroeconomy. It is precisely they who are the initiators of command-economy-type "routine" behavior.

Having taken advantage of their old contacts, *post-deltsy* succeeded in making a way into the governmental structures (parliaments, executive authorities) where they have been doing their best to politically justify and extend the life of necroeconomy.

There is no doubt that necroeconomy is only in the interests of *post-deltsy* and until (as a result of institutional reforms *post-deltsy*) it is replaced with entrepreneurs, there is no reason to believe that necroeconomy will ever come to an end.

3.5. THE END OF POST-COMMUNIST TRANSFORMATION OF THE ECONOMY

The negative impact of necroeconomy on the development of post-Communist nations is obvious. Consequently, what one needs to do is identify and utilize a mechanism that would enable us to cope with the problem of dead enterprises in an "automatic regime" characteristic to market economy. In other words, one must take advantage of said mechanism in order for the market economy to be established.

The key to a successful solution to the problem consists in the aforementioned evolutionary theory of economic change.

Routine, which would be commensurate with market economy, must be shaped primarily in the fifth group, namely, a newly established private sector. The state has to focus exactly on that group and to assist it in overcoming the embryonic phase, both expanding and developing. The state has to provide for creating stable political and microeconomic environments, which would facilitate the formation of new firms based on private investments. The post-Communist state, in defining its economic policy, must give priority to the overall development and expansion of the fifth group at the expense of the first and third groups.

Even secondhand-investment-based companies of the fifth group, irrespective of their poorer appearance, under the conditions of a favorable legal framework cannot practically underpin necroeconomy, as the very style of establishment and operation of such companies is market-driven. For this reason the market routine of such companies, in case of the loss of competitive capacity of the company's products, can ensure the company's withdrawal from the market with the aid of market mechanisms.

As per the enterprises in the second and the fourth groups, no matter who is owner—the state or private companies that took over as a result of privatization—all of them need to attract new investments through privatization or long-term concession of a certain portion of their assets to strategic investors. Otherwise, there is a strong likelihood that the vitaeconomic potential of these groups will be transformed into the necroeconomy of the first and the third groups.

As was noted above, mere privatization, as such, cannot eradicate necroeconomy. For this reason, to revitalize the dead but strategically important enterprises of the first group, the government has to take the following step, which is the only solution to the problem: Hold, as soon as possible, open international tenders for the selection of strategic investors to whom these enterprises will be conceded on a long-term basis (perhaps it would be fairer to speak about the concession of a right to start strategically important production in a dead body). It is very likely, however, that such a step will not be acceptable to strategic investors. In that case, the government will have to privatize such enterprises at symbolic starting prices, because dead enterprise cannot cost much.

One can have absolutely no hopes in regard to the third group—the privatized necroeconomy. The only true label that could be attached to the necroeconomic assets is "scrap metal." One of the most effective ways to get rid of necroeconomy is to sell scrap, including oversees—this would enable the owner of the scrap to accumulate foreign currency resources and use them for the creation of vitaeconomy.

The routine of command economy resists the recognition of dead machinery as scrap metal, creates barriers to the selling, especially exporting of scrap metal, and thereby extends the life of necroeconomy.

Theoretically, the bankruptcy law must be an effective tool against necroeconomy. Although several years have elapsed since the parliament of Georgia adopted the bankruptcy law—the one that had been developed on the basis of international experience and with the assistance of international experts—unfortunately, the law turned out to be a "stillborn child," or a necrolaw. Under this law no single, actually bankrupt enterprise has been recognized as legally bankrupted up to now. The reason is that the law failed to "fit" the institutional environment existing in the country.

The law is completely commensurate with international standards; it was approved by all international experts who had examined it. However, it is in fact not a viable law. I would call it a "sleeping beauty" from fairy tales.

The Georgian bankruptcy law is good evidence that throughout post-Communist nations new institutions, under the pressure of international financial organizations, are formed by analogy with and purposeful and direct reproduction of the Western originals (Shavans and Manyan, 1999, p. 43). As a result, the institutions that fit well developed market economies, after their transplantation into the post-Communist economies in transition, are often ineffective and sometimes even harmful. In this regard, one has to keep in mind that the IMF is often justly criticized for its accelerated, simplistic approach to institutional reforms, and for this reason the process of formation of market economy is slowed down (Stiglitz, 1999a).

Market economy routine can only be underpinned through creating market-driven institutions, replacing *post-deltsy* with entrepreneurs, and ultimately eradicating necroeconomy. The end of necroeconomy is the only true indicator of the end of post-Communist transformation (Papava, 2003b).

4

Institutional Foundations of the "Shadow Political Economy" of Post-Communist Capitalism

VLADIMER PAPAVA AND NODAR KHADURI

Any institution which does not suppose the people good...is evil.

Maximilien Robespierre
(1758–1794; French revolutionary)

4.1. ON THE "SHADOW POLITICAL ECONOMY"

Any economic system in any country in the world is a unique synthesis of legal and illegal (or shadow) economic activity. The illegal, hidden economy functions on par with the legal economy, has enormous dimensions, and in some countries does not yield to the legal economy in its dimensions.

The shadow economy as a phenomenon originated in ancient times and functions successfully up to the present, at a time when its scale is not only expanding in practice but also assumes myriad forms. Despite its centuries-old history, the shadow economy has not yet become a subject of special, comprehensive political-economic study. In its investigation of general economic principles, political economy has almost never focused its attention on problems of the shadow economy. It has either ignored them or believed that the economic mechanisms in a shadow economy are the same as those operating in a legal economy. An unfortunate consequence of such an artificially simplified view of shadow economy is that there is still not a very clear understanding of the mechanisms of a shadow economy. As a result, the steps that are taken to eradicate it are frequently ineffective.

Proceeding from what has been said heretofore, it seems necessary to carry out a comprehensive political-economic study of a shadow economy on the basis of available empirical material. I shall tentatively call the political economy of a shadow economy *shadow political economy* (Papava, Khaduri, 1997).

The shadow economy uses the same resources and markets as the legal economy, with the sole distinction that it takes place without the recognition of the state and, indeed, in some cases even without its knowledge. Although economists do not dispute this fact in principle, there is still no consensus among them on the definition of a shadow economy.

There is a widely held concept of the shadow economy as secret, illegal activity that is not taken into account. It is frequently associated with criminal ways of obtaining income, that is, with economic infractions and crimes as well as with organized crime, corruption, and lobbying of various organs of state power to influence political decisions. However, concentrating solely on the criminal manifestations of the shadow economy means not getting to the heart of the problem and making it impossible to find ways to reduce its dimensions. One should not delude oneself with the notion that a shadow economy is solely connected with criminal activity; this sphere frequently also includes activities that are entirely respectable and beneficial to society.

Unfortunately, levers that are in any way effective in influencing the shadow economy to any degree have not yet been created, and the entire arsenal of methods for combating it is usually confined to administratively or criminally punitive measures, which, of course, cannot by any means always lead to the desired results.

The shadow economy as a phenomenon has been relatively well studied for countries with developed market economies (Bhattacharya, 1999; Svensson, 1983; Tanzi, 1999; Thomas, 1999). Works are appearing on the study of the shadow economy in developing countries (e.g., Adams, Fitchett (eds.), 1992). Despite ideological barriers, in the 1980s it began to be openly studied in formerly communist-type countries (e.g., Shokhin, 1989). However, little is known about the shadow economy in countries in which post-Communist reforms are being carried out (e.g., Ékes, 1994; Papava, Khaduri, 1997).

The purpose here is to present a theoretical picture of the essence of the shadow economy, to reveal the principles of its transformation in post-Communist development.

4.2. THE INSTITUTIONAL ANALYTICAL FRAMEWORK OF ECONOMIC TRANSFORMATION

In revealing the essence of the shadow economy, the use of the approaches of the "New Institutional Economic Theory" (North, 1997) is especially effective.

According to this theory, the actions and interrelations of people are outlined by the institutional structure of society, which, within the framework of a given period of time, determines the various boundaries of human behavior. The institutions themselves are the aggregate of formal and informal (commonly accepted norms of behavior, verbal agreements, etc.) restrictions and mechanisms of coercion (through education in the spirit of these restrictions and punishment for their violation) to observe these restrictions. Formal institutions (FIs) are usually presented in written law.

It must be noted that FIs and informal institutions (IIs) are characterized by a high degree of reciprocal influence: FIs are those already in existence or desired IIs that have been reflected in written law; the developmental trends of IIs are influenced by newly emerged FIs. As the most graphic example of the impact of IIs on FIs, developed market systems in which many legislative acts regulating the economy were adopted on the basis of commonly accepted norms of human behavior in a competitive environment should be acknowledged. No less graphic an example of the reverse impact of FIs on IIs are economic systems of the Communist type, in which FIs were created from good intentions to artificially transform and "improve" people, as a result of which certain IIs atrophied.

In order to depict the relationship between FIs and IIs, let us examine Figure 4.2.1, in which they are conditionally represented in the form of a Venn diagram.

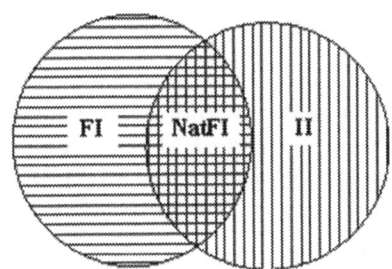

Figure 4.2.1. Correlation of Aggregates of Formal Institutions and Informal Institutions

Because some FIs form on the basis of the reflection of certain IIs in written law, sets FI and II intersect. This part of the FIs is referred to as natural FIs (Nat-FIs). The NatFI set is the intersection of sets FI and II. The larger the NatFI set, the more FIs correspond to human nature. It must be noted that sets FI and NatFI can never coincide entirely: first, not all IIs can be reflected in written law (nor, indeed, is this always necessary); and, second, FIs will also always contain some that, based on the developmental goals of a given society, reflect not only existing IIs but also necessary restrictions and mechanisms compelling their observance (i.e., unnatural FIs—UFIs).

In non-Communist-type countries, UFIs exceeded NatFIs many times, which, other things being equal, determined the lack of viability of such economic systems. In countries with developed market democracies, on the other hand, the share of NatFIs in the FI aggregate is significantly greater.

FIs, above all else, are the basis of the legal economy in any society. The defining principle of the shadow economy is the ignoring of FIs, when the actions of people are in no way subordinate to the demands of these institutions and are regulated exclusively by IIs. Here, too, the logical question arises: Are all informal institutions at the basis of the shadow economy?

Of course, the answer to this question is negative. The explanation is that a certain part of the IIs complement the FIs. These IIs, together with the FIs, create an environment for the legal activity of people, including economic activity. From the positions of FIs, such IIs appear to be *rational.* Accordingly, I shall call those IIs that complement FIs and thereby create a basis/or the legal activity of people rational informal institutions (RIIs).

Out of the entire aggregate of IIs, the shadow economy is primarily based on those that ignore FIs. From the positions of the latter, such informal institutions may be called *irrational.* Accordingly, those IIs that ignore formal institutions and thereby create an environment for the illegal, shadow activity of people will be called irrational informal institutions (IIIs).

Can it be said that the sum of all RIIs and IIIs compose the entire aggregate of IIs? To all appearances, it cannot. The fact is that both aggregates of RIIs and IIIs simultaneously include in their structures the same IIs that with equal success do not contradict FIs and complement those IIs that essentially contradict FIs. In other words, both aggregates of RIIs and IIIs contain the same subset of IIs that by their nature are *neutral* (NeutIIs). These last include in their structure the most commonly recognized elementary norms of behavior that have formed in society over quite a long period of time (sometimes even centuries), for example, behavioral norms that include elements of compassion on the part of the strong for the weak, who acknowledge this.

In order to depict the interrelations of RIIs, IIIs, and NeutIIs, let us examine Figure 4.2.2.

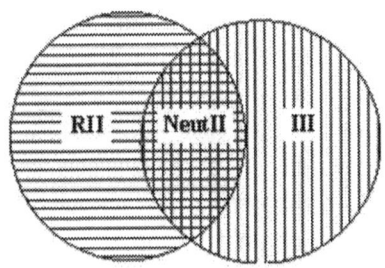

Figure 4.2.2. Correlation of Aggregates of Rational Informal Institutions, Neutral Informal Institutions, and Irrational Informal Institutions

The intersection of sets RII and III is the aggregate NeutII.

The mechanisms of change of various IIs differ from each other.

NeutIIs are the most stable; they are the least subject to the influence of FIs. NeutIIs are closest to the very essence of humanity and are therefore more "conservative."

Some NeutIIs are reflected in natural FIs, as a result of which the latter are most stable in the structure of the natural FIs and all the more so in the entire aggregate of FIs. This part of the natural FIs may be classified as *neutral* FIs (NeutFIs).

Combining Figures 4.2.1 and 4.2.2, gives the depiction of the correlation of all FIs and IIs (see Figure 4.2.3).

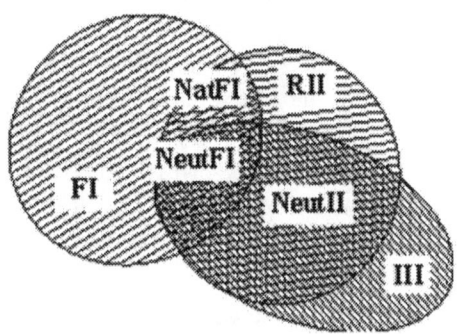

Figure 4.2.3. Correlation of All Types of Aggregates of Formal Institutions and Informal Institutions

When various changes take place in the economic structure of society, they are first of all reflected in FIs. When these changes are relatively insignificant, some FIs appear to be smoothly replaced by new FIs. But when the changes are significant, the majority of the FIs are destroyed and it is not always possible to create new ones to take the place of the old. It should be noted that, even in the ideal case in which the goals of transformations in the economic structure of society are clear, and even with the most complete knowledge of which new FIs are needed and how they should be created (which in itself is by no means always obvious), there is no assurance that these new institutions will be created in good time. This is above all impeded by the inertness of economic and social processes.

The vacuum that forms in the structure of FIs exerts a direct negative impact on RIIs: A portion of them disappears as the corresponding FIs are destroyed. This vacuum in the structures of FIs and RIIs is filled with proliferating IIIs. This is precisely the reason that—in countries making the transition from one economic system to another—the scale of the shadow economy grows significantly. The most graphic example of the total destruction of old FIs, simultaneous with the disappearance of the corresponding RIIs, and the subsequent replacement of both of them by proliferating IIIs is Georgia in 1993–95, when the scale of the shadow economy increased to eighty percent (Papava, 1996b). An example of the most purposeful and sensible transformations is post-Communist Hungary, where the scale of the shadow economy reached twenty-five percent (Ékes, 1994).

Thus, during the transition from one economic system to another, the area of circle FI in Figure 4.2.1 is reduced, while the area of circle II expands. Similarly, the area of circle RII in Figure 4.2.2 diminishes and the area of circle III expands. During this transformation of the economic system, NatIIs are the most stable and remain virtually unchanged, which guarantees a relatively more stable position of UFIs (unnatural formal institutions) in the entire aggregate of FIs. If any types of UFIs are nevertheless destroyed, it is not so bad, because the corresponding NatIIs regulate the given processes without detriment to the interests of all society. Those natural FIs that are not a part of NeutFIs are more subject to change than the latter.

Significant destruction in the structure of FIs and RIIs and their replacement by IIIs (which do not and cannot in principle belong to NeutIIs) is fraught with the most serious manifestations of the criminalization of the economy and its management.

The special role of the portion of NeutIIs that does not belong to NeutFIs, when, at the same time, they compose part of the two aggregates of RIIs and IIIs, results in some types of shadow activity that are inoffensive and not of an antisocial, antihuman nature. The legalization of these types of shadow activity is impeded by imperfections in FIs; any improvement in them promotes the greater legalization of the given types of activity, but since absolutely perfect FIs cannot be created, in any society certain types of entirely inoffensive types of economic activity will always remain in the shadow economy.

Based on institutional analysis of the shadow economy, it is easier to examine forms of manifestation of the shadow economy in countries with developed market orientations and with communist-type economic systems.

4.3. CHARACTERISTICS OF THE SHADOW ECONOMY IN DEVELOPED COUNTRIES AND COMMUNIST-TYPE ECONOMIC SYSTEMS

In order to study the characteristics of the shadow economy in countries undergoing post-Communist transformation, it is necessary to know where they have come from and where they are going—that is, the characteristics of the shadow economy in countries with developed market systems and in countries with communist-type economies.

It must be noted that, according to experts' estimates, in countries with market systems the shadow economy accounts for 5–20 percent of gross national product (e.g., Svensson, 1983, pp. 92–95). Of course, these indicators cannot be precise, but it is possible to obtain an approximate understanding of the size of the shadow economy.

It is widely believed that the shadow economy operates exclusively with cash; checks, bills of exchange, and other means of payment are not as liquid and may be detectable; in a shadow economy there are practically no payments through banks. It can definitely be stated that tax evasion is almost always possible when cash is used. Here it is appropriate to emphasize that the concealment of income with the intent to evade paying taxes is one of the principal features of the shadow economy.

Theoretically speaking, every tax is interference by the state in the functioning of a market economy, and it limits the market's potential to make maximum use of resources. At the same time, taxes are the price paid for the possibility of enjoying social goods in reality. However, in many cases, tax evasion is attempted regardless of the size of earnings. The reason is clear and understandable: There is hardly anyone who will not try to obtain goods or services free of charge or at least for a lower price. And here, administrative methods alone—or patriotic appeals that the power of the state, well-being, security, and protection of civil rights depend directly on national budget receipts—are insufficient. The ideal salvation from the "disease" of nonpayment of taxes would be the creation of a system in which the taxpayer would be interested to the maximum degree in paying taxes in full and on schedule rather than in evading their payment (e.g., Papava, 1997).

The shadow economy brings about the lowering of state and local taxes. But it should be noted that if it were entirely eliminated, some work would not be performed at all or would be performed by customers themselves (once again, without the payment of taxes). It must be remembered that, because money earned in the shadow economy as a rule ends up in the legal economy, everything is nevertheless indirectly taxed. Thus, "shadow figures" also "pay" taxes, but do so indirectly. And it has been established that if tax agencies curb the concealment of income in the early stage of functioning of such a shadow figure, the budget may lose more than it gains (Svensson, 1983, pp. 63–64). This segment of the shadow economy is regulated by NeutIIs, and some of them even by NeutFIs as well.

It is usually difficult to say what money is shadow money and what money is not. Shadow money is money that circulates in the shadow economy. Money that is criminally obtained (from robberies, drug and arms trafficking, illegal prostitution, etc.) is also considered shadow money. As a rule, part of the shadow money is left for the expansion of "shadow business," which is natural because it is the principal source of financing of the shadow economy. Unfortunately, capital from the legal part of the economic system is frequently invested in the shadow economy. This may be due to the state's inability (and sometimes also reluctance) to fight against it.

Relations with the shadow economy in former communist-type countries were particularly painful. After 1917, an experiment to build communism on an unprecedented scale began. An unprecedented fight against private property began. It was specifically private property that was recognized as mankind's principal misfortune. The economy began developing in an unnatural way and as a result there was also great distortion of its component part—the shadow economy, which went virtually unrecognized until Gorbachev's perestroika began.

If those going into the "shadows" in countries with market economies did so primarily in connection with tax evasion, in communist-type countries things were much more complex. The most prevalent types of shadow activity were the padding of performance figures and other distortions of plan fulfillment data; the production of inferior, substandard, or incomplete products; theft on the job;

misappropriation of state property through the abuse of one's official position; and bribe-taking. All society was drawn into the shadow economy. However, any manifestation of this activity was for quite a long time treated as being the result of individual asocial inclinations of individual citizens, against whom various punitive measures were applied. But, most importantly, the question of combating the roots of this disease was never raised once. Nor could it be raised in connection with the very essence of the communist-type economy.

The existence of the shadow economy was entirely determined by the FIs of the administrative-command system of economic management, which was manifested in the strict planning of the production of goods and services and in the distribution of resources. In my opinion, the most successful and, moreover, the most complete classification of the shadow economy in communist-type countries was made by Shokhin (1989, pp. 69–83). In particular, he believes that the shadow economy consists of the illegal segment of the "second" economy, the informal economy, the fictitious economy, and the "black" economy.

The second economy is understood to mean all those forms of production activity that, as a rule, were previously considered as having no prospects—individual labor activity and small-group production. Consequently, the "first" economy is understood to mean large-scale state and collective farm production.

The second economy is frequently compared with an iceberg: Only a small part of it is registered and taxed. The bulk of the second economy is hidden from regulatory agencies (note that it is hidden from regulatory agencies, but not from various kinds of inspectors and law enforcers). And this is despite the fact that no one has officially prohibited individual labor activity. However, discriminatory taxation and society's attitude toward it as a "rudiment" forced those engaged in individual labor activity to work illegally. Furthermore, they harbored a fear of *dekulakization*. The second economy is primarily regulated by RIIs.

When the reasons for the preservation of the shadow economy are examined, it is usually noted that in communist-type countries some of the shadow figures of the second economy were not interested in legalizing their activity for both psychological and purely financial considerations. Here it is necessary to consider not only legal taxes but also the system in the form of illegal taxes that forced entrepreneurs to pay much larger sums "on the side" to local (but not *only* local) authorities and to the police (starting with the district inspector and moving higher). In other words, the result of the illegal state of the second economy was that some IIIs also edged their way into its regulatory mechanism in the form of RIIs.

The basic mechanism of functioning of the second element of the shadow economy—the informal economy—is the system of centralized planning and the practical exclusion of economic methods of management from the work.

Administrative-command methods of management almost always compelled workers to act within the framework of the adopted procedures for implementing managerial and planning decisions. Such actions originated as a mode of adaptation. They frequently became distorted and thus distorted the management system itself.

The system of planning was built on the principle "from the achieved level." This in turn generated a system of "tenders," whose participants were, on the one hand, enterprises and branch departments and, on the other hand, central planning organs in the form of Gosplan (State Planning Committee). The formulation of a plan that pleased all participants was the subject of the tenders. The "status quo" principle was the means that Gosplan used to place pressure on a branch or on enterprises.

The possibility of obtaining a good plan opened up broad opportunities for using material resources to obtain illegal income. Accordingly, managers of enterprises did their utmost and used fair means or foul to make sure that the plan did not correspond to enterprises' real potential.

The most characteristic feature of the Soviet economy was overfulfillment of the plan. Overfulfillment of the plan offered a number of appreciable gains and advantages. Precisely this overfulfillment of the plan was the principal factor in incentives and professional advancement. It also encouraged enterprise managers to strive to obtain a lower plan. Clearly, agreements regarding a lower plan were usually dictated by selfish motives.

Sometimes the plan could also be raised at the "request" and desire of producers, whereupon it was fulfilled at any price to the detriment of both the environment and state interests. However, it was specifically this detriment that yielded superhigh shadow income.

The informal economy was manifested not only in manipulations of the plan, but also in the functioning of the system for the distribution of the means of production. Every enterprise director tried to obtain the maximum quantity of means of production from central distribution organs of economic management, and, therefore, most enterprises had huge, above-norm inventories of raw materials, equipment, and other scarce resources. This excess formed on the basis of informal deals and, of course, was by no means devoid of selfish interests. Given the use of a system for writing off supposedly worn-out equipment and spoiled raw materials, this excess was a significant source of illegal enrichment.

All these selfish actions were based on the bribe-taking mechanism, which in countries with developed market economies differs radically from that in countries with communist-type economic systems. In particular, while in the former bribes are usually given for actions that the law does not allow, in the latter bribes in the great majority of cases are given for entirely lawful actions.

The informal economy is realized by IIIs, including both NeutIIs and UFIs.

The padding of performance figures and other violations of plan and financial accountability were one form of manifestation of the shadow economy. Thus, an entire sector of the shadow economy existed—the fictitious economy. It made it possible to obtain unlawful income by seemingly entirely lawful means. This applies above all, to padding.

Padding was used to obtain unearned income in the form of wages, bonuses, or material rewards. One type of the fictitious economy, and thus of obtaining unlawful income, has been the sale of resources obtained after the violation of standards due to the worsening of quality and the production of incomplete products. The communist-type economy "specialized" in the production of inferior-quality products. The production of products for "export" was the peak of cynicism. The same enterprises that produced inferior products for domestic consumption also produced far better products for delivery to foreign countries. This created conditions enabling enterprise managers to earn considerable money by padding and falsifying reports.

Padding was also used to attract and retain workers. It was frequently the practice to offer unduly high wages and to misuse various funds. Such practices were often used to maintain production because personnel turnover at most enterprises not only made it impossible to expand production but even to maintain it at the same level. All this was done with only one goal—to obtain superhigh unlawful income. Such violations have been particularly frequent in construction.

The principal regulators of the fictitious economy were IIIs, with the exception of the part of NeutIIs that did not belong to UFIs.

The peak of the shadow economy in communist-type countries was the black economy. Even when the strictest management techniques were employed, when everything "noncommunist" was persecuted, fee proportions of fee underground economy attained enormous scale. Entire enterprises or parts of them were left out of fee reckoning and worked exclusively for "fee" black economy.

Virtually all state enterprises produced both officially known, planned, often inferior and substandard products, as well as products "on fee left" that are concealed, primarily quality products, and, most important, that are in short supply. An underground study was made of fee consumer market and, unlike the state, which planned the production of consumer and producer goods according to the administrative principle (without any study of the market, thus later forcing enterprises to produce products no one needed and consumers to buy them), illegal production was limited to what was required by consumer demand.

Considerable economic detriment to the population resulted from products that did not satisfy requirements. Such a segment of the economy in communist-type countries was not officially considered an integral part of the shadow economy, but considering the damage it inflicted on the population, this activity should also be viewed through the prism of the shadow economy. The sale of inferior products was due to the abnormal status of trade, the "rightless" position of the consumer, and disproportions in supply and demand. These processes were for the most part regulated by UFIs.

Thus, the state inflicted more damage on all of society than the black economy.

This part of the black economy was regulated exclusively by RIIs, including NeutIIs and UFIs; certain IIIs that did not belong to the NeutIIs occasionally also found their way into this regulatory system.

One of the component parts of the black economy is the black market. The black market specialized exclusively in the consumer sector. Speculation and all manner of machinations involving scarcity were related to it.

In the black market, there was a segment in which, despite the strictest prohibitions, wholesale and retail trade (primarily in imported products) was organized. For these purposes, places known to everyone were used, to which people who had money came and bought what they wanted; that is, in the "desert" of the communist-type economy, there were small market "oases."

This activity was regulated by NeutIIs.

The black economy also included officially prohibited types of activity like prostitution, the use of the services of hired killers, the drug business, and so forth. All these types of activity were regulated exclusively by IIIs. It must be noted that in this part of the black economy, there may also be a certain degree of intersection with the second economy when, for example, drugs are produced as a cottage industry.

Thus, in a shadow economy it is possible to tentatively identify two frequently closely intertwined spheres of activity: (1) *shadow entrepreneurship*, which embraces illegal activity in the production, sale, and servicing of products; and (2) *parasitism*, speculation, and various types of activity in the form of padding, extortion, and the like (Papava, 1990). It should be noted here that the bulk of the second economy, with the exception of socially unacceptable types of activity (for example, the production of drugs), falls under the heading of shadow entrepreneurship. Part of the informal economy in the form of interpersonal relationships within the framework of administrative-command procedures of planning-managerial activity is related to parasitism while the other part—in the form of illegal economic methods of management—is related to shadow entrepreneurship. Part of the black economy in the form of its formal links is related to shadow entrepreneurship, while the remaining part of the black economy is related to parasitism.

With some reservations, it may nevertheless be considered that shadow entrepreneurship was of a progressive nature as the embryonic state of market interrelations in the communist-type economic system.

4.4. CHARACTERISTICS OF THE SHADOW ECONOMY IN COUNTRIES WITH POST-COMMUNIST CAPITALISM

Several years ago, most communist-type countries launched democratic reforms with the aim of returning the economic system to a natural channel of development. In the course of several years, these countries had to travel the same road that had been traveled by countries with developed market systems.

In this short period of time, there had to be changes both in the economic system itself and, above all, in people, who had to change this system. The restructuring of the way of thinking is the most difficult-to-surmount fruit of the reform.

In communist-type countries, an image of humanity has formed that the literature calls *homo soveticus*, or a person who is entirely dependent on the state and who fears the state. The classic image of "man" in a market economy is Adam Smith's *homo economicus*, who tries to improve his lot gradually and to realize maximum gain. Considering the special impact of FIs and IIs on human behavior, it may be stated conditionally that modem man in countries with developed market systems is an *institutional economic man* or, more briefly, an *institutional man* (Williamson, 1985, Ch. 2).

But man in countries that have undergone the post-Communist transformation is no longer entirely *homo soveticus* and but are still not entirely *homo economicus*. In other words, he is *homo transformaticus* (see Ch. 3).

Homo transformaticus is a vigorously active person both in a legal and in a shadow economy and practically all questions of post-Communist transformation should be viewed through the prism of his behavior.

The principal difference between shadow economies in countries with market systems and communist-type economies stems from the very essence of these two fundamentally different economic systems, and in particular, the prevailing forms of ownership. In communist-type countries, the shadow economy developed on the basis of state ownership, while in countries with developed market systems, it developed primarily on the basis of private, but also on the basis of state, ownership.

The process of privatization of state property in post-Communist countries may become the basis for the transformation of the shadow economy that is characteristic of communist-type countries into a shadow economy that is characteristic of countries with developed market systems.

Before mass privatization began, the authorities frequently believed that in the privatization process it would be possible to invest shadow capital in legal structures undergoing privatization. Unfortunately, these expectations by no means *always* materialized. After shadow capital was invested in enterprises scheduled for privatization, some of these enterprises were drawn into the shadow economy.

The privatization of state-owned property is not only and not merely the act of buying and selling the latter but is also essentially a process that has pretensions to forming a social stratum of entrepreneurs.

Many of those who call themselves entrepreneurs in post-Communist countries are former communist party figures and former directors in whose behavior it is very difficult to find the merits possessed by Western entrepreneurs.

But the majority of those in charge of enterprises today behave just as they did before, when they were appointed directors of state-owned enterprises. To date, work methods like padding or other distortions of financial accountability, the production of inferior, substandard products, theft on the job, bribe-taking, and so on, have not been eradicated. Today, too, they try to live at state expense: They are becoming parliamentarians, forcing their way into the government or pushing their proxies forward so the state will pass laws and perform other legislative acts that will enable them to reap economic gains at the expense of the interests of individual citizens and all of society.

Before the post-Communist transformation began, persons in this category were called *deltsy*. In the initial stage of the post-Communist transformation the *delets* could by no means always be transformed into entrepreneurs. The *delets*, as one of the representatives of *homo transformaticus*, took on market-democratic forms, albeit remaining essentially the same. Therefore, it is more accurate to call entrepreneurs who emerged in countries undergoing post-Communist transformation *post-deltsy* (see, Ch. 3).

The *post-delets* phenomenon is one of the principal keys to understanding many problems of post-Communist transformation, including the transformation of the shadow economy.

The most inoffensive of the parts of the shadow economy in communist-type countries was the second economy. Following the collapse of the communist-type economy, almost all small business, which was also the basis of the second economy, was left in the shade. Whereas in the past, representatives of the second economy did not register officially because of discriminatory taxation and a sense of fear, they are now prevented from doing so by racketeering and corruption in the registration process.

In the majority of the post-Communist countries the informal economy should have disappeared with the abolition of centralized planning. Unfortunately, it still remains, albeit in modified form. If heads of state enterprises in the past tried to lower the state plan so as to be able to overfulfill it, at the present time, heads of private enterprises (they are for the most part the same people) try to officially reduce the volume of production so as not to pay taxes: in their official reports, they reflect only a small part of their output.

These *post-deltsy* do not hide from the public. On the contrary, they often voice demands for the creation of favorable conditions for their work in the mass media. These voices are often heard in the higher echelons of state government, *inter alia*.

The lobbying of decisions advantageous to the *post-deltsy* in the legislative and executive branches has become commonplace.

The name *businessman* no longer applies to many *post-deltsy* and, as already noted, they are trying to bolster their influence in the political arena to be the "chosen ones of the people" in the highest legislative body. Thus, the probability that the "roots" of the shadow economy will grip parliamentarians in the post-Communist countries is very high.

In the economics of post-Communist capitalism, the so-called gentleman's agreement has acquired a large scope. Economic agents try to downplay quantity and the price of the product in a contract or to steer clear of contracts altogether. Clearing transactions are carried out exclusively with cash.

In particular, smuggling should be discussed. It should not be thought that smuggling was totally nonexistent in communist-type countries when the state border and the customs service were at a high level; it existed, but it was of a primarily political or purely criminal (drugs, arms) nature. In countries that have undergone the post-Communist transformation, contraband also includes ordinary commercial goods. These goods are contraband only because they cross the border without customs being paid for them. However, in the majority of instances, this does not mean that smugglers pay nothing; customs officials accept bribes from them for their "services."

The fictitious economy also remains in force, although the mechanism of its functioning has undergone fundamental changes. While in the past, *deltsy* artificially increased the pay of their workers or hired fictitious workers, dividing pay increases in the former instance and pocketing all pay in the latter, the official wage in almost all commercial structures today is several times lower than the sum actually paid or workers' employment is not formalized at all—officially, they receive no pay whatsoever. Both employers and workers benefit from this arrangement. The former pay the state almost no social withholdings—they are charged against the wage fund—while the latter pay no income tax or pay only a meager part of it.

The *post-deltsy* and their successors have not forgotten the art of producing inferior, substandard, and even unsafe products. By offering these pseudoproducts for lower prices, they capture considerable segments of the market and receive significant incomes, to the detriment of consumers' interests.

Post-deltsy demand state assistance, citing many reasons; enterprises are now getting back on their feet. As a result of severed economic ties, they cannot sell their products. The government, acting "under the dictates" of the IMF and the World Bank, has allowed foreign capitalists to seize domestic markets, and so forth.

The *post-deltsy* indeed proved to be unready to work under the new conditions. They did not understand that on the same counter next to inferior and high-priced goods there can be goods that are priced the same or lower and of much higher quality. In order to be victorious in the competitive struggle, they must either lower prices and improve quality of goods produced or else erect a "Great Wall of China" against their competitors. Unfortunately, very few post-Communist businessmen think about the first path. It is much easier to persuade the authorities to pursue a strong protectionist policy, thereby restricting competition on the part of foreign producers. The "patriotism" of the *post-deltsy* and their followers bodes significant losses in the level of well being of the citizens of post-Communist countries.

One type of state support for domestic production in all countries, including post-Communist countries, is state purchases. Here, too, the *post-deltsy* have found a loophole for their shady plans. Naturally, this is not done without the help of state officials. The transaction is simple: The state buys the products of a given enterprise for artificially inflated prices, and this increase in price is divided between participants in the transaction.

A number of post-Communist countries entering the transitional economy are preserving types of shadow activity, such as the thefts of materials, resources, and other means of production. If some kind of explanation can be found with respect to state enterprises that have not yet been privatized, the situation in which the enterprise owner himself steals his own property seems paradoxical. This is done so that products can be produced on the side and will be left out of the reckoning. Thus, to the *post-delets* way of thinking, one of the principal ways of earning money continues to be theft, even if it is of one's own property.

Many enterprises continue to work using resources accumulated earlier, in excess of the norm. It should hardly be considered that the *deltsy* knew that, in principle, the end of a communist-type economy was possible, but if these enterprises also work, then this would be at the expense of the recent shadow activity of *deltsy*.

The formation of new independent states reveals the need to form new economic institutions of statehood and to pursue appropriate economic policy. In the process, it frequently becomes possible for *post-deltsy* to earn illegal money. The licensing and establishment of quotas for export-import transactions graphically exemplify this. It is generally recognized that some goods and services (especially arms, drugs, etc.) should be produced and delivered under strictest state control, but there is no economic substantiation for controlling exports and imports of conventional goods, and, most importantly, this creates favorable conditions for corruption and extortion.

In the period of post-Communist transformation, the state quite often meets the newly made businessmen half way, offering various benefits, especially in the area of taxation. This step directly promotes the emergence of shadow activity.

Obviously, the state cannot grant benefits to everyone, lest it be left without means to exist. Therefore, only a very limited group of people enjoys these benefits. Let us assume that the authorities have decided to extend tax privileges to a particular firm. Losses in national budget revenues must not be high. However, after the privileges have been introduced, the *post-deltsy* try to extend these benefits to any activity, and as a result of underground deals, virtually the entire economy is swallowed up in this hole.

The most complex part of the shadow economy remains the black economy.

It must be noted that, despite the possibility of legalizing their activity, the majority of "black," unofficial enterprises found themselves in a difficult situation; many of them simply ceased to exist, which once again demonstrated the inability of the *post-deltsy* to work without state support, when resources were centrally distributed.

After the communist-type economy collapsed, there was a major chance for goods produced in the black economy to emerge from the shadows. However, at the beginning of post-Communist economic reforms, stores in many countries were almost entirely bare. If only one part of trade (trade in scarce, primarily imported products) had hitherto been part of the black market, with the beginning of the reforms, the entire market became black. So-called merchandise markets, where practically everything could be purchased, were legalized, but almost no one officially paid taxes.

Nor do large trade facilities that have either already been privatized or are in the process of being privatized relinquish their positions. They continue to carry on both official and unofficial trade. But if there were previously only goods of a certain list price on the counter and everything else was sold under the counter (at higher prices), in the initial stage of the reforms, absolutely all goods were on the counter, even though some of them were not registered. There are cases in which products produced on the side sell for lower than officially registered prices.

Due to the lack of a corresponding legislative base and with the tacit consent of the authorities, some post-Communist countries have created private companies, which, according to the pyramid principle, attracted the population's money (interest was paid to investors from newly attracted money). After pocketing large sums of money, the heads of these companies either fled the country or landed in prison. As regards financial responsibility to the numerous investors, in some post-Communist countries it had to be assumed by the state.

One of the "novelties" of the economy undergoing transformation was a return to cash money. The reason for this was not only tax evasion but also interruptions in the work of banks when ordinary remittances of money were carried out with long time delays. Therefore, many who had money in their bank accounts prefer to revive their money and pay with cash that they carry in their suitcases. Demand emerges for cash money, and together with it there is new, highly profitable business in converting bank money to cash on the basis of the bribery mechanism.

One more novelty appeared in the development of the shadow economy: free economic zones. By design, the free economic zone was intended to attract progressive technologies with the aim of promoting economic growth in a certain region of the nation. Unfortunately, it was specifically the free economic zones that accounted for the majority of international financial crimes. In many post-

Communist countries, the largest flow of "shadow" money from virtually the entire world passes through companies registered in free economic zones for its subsequent legalization.

In some post-Communist countries, in observance of "social fairness," privatization vouchers were issued to the population. Due to a lack of appropriate institutions, the great majority of the vouchers ended up in the hands of the shadow persons, who were thereby able to control the supply of and demand for vouchers and hence their prices (e.g., Papava, 1995b).

In many post-Communist countries, where voucher privatization was carried out on the black market, vouchers were purchased from the population for a price that was several times lower than the actual price. Therefore, many times more former state property ended up in the hands of shadow persons than they could acquire for its nominal value; the share proclaimed by the state of the entire population in privatized property was concentrated in the hands of crafty shadow speculators who paid no taxes.

In summary, it may be concluded that the problems of the shadow (but not only the shadow) economy in countries with post-Communist capitalism are primarily connected with the lack of some market FIs and the weakness of others already in existence. Therefore, the creation and strengthening of FIs seem to be the top-priority tasks of the post-Communist transformation.

4.5. AN ECONOMIC APPROACH TO THE RESTRICTION OF CORRUPTION IN POST-COMMUNIST COUNTRIES

Corruption is one of the most pressing problems of modern society. It has become a priority for consideration by international organizations and more generally among politicians and scientists (Adams, Fitchett (eds.), 1992; Elliott (ed.), 1997; Klitgaard, 1998; Mauro, 1997a, 1997b; Negru, Ungurean, 2001; Rose-Ackerman, 1997; Tanzi, 1995, 1999; Thomas, 1999; Tullock, 1996; Waller, Verdier, Gardner, 2002; WB, 2000). It should be mentioned that the scientific analysis of this problem is often of secondary importance and gives way to political approaches to ways of suppressing corruption, not to mention proposals intended for populist effect.

It should be made clear from the very beginning what kind of event the corruption is from the economic point of view in post-Communist countries. This will help in the creation of an effective mechanism for its restriction.

It should be mentioned that corruption, as such, is a *secondary* phenomenon and it will be practically impossible to elaborate an effective mechanism for its restriction without revealing the economic reasons causing it.

One terminological aspect should also be discussed. Namely, as a general rule, in respect to corruption the word combination *to combat corruption* is used for what—in public opinion—is unacceptable *in principle,* because there are economic preconditions causing corruption, the fight against which, or against economy, is just nonsense. It is true that the various manifestations of corruption could be combated, which in a short period of time will have a camouflage-type pseudo-effect, but actually nothing will be changed. The main perpetrators of corruption will change, but the economic reasons causing corruption will remain untouched. At the same time, if one considers that the full disappearance of corruption in principle is impossible, then the right approach to the problem from a terminological point of view will be the word combination *the restriction of corruption.*

The nature of corruption in post-Communist capitalist countries differs from that of developed countries. This process is itself unique, as the corresponding economy is no longer a command one, but is not yet fully a market one either; and it is this that is directly reflected in the causes of corruption and its various manifestations.

In order to study the economic nature of corruption in countries with post-Communist capitalism, it will be appropriate to remember that the process of transition to a market consists of two complementary sub-processes. The first is *the achievement of macroeconomic stability* and the second is *the formation of the institutions appropriate to a market economy.* Unless these subprocesses reach their logical end, both of them may (and it is generally the case) become the cause of corruption in the post-Communist transformation of the economy (Papava, 2000c).

If the macroeconomic stability of the country has not been achieved, which can be revealed in a high rate of inflation and devaluation of the national currency and/or in considerable failure to collect tax revenues, then this creates the possibility of rapid earning of dirty money.

In this case, the management of the state banking system and persons close to them, having access to the state credits, are given "legally unlimited" opportunity to become rich through rapid currency or commodity transactions, with the help by means of devaluation of national currency and increases in prices. Unfortunately, Georgia has had a bitter experience in this respect, when in 1992–1994 the main form of corruption was rapid earning of dirty money (Gurgenidze, Lobzhanidze, Onoprishvili, 1994; Papava, 1996a; 1999).

Failure to collect revenues to finance the national budget is nothing other than directing them to the pockets of the tax collectors and their protectors. Conversely, an incomplete budget creates the productive grounds for the authorities of the state treasury to give priority to those persons who give a larger bribe while financing the budgetary expenses approved by the law. Low tax revenues are not able to ensure the relevant level of payment of the employees of the budgetary sector, and this is an objective reason for initiating corruption in high-level officials.

Therefore, post-Communist macroeconomic instability is quite a strong nourishing source for corruption.

As far as control of inflation, the achievement and maintenance of exchange rate stability is possible within quite a short period of time, this makes it possible to not only restrict but also to practically eradicate corruption in this field. The IMF has much experience with this and post-Communist countries, which have cooperated intensively with the IMF and achieved the positive results in a short period of time.

Georgia is one of the better examples of this. In 1994 cooperation with the IMF resulted in the successfully implemented money reform of 1995 (Papava, 1996a; 1999; Wang, 1998; Wellisz, 1996).

It is far more difficult to establish perfect order in a fiscal system. As proved by the international experience, there is practically no country in the world where concealment of revenues does not take place with the aim of evading the payment of taxes. Tax evasion is the main element of illegal activity in any country with a developed market economy (Svensson, 1983). In order to restrict corruption in this field the following is necessary: continuous improvement to the administration of taxation and customs systems; the development of taxation and customs legislation relevant to this process; and continuous education of the public in taxation and customs matters (Acconcia, D'Amato, Martina, 2003; Chander, Wilde, 1992; Papava, 2001d; Sanyal, 2000; Sanyal, Gang, Goswami, 2000; Shevardnadze, Chechelashvili, Chocheli, Khaduri, 2000; Wane, 1999).

As proved by the international experience, the reformation of a fiscal system requires much more than one year. A longer period is needed for the second constitutive subprocess of post-Communist transformation of the economy—the establishment of the institutions appropriate to the market economy. At the same time, the lack or imperfection and weakness of such institutions create possibilities for corruption. It should also be stressed that the creation of some institutions in a hasty way—for which, as a general rule, the direct copying of Western analogues is performed—does not prove right in most cases, not to mention the obvious adverse effects revealed in some cases. One of the relatively harmless examples of this in Georgia is the bankruptcy law, which is practically a copy of the German legislative model, drafted with the help of German experts and then adopted by the Georgian Parliament. Despite the general approval of foreign experts the law was *stillborn* from the very beginning, inasmuch as according to this law none of the *de facto* bankrupt enterprises was *de jure* bankrupt. After the improvement of this law its enactment was halted for an undetermined period of time by the Law on Tax Arrears Restructuring, the draft of which was prepared with the help of World Bank experts and which expresses the nationally detrimental interests of the most anti-reformatory wing, the industrial lobby of Georgia. It tries to demonize bankruptcy. Yet, it should be stressed that prolonging the operation of a bankrupt undertaking is equivalent to maintenance of bad management without any changes (something that destroys the developmental prospects of an undertaking). The tax arrears restructuring procedure is of a corrupt nature for enterprises, because the preparation of the draft of the approval on restructuring, consideration of deadlines, and other conditions in this draft are dependent upon a public official. Furthermore, the aforementioned lobby has been trying for years to introduce a mechanism for writing off the tax arrears, which will obviously be a step forward toward corruption in this field (unfortunately, the Law on Tax Amnesty was adopted by the Parliament of Georgia after the Rose Revolution).

In order to restrict corruption caused by the institutional vacuum that is characteristic of the post-Communist economic transformation, it is necessary to choose that main institution without which the establishment of a market economy will be impossible: the institution of private property.

The difficult process of establishing the institution of private property in a post-Communist transformation is the main cause of corruption and thus differentiates itself from the reasons for corruption in Western countries.

The creation of a liberal legal environment, necessary for the development of entrepreneurship, is the basis for the reinforcement of the institution of private property. It is also necessary to place all of the entrepreneurs, both local and foreign, in equal conditions in order for fair competition to be the only way of revealing the winner.

Primary accumulation of capital is taking place in the post-Communist capitalist countries. This process took place a long time ago in well-developed Western countries; without it, transition to a market economy is impossible.

History does not show any example of carrying out the process of primary accumulation of capital with "clean hands" and legality. This process is usually based on the phenomenon that today is considered corruption.

There is no (or almost no) objective economic basis for the corruption in the developed countries, because, first of all, high officials are provided with rather high wages and what is most important, they, as a general rule, already have capital accumulated by their ancestors, which, other things being equal, is a guarantee for their respectable existence and practically perfect institutions are already established in these countries. Despite this, it is still necessary to expose corruption in the ministers of the European Union (EU) or of any of its member states, the US, or Japan. In these countries they usually use *administrative methods* for the restriction of corruption, which is fully justified.

In the process of primary accumulation of capital, the use of mainly administrative methods with the purpose of restriction of corruption will inevitably fail. The introduction of a rule that every official should prove that his property has been legally acquired, and that in the absence of documentation of the origin of the property, its owner should be fined, or the property should be seized, et cetera will finally result in returning of the process of primary accumulation of capital to its point of origin. Launching this process all over again will prolong the "life" of corruption. Besides, as a result of imposing punitive measures a renewed process of primary accumulation of capital will be carried out in an even more disguised manner and will accordingly develop as a more hideous event. The main means of transformation of newly accumulated capital into property terms in post-Communist capitalist countries is home construction, or the creation of other immovable property. In this manner many people are employed and get remuneration for their work, construction materials are bought, and creates further employment to the workers of contingent enterprises, and so forth. If only punitive measures are introduced, the rate of bribery will be increased because of the increased possibility of disclosure (or risk-factor), and illegally gained money will not be transferred into property in these countries, but it will flow out abroad. In other words, corruption will not be restricted, but its main perpetrators will change and the society will be deprived of the indirect effect of the primary accumulation of capital.

In order to restrict corruption and establish the institution of private property, it is necessary to legalize the existing results of primary accumulation of capital, which will let it "act" in the public interest.

Such an approach does not exclude the punishment of all the lawbreakers according to the law, provided the very important constitutionally recognized principle of presumption of innocence is not violated.

Measures for restricting corruption should be carried out in law enforcement agencies with particular care, and to this end institutional reforms should be carried out together with the financial stimulation of the officers. Otherwise, the agencies intended for the maintenance of order may become the initiators of an extension of corruption or, in an even worse case, institutions of political settlement (e.g., the epoch of Stalin, when—because of the well known events of 1937—many persons who had divergent thoughts, a veritable army of innocent people, were subjected to repression and worse).

From this point of view, special care is needed in regard to the establishment of any anti-corruptive institution, or institution having special rights (namely the right of criminal prosecution and investigation) for combating corruption. In conditions of weakness in the institutional arrangement of the state, such an institution may very well become a shelter for corruption. Unfortunately there are many examples of this in the world. Only the creation of an institution with coordinating functions is acceptable, which at the same time can monitor the measures to be carried out for the purpose of restriction of corruption.

With a view to the restriction of corruption, it is very important to comply with the principle of publicity, which should ensure the provision of society with maximum information regarding current processes in order to increase the efficiency of the measures to be carried out.

Corruption is a contagious disease with which a whole society may be more or less sick—the appropriator of collected taxes, the thief of the treasury, or the ordinary citizen who does not pay for electricity. Unfortunately, even media cannot avoid this disease, when financially powerful clans (some of them political in nature) can bribe them and dictate the dissemination of information to the public. This is caused by the existence of disorganized state institutions and by grave economic conditions in a country, when the press and television have difficulty surviving independently. Despite this, only the press and the television are efficient instruments that could be used for exposing corruption, through the state promotion of competition between them.

Finally, as corruption is a secondary phenomenon, overcoming poverty by means of economic growth should be the main objective of the country. This is the precondition for restricting the economic basis of corruption.

5

The Theory of Market Equality and Its Application to the Process of Post-Communist Transformation

Those who attempt to level never equalize.

Edmund Burke
(1729–1797; Irish-born Whig politician and man of letters)

5.1. ON THE CONCEPT OF EQUALITY

The cornerstone of social policy is the achievement of equality, or at least an approximation thereof. However, there is no single, generalized, widely accepted definition of equality. Several aspects of equality are distinguishable: equality before God, equality of opportunity, and equality of outcome (Friedman, Friedman, 1990, Ch. 5), among others. The term *inequality*, which reflects a widespread public perception of the actual state of affairs in regard to equality, is more often practiced. Socially, inequality may be taken to mean conditions under which people do not have the same access to public goods, money, prestige, and power as others.

It should be also emphasized that the term *equal* does not mean "the same." The same is always equal, but equal can mean the same only in exceptional cases.

We know that absolute equality among people is fundamentally impossible because people differ from each other in their physical characteristics, opportunities, and mental capabilities; that is, people are different by nature (e.g., von Mises, 1981, Ch. 3). At the same time, as individuals they are equal before God, in that each is his own master insofar as he does not infringe upon the analogous rights of others (Friedman, Friedman, 1990, pp. 129–131). Posing the question this way leads to a definition of equality of opportunity (Friedman, Friedman, 1990, pp. 131–134) in which no one has the right to arbitrarily prevent others from taking advantage of their opportunities to achieve their goals. And these opportunities should be determined exclusively by their capabilities, regardless of origin, nationality, skin color, religion, gender, and so forth. In practice, equality before God and equality of opportunity are protected by policies that defend the principle of equality before the law (Friedman, Friedman, 1990, p. 132).

The idea of equality of outcome became especially popular in the twentieth century (Friedman, Friedman, 1990, pp. 134–146). The concept of fair distribution can be very hard to define, and the only way to explain its content is unrealistic in practice: when all members of society receive the "same share," which they will perceive as their "fair share." Generalizing all of the possible approaches to defining equality of results, it can be concluded that it is understood not as identity but proportionality of goods to the merits of each individual (Sorokin, 1959). In my opinion, such a definition of equality of outcome harbors a veiled uncertainty: It can be just as hard to define the concept of proportionality of distribution in the social sphere as it is to define the concept of fair distribution mentioned above.

At the theoretical level, contemporary economists understand equality as equality of opportunity (Roemer, 1996, p. 179), despite the fact that, for ordinary people, equality is primarily about equality of income and property. So it should not be surprising that, for the person on the street, reform involves redistributing wealth in order to make the distribution of income and property more equal (von Mises, 1981, Ch. 16). The danger is that such reforms and their associated rhetoric can ultimately destroy the economy. Measures to promote equality are typically followed by some people squandering their share, while others get rich, so that the problem of restoring equality is placed on the agenda once again, and so on. People with an improvident attitude toward their property in such circumstances have no incentive to change their behavior, and those who are frugal and industrious will not want to preserve these qualities (von Mises, 1981, Ch. 16). International experience shows that, in the end, there is no way, not even terror, to establish equality of results in society. This has created an atmosphere of hopelessness, a recognition that people are unfair, that it is not in the government's power to correct inequality, and that there will always be inequality. According to von Mises (1981, Ch. 30), equality of outcome can only be evaluated subjectively.

The market, as one facet of the economic foundation of capitalism, is often asserted to be the basis of inequality among people (Friedman, Friedman, 1990, pp. 146–148). Not only were Karl Marx and his (conscious and unconscious) successors (communists) convinced of this but it can also be said to be held as truth in the contemporary Western economic worldview. Economics textbooks are the evidence of this. The market is characterized as a dispassionate mechanism that has no conscience or moral standards. It has been argued that markets lead to high levels of income inequality (McConnell, Brue, 1990, Ch. 37), that equality of opportunity is just some fine talk of modern democracy, while in real life market conditions create rich and poor (Samuelson, Nordhaus, 1995, Ch. 20), that the market distributes wealth unevenly and inequality is a consequence of capitalism, even though it is pointed out at the same time that the citizens of communist countries are also not equal (Milanovic, 1998, pp. 12–22). However, I assert that their inequality is due to these countries' political systems. It is therefore not surprising that current economics textbooks (e.g., Fischer, Dornbusch, Schmalensee, 1988, Ch. 20; Mankiw, 1998, Ch. 20; McConnell, Brue, 1990, Ch. 37; Samuelson, Nordhaus, 1995, Ch. 20), not to mention textbooks on economic development (e.g., Todaro, 1994, Ch. 5) or labor economics (e.g., Ehrenberg, Smith, 1994, Ch. 15) place special significance on problems of income inequality.

This approach to the issue of equality is even more problematic in post-Communist countries, where the person in the street has trouble figuring out how much equality there should be in a market system (Milanovic, 1998, pp. 40–59). There is therefore the need to analyze whether the market mechanism really is antithetical to the idea of equality, or just to the principle of equality of outcome. Rethinking this problem will make it possible to establish a new theoretical and political construct—*a doctrine of market equality* (Papava, 2004), which, among other things, is particularly important for the post-Communist transformation. As is known, there are two types of markets in economic theory: free and real. In my opinion, a *pseudoreal market,* in which the "visible hand" of the state operates ideally, needs to be separated from the category of real markets. This question will be addressed in detail below. While the free-market model is only an abstraction (i.e., a theoretical construct crystallized for research purposes), it is on the basis of this ideal model that the initial concept of market equality ought to be broken down.

5.2. MARKET EQUALITY IN THE FREE-MARKET MODEL

In their most concise form, the basic criteria of a free market can be formulated as follows:

1. Absolutely unimpeded access to the market for buyers and sellers, and equally unimpeded departure from it, which is equivalent to having an unlimited number of participants in competition;

2. Absolute mobility of all types of resources (labor, material, financial);

3. Complete market information (on supply and demand, prices, etc.) for each competitor;

4. Absolute uniformity of similar products (there are no trademarks or any individual quality characteristics of goods);

5. Inability of competitors to influence the decisions made by other market participants.

The basic principle in this system is *laissez faire* ("let it be"), as a result of which the efficiency of interrelations among businessmen, between businessmen and consumers, and the dynamics of private and public interests are governed, in Adam Smith's terminology, by the "invisible hand," and which can be described as the theorem of efficiency thereof (Barr (ed.), 1994, Ch. 2). These criteria allow us to analyze the equality of market agents and whether or not they interact with each other on equal terms.

According to the first criterion, all buyers and sellers are *equal* in terms of access to the market and departure from it, since each of them can do this absolutely unimpeded. Consequently, in free-market conditions, all buyers and sellers are equal from the point of view of being *in* the market. Absolute mobility of all types of resources *equalizes* free-market agents from the point of view of market-dictated change in their type of business. Complete market information for each competitor is no less important from the point of view of their *equality*, since this precludes the possibility of erroneous actions on their part due to incomplete information. Absolute uniformity of products of the same kind puts all business-men on equal footing in selling their products, and all consumers on an equal footing in making their purchases. Because none of the competitors can impose their terms on other market agents, they have equality from the point of view of making decisions.

Thus, the free market model implicitly posits complete equality of opportunity for the agents participating in it. That is, *in free-market conditions, market equality means equality of opportunity for each agent from the point of view of being in the market, changing his type of business, access to complete information, production and purchase of products of the same kind, and decision making*. In short, I can say, that a free market is a system of equality of opportunity. Market equality could naturally be realized in practice in conditions of market equilibrium, if all of the opportunities that this equality offers are used to the fullest extent. Since such a free market is a theoretical construct, market equality in free-market conditions is also an ideal state, to which market regulation should aspire.

5.3. MARKET EQUALITY IN THE PSEUDOREAL-MARKET MODEL

In spite of the attractiveness of the free-market model, it is not capable of solving some very important problems, known as market failure. Among these problems, there are three that are primary:

1. Externalities;
2. Public goods (as well as significant quasi-public goods);
3. Providing the economy with the necessary quantity of money.

Externalities are present when the actions of one person affect the welfare of others, in either a positive or negative way. When a person makes a decision to renovate the facade of his house, the result has a positive externality for others who receive aesthetic pleasure from the building's appearance. On the other hand, environmental degradation from chemical production creates negative externalities.

In both cases, the principle of equality of market agents is violated:

- In the former case, the person whose actions create the positive externality suffers a loss, insofar as the positive effect that is redistributed to others does not involve any effort on their part;

- In the latter case, everyone affected by the negative effect suffers a loss, insofar as whoever creates this negative externality (e.g., in the form of chemical production) receives an economic benefit, while the others are left in a worse situation (e.g., due to chemical wastes).

In order to minimize inequalities due to externalities, the government interferes in the market because the market is incapable of solving this problem on its own. In this situation, the government may use administrative regulation or internalization of the externality. According to the first method, a special government agency could either completely prohibit a certain negative effect (e.g., a prohibition on allowing chemical wastes to get into the drinking-water system, thus criminalizing such acts), or set an upper limit on it (e.g., establishing maximum limits of chemical wastes for each chemical enterprise). The second method uses economic incentives to impose private costs on the originators of externalities. Internalization of negative externalities can take the form of special per unit taxes charged (e.g., per ton of chemical waste), which are known in the economic literature as Pigou taxes. Such taxes give the producers of negative externalities an incentive to reduce this effect. As for internalization of positive externalities, the government can put subsidy mechanisms in place for this purpose, which provide an incentive for producers not to curtail them. By using these methods to reduce inequalities due to externalities, the government can make the inequalities less severe, although it cannot achieve full equality.

As I pointed out above, a free market is not capable of producing public goods, since the marginal costs associated with additional consumption of these goods are zero. Public goods can therefore be used without incurring any cost in doing so. Since the private sector has no direct interest in producing them, this has to be done by the public sector. Consequently, public goods are carriers of positive externalities, which contribute to inequality. Noncompetitive or nonexclusive goods (e.g., streets and highways, police and fire departments, libraries, and museums) are known as quasi-public. They can be produced by the private sector, but in insufficient quantities due to the positive externalities. This forces the public sector to join in the production of quasi-public goods. Club goods, where a club is understood as a voluntary association of people to obtain common use or benefit on a shared basis, are one type of quasi-public goods. By their nature, club goods are public (because they are used equally by all of the club members), but membership fees or dues and other possible restrictions make it possible to localize these goods within a given private group, which in principle precludes the need for the public sector to interfere in the production of these goods (Cornes, Sandler, 1996, pp. 33–34).

Equality ought to be the government's basic principle in the production of public (and quasi-public) goods: these goods should be equally accessible to all members of society. Public goods associated with egalitarianism (see Ch. 6, 5.6), that is, the social solidarity that is associated with supporting the disadvantaged, are particularly important in this respect (Papava, 1993, 1994). The attainment of so-called vertical equality (Barr (ed.), Ch. 2) through social transfers that provide for a social safety net, unemployment, and veterans' benefits, government programs for free health care, public housing, and the like is a justification for producing egalitarian public goods (Papava, 1993).

The third important, generally acknowledged problem is that the free market is incapable of providing the economy with the necessary quantity of money; although it has been shown theoretically that it is not only possible but also economically more efficient to transfer this function from the government to the market (Hayek, 1976).

In addition to these three basic problems, the government is obliged to promote free competition by eliminating barriers to market entry, in order to promote the free dissemination of market information and unobstructed flow of capital. The government has particularly important functions here, such as creating a legal framework and social atmosphere that support the functioning of the market system and stabilize the economy (primarily by achieving low levels of inflation and high levels of employment). The government also regulates international economic relations, prevents potential conflicts between economic agents within the country, directly manages the economy in emergency situations (e.g., during a war), and devises long-term development programs. Consequently, in the conditions of a real market, Adam Smith's invisible hand is replaced by the visible hand of the state (Sirkin, 1968).

Externalities, inadequate supplies of public goods, and restrictions on flows of information and capital by monopolistic entities prevent markets from ensuring equality of opportunity for its participants. Market equality is thereby disturbed. In this case, the state should minimize deviations from free-market principles and maximize market equality. Since in reality the visible hand of the state itself may often impede market equality, policies devoted to achieving market equality are the same kind of theoretical construct (and just as necessary) as the free-market model. To differentiate the market model described above from the real market, I will call the former a model of a *pseudoreal market* in which the visible hand of the state is not only called upon to minimize market inequality, but actually does so.

5.4. MARKET EQUALITY IN THE REAL-MARKET MODEL

There is more than one textbook on the activity of the visible hand of the state that presents the generalized rich experience of studying this problem in a concentrated form (e.g., Atkinson, Stiglitz, 1980; Stiglitz, 1986). The best tool for analyzing the capability and efficiency of the visible hand of the state is "public choice" theory (Buchanan, Tollison (eds.), 1972; Buchanan, Tullock, 1962), which explains why a pseudoreal market differs from a real one. The underlying principle of public choice theory is that people act the same in their roles as public figures as they act as individuals. The visible hand of the state is seen as the visible action of high government and political officeholders. If the actions of this visible hand do not minimize inequality, then, other conditions being equal, this is due to the people who took up the burden of performing the function of the visible hand of the state, and—in so doing—have disgraced it.

The term *homo economicus* (economic man) has been adopted in the economics literature to describe a human action in a market economy (Avtonomov, 1998; Becker, 1976; von Mises, 1996).

Public choice theory argues that public officeholders are also motivated primarily by considerations of personal gain. This implies political rent seeking, which means seeking and protecting economic rent (i.e., payments for a share of some production factor exceeding its opportunity cost). Subsidies are the most graphic example of political rent. Subsidies allow *homo economicus* holding public office to obtain support in elections from voters who are the recipients of these subsidies and thus to receive political rent. This is despite the fact that these subsidies are intended to internalize positive externalities, which should signal their creators not to curtail these externalities. Political officeholders' restrictions on competition by imposing certain taxes, as well as systems of bans, quotas, and licensing on imports, are also striking examples of political rent seeking. These policies may distort market prices and create political rent, thereby potentially disturbing market equality. According to Becker (1971), the most inhumane example of disturbance of market equality is economic discrimination, which is manifested in the fact that individuals of different race, nationality, gender, and/ or age have different opportunities to get jobs, be promoted, receive adequate pay and raises, get an education, and so forth.

Theories of economic discrimination differ according to the perceived source of discrimination. According to one theory, discrimination comes from personal bias; according to another, from statistical bias; and to a third, monopoly power (Ehrenberg, Smith, 1994, Ch. 14). Still, it is widely understood that discrimination is associated with buyers and with the visible hand of the state. Discrimination by buyers is based on prejudice, and it is difficult to justify on economic grounds because discrimination as such is economically unprofitable for businessmen (Ehrenberg, Smith, 1994, Ch. 14). For example, catering to racist buyers may mean that an employee of one race has to be paid more than an employee of another, which can in turn distort market prices and take away part of the businessman's profits. This would ultimately harm the economy as a whole.

When public officeholders introduce policies on the basis of such prejudices in order to seek political rent, they are legitimizing discrimination. The recipients of political rent in a racist government may be, for example, the white members of the population. Although the existence of racial discrimination was formally denied in the formerly communist countries, it is now understood that this was not the case, due to gender and ethnic inequality; in addition to other problems, this one needs to be resolved in the process of post-Communist transformation (Meurs, 1998).

Among the ways of obtaining political rent, lobbying (when, based on propaganda for a certain policy, people in power put into practice measures that favor the interests of their backers, i.e., voters), and logrolling (when legislators trade votes in order to reach particular outcomes) are worthy of particular attention. Consequently, in the final analysis, realization of the government's official goals leads to both predicted and unforeseen consequences.

The theory of public choice explains why the visible hand of the state is incapable, in many cases, of accomplishing one of its basic purposes: eradication of market inequality. When local authorities initiate particularly unacceptable manifestations of market inequality, the "invisible foot" effect (Gordon, 1983) (as well as the Tiebout (1956) model) begins to operate in the form of people changing their place of residence in order to improve their living and working conditions (Fischer, Dornbusch, Schmalensee, 1988, Ch. 21). The situation is somewhat more complicated when unacceptable manifestations of market inequality are initiated by central authorities, but now even this can be overcome, because the invisible foot effect is also manifested at the international level when people migrate from one country to another for such reasons.

In conditions of the real market, market mechanisms are key to overcoming market inequality. Market equality can only be established on the basis of market democracy. So the key function of the visible hand should be to weaken as much as possible the forces obstructing the free market, via the establishment of democratic institutions. This is a rather difficult task, involving not only economic issues but also national, historical, cultural, and social ones.

5.5. MARKET EQUALITY IN THE POST-COMMUNIST TRANSFORMATION

The issue of market equality is especially critical for countries in the process of post-Communist transformation, because the market as such is itself in the formative stage. And because the market is not yet fully formed, it is almost impossible to have market equality. At the same time, because the market is in the formative stage, steering a proper course toward the ideals of market equality from the very beginning is particularly important.

The quest to achieve equality of outcome was a distinguishing feature of the communist period. Realization of this principle was seen as the highest achievement of the economic system, and all state institutions promoted equality of outcome and the creation of a "new man" to this end (O'Brien, 1989), even though, in reality, there was no equality of results. Indeed, as I pointed out above, there can be none in principle.

Partially because of privatization, but mostly thanks to newly created private organizations, *homo economicus* gradually began to appear in the course of the transition. Such people, unfortunately, do not constitute the majority in post-Communist society, and do not set the political and economic climate. The majority is instead represented by those who subconsciously fear the state and expect it to help them, while at the same time demanding freedom of action and a democratic government. These are individuals who have not been able to completely free themselves of the principle of equality of outcome while beginning to aspire to the principle of equality of opportunity. Such a man, *homo transformaticus*, is the driving force in the process of post-Communist transformation. The entrepreneurs that did appear in post-Communist countries as a result of "nomenklatura privatization" are more accurately called *post-deltsy* (see Ch. 3, 3.4).

In conditions of more or less mature market relations, public office is generally held by people of the *homo economicus* type. By way of contrast, in post-Communist societies these officeholders are of the *homo tranformaticus* type. Since, during the post-Communist transformation, the new institutions needed for a market economy are still in their formative stage (see Ch. 4), the political rent-seeking mechanisms that take hold during this time diverge from those found in mature market systems. In a post-Communist society, political rent seeking takes four basic forms: speculation, subsidization of imports, soft credits, and *nomenklatura* privatization. Together they determine the "rent-seeking behavior" (Åslund, 1996) of *homo transformaticus*. These four types of behavior are characterized as follows (Åslund, 1996, pp. 101–102):

1. From the beginning of the post-Communist transformation, when not all prices had yet been freed, public officeholders and/or their representatives bought up cheap goods in short supply and resold them at the market price;

2. At the beginning of the transformation, due to the multiplicity of exchange rates, public officeholders and/or their representatives bought foreign exchange cheaply and then sold imported goods at the market price;

3. In the initial stage of the transformation, the system of soft government loans was still in place. The only people who received these loans were public officeholders and/or their representatives;

4. Public officeholders artificially lowered the prices of assets being privatized in a non-transparent manner, thanks to which these very people or their representatives, or those who paid them a bribe, became the new owners.

The economic roots of this rent-seeking behavior lie in the fact that the communist system itself was by nature a peculiar form of kleptocracy (Åslund, 1996, p. 104).

According to the well-known Peruvian economist Hernando de Soto, a state that is excessively bureaucratized, ignores laws and practices, and is engaged in redistributing national income (rather than creating the conditions needed for its production), can be classified as mercantilist (De Soto, 1989). Since the visible hand of a mercantilist state was needed to begin the post-Communist transformation, prospects for market equality were not good from the very beginning. As the transformation develops and the institutional vacuum begins to be filled, these types of political rent seeking give way to types more typical of a market economy. After prices are liberalized, exchange rates unified, the system of soft loans abolished, and mass privatization completed, these sources of political rent cease to exist. Progress toward attaining the ideal of market equality depends on the extent to which free market and democratic principles are observed.

5.6. Egalitarian Goods, Egalitarianism, and Privatization in Post-Communist Countries

According to the opinion established in economic theory, transfer payments are not connected with production; they only redistribute income and thus they appear as nonproductive transactions (e.g., McConnell, Brue, 1990, Ch. 8).

But this problem may be viewed in a different way. The market mechanism results in great property inequality: owners of large capital, landlords, highly paid persons, and rich heirs possess considerable amounts of wealth. Beside them are the unemployed, aged, et cetera whose incomes in the market system are either very small or nonexistent. The division of society into rich and poor is not the result of the market system alone. In the history of humanity many there have been many cases in which market restrictions led to the property stratification of society: medieval Europe, India under British occupation, and the FSU are prime examples of this (Friedman, Friedman, 1980).

Nobody is protected from future disability, unemployment, and so forth, to say nothing of old age. These are the main motivations of well-off people ready to help those with the lowest standard of living. It must be noted that, in the history of the family, there are no firm tendencies toward enrichment and impoverishment and that all these tendencies work in a specific period of time (Sorokin, 1959).

The government pays benefits to all those people (unemployed, aged, etc.) through transfer payments. All these means are obtained from taxes on people with sufficiently high incomes. In this way, it can be said that the "Robin Hood effect" is created. What is the government's motivation in this case?

Friedrich Hayek (1988) asserted in theory that if this is done to achieve socialist aims, it is unjustified because they cannot be realized. I would assert that it has been practically demonstrated in the East European countries, and the latest proof is the breakdown of the USSR.

Especially in Western Europe, the highly developed countries of the Americas, Asia, and also in many non-Communist countries, the aforementioned activity is motivated to provide social security by overcoming poverty and decreasing inequality of income.

Modern—even the most developed—societies disintegrate into separate social groups according to income level. The result is that there are the well-off as well as the poor. Unemployment is one of the undesirable results of the market, among others.

Wars cause the survivors different problems (loss of health, time, etc.). I could easily continue listing similar groups of people.

The market mechanism is unable to solve the economic problems of these social groups. The latter can cause social upheaval in aiming to redistribute wealth. Society is interested in avoiding such social cataclysms no less than in providing national defense or purity of social environment.

Both national defense and purity of environment are public goods. It is possible to say that transfer payments resulting in public goods are, to my mind, of the egalitarian type. *Egalitarian goods* are a social security achieved by overcoming poverty and decreasing inequality of incomes. Creation of this good is based on the development of social insurance and benefits to war veterans and the unemployed, a state program of free medical aid, state housing construction, et cetera. Egalitarian goods as well as national defense or purity of environment are noncompetitive and nonexcluded goods; they meet the criteria for determination of this or that good's affiliation to public goods (Papava, 1993, 1995).

Overwhelming diligence in overcoming poverty by means of redistribution of wealth, not to mention production efficiency, may mitigate against social security. This was experienced in England in the 1970s (Friedman, Friedman, 1980).

Therefore, only reasonable redistribution of wealth carried out by government secures social tranquility (i.e., production of egalitarian goods as a form of social goods).

Proceeding from the fact that egalitarian goods are a form of social goods, expenses for the latter are productive. Consequently, transfer payments, to counterbalance the widespread view, are productive transactions according to their nature (Papava, 1993, p. 60).

The state, as monopolist-feudal-lord (see Ch. 1), for decades advocated the idea of egalitarianism in the most deformed (i.e., equalizing) forms. It was reflected in post-Communist privatization (i.e., gratuitous distribution of the whole or part of property that has to be privatized). Such a way of privatization was chosen by many post-Communist countries.

Free distribution of property without change may have grave consequences for some people and also for the whole of society. The thing is that, if a person has not earned the property, but received it by means of expropriation from the state, then the property is considered to have been obtained for nothing, and thus the individual never worries about it. It must be taken into account that those who have been working hard all their lives can find themselves in a very unfavorable situation; namely, on seeing that everyone can possess property equally, regardless of their working ability, they can think that their work has not been properly recognized by society (because they receive the same amount of property as someone who did nothing), and therefore they lose the incentive to improve their work. Expropriation is inadmissible, both between individuals (as happened in the 1920s and 1930s in the FSU), and by the state.

Recently a "new" idea was put forward. It is a proposal that workers have already redeemed their share of state property and, thus, it must be given to them free of charge. One cannot exclude the possibility that some people, by their intensive work and low wages, could have redeemed some shares of state property. The problem lies in determining this share. It is indisputable that the number of working years cannot be the criterion for it. In the period of Soviet communism it was possible to do nothing at work and receive equal remuneration with others in most enterprises and organizations. Thus, it was practically impossible to give individuals real shares of property. And as it was practically impossible to determine the individuals who really redeemed their shares, there was an obligation to distribute state property to everyone free of charge.

Thus I have to admit that the principle of distributing the state property redeemed earlier was a concealed form of appropriation and, therefore, was not acceptable. This type of privatization of capital was unacceptable because it was practically impossible to choose any realistic principle according to which state property should be distributed. The use of the principle of equality, whether it concerns produced goods or property, cannot be accepted because it undermines any kind of economic incentive. Fundamental difficulties appear in a given scheme, when it is necessary to solve the problem of the property of those who in the near future will become adults and, therefore, will demand the same share of property for private use. Proper possibilities may be found for this, which means that distribution of equal, obtained for nothing (and therefore not economic) property would be repeated indefinitely and in turn would be the most unfavorable factor for establishing the attributes of a market economy.

In spite of the aforementioned deficiency, in many countries with post-Communist economic reforms, different systems of special official documents—called vouchers for privatization of state property—were actively used. A voucher gives all members of society the right to obtain, free of charge, an equal share of the value of privatized property. It was done in order to achieve social justice and social equality. Thus, this was an example of renewed communist ideas, and post-Communist economic reforms use the communist ideology in the most distorted forms of egalitarianism. Such "Neo-Bolshevism" promotes the formation of a deformed, quasi-communist market system.

Some Western countries have enjoyed good experiences of privatization. Unfortunately, most of the post-Communist countries could not use this experience immediately, because there was considerable discrepancy in the initial conditions of privatization between Western and post-Communist countries. In Western countries, where privatization has been realized, a well-developed market system, based on both private and state properties, has been included in the initial conditions. Consequently, the privatization policies of these countries have supposedly been founded on increasing the share of the private property to raise the efficiency of the market system.

The economic system of state-monopolistic feudalism, as mentioned earlier (see Ch. 1) was based only on state property. At the same time, the ideas of social equality permeated the mentality of most of the population of these countries; hence, it had considerable influence on the privatization policy of such countries.

In the system of voucher privatization, any owner of a voucher can exchange it for a share and become a shareholder. It is necessary to emphasize that this type of privatization policy has not been used in East Germany because of its unification with West Germany. Does this privatization policy (using vouchers) guarantee equal opportunities for all? Of course it does not.

First, some people already had considerable property and the distribution of vouchers equal in value to the whole population cannot erase the property discrepancy between the rich and the poor. Second, the total nominal value of the vouchers was equal only to the part of state property exposed to privatization. This means that in the best case, if all citizens exchange their vouchers for shares, most of them will become the owners of very little property. Consequently, the creation of equal opportunities for the whole population (in other words, the communist tendencies toward equality) as the main target of privatization has been unattainable point. On the other hand, this tendency was highly likely to lead to the undesirable consequences of increasing rates of inflation.

Most of the citizens of post-Communist countries are poor. These people have no ambition to become shareholders. They only need to buy some additional consumer goods. Hence, they were going to sell their vouchers to the rich, and the latter would become the owners. The sums of money held by the rich would change hands, because they would transfer to the poor. As a result, the structure of consumer demand would necessarily change: If the rich are ready to spend the sums of money on buying the shares, now their new holders, the poor, will spend these sums on buying consumer goods. Consequently, these sums of money will increase prices of consumer goods, which will give rise to inflation.

In many post-Communist countries, the market system has not been perfectly founded yet. There is a shortage of most consumer goods. In this case, the afore-mentioned inflation was going to become considerably higher. As a result the poor were going to become poorer. Unfortunately, the realization of such a privatization policy in post-Communist countries confirmed the situation described above.

5.7. Economic Policy for Market Equality in the Post-Communist Transformation

Economic policy is very important for achieving market equality. Economic policy is based on particular schools of political philosophy, among which can be distinguished utilitarianism, liberalism, and libertarianism. All three of these schools rule out the principle of income equality, although—according to the first two—economic policy should be aimed at bringing incomes toward a certain optimal level.

As a political philosophy, utilitarianism stems from the principle that the state should try to maximize total social utility, where utility is understood as a specific person's level of happiness or satisfaction, and is expressed in units of welfare. The assumption of diminishing marginal utility suggests that taking one dollar away from a rich person reduces his utility less than giving it to a poor person raises the latter's utility. Consequently, such income redistribution can raise total social utility. The greatest difficulty in this scheme lies in finding the optimal limit of redistribution, beyond which a person loses the incentive to create wealth, causing the whole society to suffer. Repeated violations of this limit on the part of the government are, unfortunately, not so rare. This suggests that pursuing utilitarian redistributive policies during post-Communist transformation—when the state has no relevant practical experience in utilitarian redistribution, and, when *homo transformaticus* still harbors nostalgia for the former pseudo-equality of incomes—is very risky. The likelihood of violating the optimal limit of income redistribution is very high.

According to the underlying principle of liberalism, the state should pursue a policy of supporting fairness. But since defining fair distribution is impossible, the practical implementation of liberal economic policies generally reflects an emphasis on maximizing the welfare of the poorest members of society (the minimax criterion). (By contrast, utilitarian economic policies seek to maximize the average utility of members of society.)

Libertarianism as a political philosophy (Boaz, 1998) is based on the principle that the state's primary duty is to punish criminals and assist in the implementation of voluntary agreements, but *not* to redistribute wealth. The goal of a libertarian economic policy is to protect human rights and provide equality of opportunity. *Economic policies in support of market equality are therefore based on libertarianism.*

The advantages of libertarian economic policies are apparent in the case of discrimination. A libertarian economic policy argues that the best way to overcome discrimination is through a competitive market, because in this case, in order to make more profits, businesses will hire those who will work most cheaply. This will ultimately raise their pay, thereby eliminating the discrimination.

One may ask, does a libertarian economic policy rule out social protection of the population? It is true that in conditions of a competitive market the poor have far more limited opportunities than the rich. At the same time, in theory free competition in no way precludes the realization of social and cultural goals, either in the form of private charitable activities or via special governmental assistance. The main thing here is for the government to focus on equality of opportunity rather than on wealth redistribution, while at the same time providing the public good of social stability.

Is pursuit of libertarian economic policies during post-Communist transformation appropriate? The fact that *homo transformaticus* is the primary actor in the process of post-Communist transformation dooms the use of libertarian economic policies in pure form to failure, because with *homo transformaticus*'s mentality *homo transformaticus* is not yet fully prepared to exist in an exclusively competitive system. *Economic policies in post-Communist countries should therefore combine elements of libertarianism and liberalism, provided that the former is predominant.* Libertarian economic policies will help the post-Communist transformation move toward the ideal of market equality, while the liberal economic policies supplementing them will allow society to avoid social tension and possible social explosions. The ultimate outcome would be the establishment of horizontal equality (Barr (ed.), 1994, Ch. 2), which in this context means:

- No businessman should experience more formal or informal support from the visible hand of the state than any other. This should be expressed in

maximum noninterference of the state in commercial activity, combined
with appropriately severe punishment for all lawbreakers;

- Social assistance from the state should be targeted at the poorest classes of
society.

Only in such circumstances can members of the middle class have the opportunity, through maximum application of their intellectual and physical capabilities, to gradually make a decent life for themselves. To do this, the government
needs to intensify its fight against corruption, legalize shadow businesses, and
accelerate the creation of democratic institutions. This will gradually move society closer to the ideal of market equality—equality of opportunity.

6

Economic Ability of a State and a Model of an Economy Without Taxes

The state is not "abolished," it withers away.

Friedrich Engels
(1820–1895; German socialist)

6.1. THE FIFTH FACTOR OF PRODUCTION

Economic theory devotes a special place to problems of the private and public sectors. When one speaks of a "market economy" in the narrow sense, one usually means the private sector, because its functioning is specifically based on so-called market principles. The public sector, however, is not based on the market: The distribution of the results of its work, that is, public (and quasi-public) goods, is not manifested in the form of their direct purchase and sale, but the financing of their production is in the nature of a forcible act because the state forces households and corporations to pay the taxes that serve as its source.

Here, to all appearances, it is appropriate to examine the terminological question of the legitimacy of using the term *state* instead of the term *government* that is often used in Western economic literature. It is easy to see that almost all the problems that the state sector must address go beyond the jurisdiction of the executive branch, requiring the participation of the legislative and, in some cases, the judiciary branches as well. For example, other things being equal, it is impossible to attain the legal base and social atmosphere needed for the market to function effectively without the intervention of the judicial branch.

Consequently, the government as an executive branch is not capable of "personally" resolving in full measure all the questions posed by the market system. It can therefore be considered more correct to say "state" instead of "government" when discussing the system's functioning.

In economic theory a most important place is given to the problem of taxes, though some economic schools have a negative attitude toward them and their role in the economic policy of state (Mill, 1976, Ch. 2; Friedman, 1982; Friedman and Friedman, 1980). It is known that taxes are intended for state expenses, which is why almost nobody doubts the necessity of taxation. At best, the question of abolishing particular types of taxation is discussed (Slemrod, Bakija, 1996). Problems of taxation are more complicated for countries that are in a situation of transition to a market system (Tanzi (ed.), 1993).

The goal of this chapter is to substantiate the fact that the state's economic activity is in reality an internal, immanent part of the market. Based on such a formulation of the question, one can take a fundamentally different approach to the problem of forms and methods of state economic activity in which, for all practical purposes, they do not differ in any way from the forms and methods of activity of other economic agents. This in turn requires rethinking the commonly accepted view of the market and the role of the state in the market system. In other words, the goal of this chapter is to substantiate the possibility of the public sector to function according to the principles of the private sector when, even if elements of force are present, they are minimal and concern only an insignificant part of society. I am talking about the construction of an economic model whereby the system of taxation may be replaced by a certain other system (which will be discussed below) that minimizes the element of force.

First of all, it is necessary to consider the results of state activity in the sphere of economic regulation, involving modification of one's understanding of the market.

In manuals there is a detailed description of the main features typical of a free market (see Ch. 5, 5.2); relations among entrepreneurs, relations between entrepreneurs and consumers, and the coincidence of private and public interests are regulated according to Adam Smith by an invisible hand.

It is known that a free market has never existed in the world and cannot exist. Such a sterile economy (as absolute competitive space) is an abstraction, a theoretical structure necessary only for research of market tendencies. A free market can only be a fragment of a real market.

In reality, the market processes (typical of a free market) are distorted under the influence of monopolistic formations (both natural and unnatural), inflation, requirements of trade unions, errors of entrepreneurs due to insufficient commercial information, and so forth. All these and other distortions of market processes are qualified as market failures.

It is generally acknowledged that state interference in market processes aims at removing market failure. As a result of this, the real market is a regulated (by the state) market.

According to views widely held in economic theory the activity of a state is not considered as an internal part of a market economy, but serves as a supplement to it. The state has to solve the economic problems that cannot be solved by a market. Thus, the economic activity of state can be considered as a forced supplement to the market. Such an approach is characteristic of both contemporary main economic trends: neoclassic and neokeynesian theories (Galbraith 1973, Ch. 3). The difference is in attitude toward the level, forms, and methods of state interference in the economy.

It is necessary to note that the mentioned goals of the state are not always reached; the more the interference of the state in the economy, the more specific behavior (e.g., lobbying or logrolling) it generates. It does not prevent market failure, but aggravates it. And it results in state failure (see Ch. 5, 5.4).

Proceeding from the definition of public goods as noncompetitive and nonexcluded it was shown that everything done by the public sector in order to regulate the market is nothing but public or quasi-public goods (Papava, 1994, pp. 38–40). Besides national defense or public order, among others, public goods include the absence or at least considerable reduction of external effects, the presence of necessary amounts of money in the economy, and abolition or at least considerable restriction of market power. Public goods also include the creation of a legal basis and public opinion to support and facilitate the market system, egalitarian goods (see. Ch. 5, 5.6), economic stabilization, goods produced by public utilities, and so forth.

It is necessary to note that, within the public sector of a country, enterprises producing private goods may also be included. They are known as quasi-public goods. For simplification I will not include the latter in my following considerations. Thus, the whole environment of goods can be divided into two main groups: public goods and private goods. Proceeding from the fact of who is the producer of these goods, the economy is divided into two sectors: private sector (producing private goods) and public sector (producing public goods).

According to the theory of factors of production, the receipts obtained from goods sold are distributed among factors of production.

Contemporary economic theory recognizes four factors of production: land, capital, labor, and entrepreneurial ability. Corresponding incomes for them are rent, interest, wages, and entrepreneurial profit (e.g., McConnell, Brue, 1990, Ch. 2). Besides these incomes the price of goods includes depreciation and indirect taxes. The latter is considered in economic theory as unearned state income (McConnell, Brue, 1990, Ch. 9) and this in turn partly calls into question the integrity of the theory of factors of production that divides the price of a good into income-producing factors: there arises a type of income (indirect business taxes) that does not have an economic basis. In order to overcome this contradiction, one must answer the question: Have all factors of production and the corresponding incomes been taken into account?

To all appearances, the answer to this question would be in the affirmative, if all interrelations among economic agents were determined on the basis of the *laissez-faire* principle, characteristic of the free market and of pure competition, and in the absence of state economic activity. In reality, however, this is how matters stand.

If an entrepreneur undertakes the initiative to include land, capital, and labor in the unified production of goods or (performance of) a service, the state undertakes the initiative of regulating the given entrepreneurial activity within the framework of the national economy. If an entrepreneur organizes the production of certain goods or services, then the state organizes the production of the entire mass of goods and services within the framework of the national economy. If an entrepreneur makes decisions (uses innovations, assumes risks in the process of running his own business), the state makes decisions on the main avenues of developing the entire national economy, uses innovations, and assumes risks in its own economic policy.

Much in the development of the modern economy and business depends on which political forces are in power within the state. For example, the assumption of power by conservatives in the USA and the UK in the late 1970s and early 1980s promoted the growth of economic activity in those countries, while seventy years of communist rule in the FSU doomed the market to a predominantly underground existence and brought the country to a state of deep crisis.

It can thus be concluded that the *economic ability of the state is the fifth factor of production* (Papava, 1993, 1994). This approach has been reflected by Griffiths and Wall (1995, p. 338; 1997, p. 358).

Notwithstanding the cited parallels, the similarity between entrepreneurial ability and the economic ability of the state is purely external; but internally there is a fundamental difference between them.

The entrepreneur deals both with material resources (land, capital) and with human (labor) resources, which he unites in a single production process; the state, however, primarily unites human resources—entrepreneurs—within the framework of the entire national economy.

By making basic decisions in the conduct of his business, the entrepreneur determines the course of activity of a specific firm. The decisions made by the state influence the strategy of development of all firms making up the national economy.

As an innovator, the entrepreneur develops the production of new products and introduces new technologies and new forms and methods of business organization. The state as an economic innovator, on the other hand, primarily introduces new forms and methods of monetary and tax policy, forms new institutional structures, and so forth.

In the process of operating his business, the entrepreneur assumes risk and, depending on how justifiable the risk is, receives an appropriate reward; bankruptcy may be the most lamentable variant of the development of events. The state, which guides the economy, also assumes risk, but of a somewhat different nature; the state does not have the right to such bankruptcy, when it is subject to self-destruction (although history contains a few examples of even this). And the receipt of as much economic profit as possible is the most significant reward to the entrepreneur for uninsured risk, whereas the reward for persons exercising state power is victory in elections in order to retain power for the next term.

Thus, if the state's economic ability acts as a factor of production, it should bring in a certain amount of revenue. This revenue is what is currently called indirect business taxes. As is known, these taxes raise the price of a product—a price that includes incomes, based on factors of production: land, labor, and entrepreneurial activity. Accordingly, I treat this price increase as revenue of the state, that is, as the fifth factor of production. *Recognition of the state's economic ability as a factor of production in turn makes it possible to give the status of state profit* (by analogy with entrepreneurial profit) *to indirect business taxes.*

In qualifying indirect business taxes as factor income, a question may arise about the state's receiving direct taxes, in addition, in exchange for its economic ability. In reality, direct taxes are part of other factor incomes and are subtracted from them after they are collected by the state. Unlike direct taxes, indirect business taxes are placed at the disposal of the state directly in exchange for the services reviewed above; indirect business taxes, like other factor incomes, are primary, while direct taxes are derivative incomes.

Proceeding from this, in the further considerations in this chapter, taxes are taken to mean *direct* taxes.

As distinct from McConnell and Brue (1990, Ch. 2), Fischer, Dornbusch and Schmalensee (1988, Ch. 8) consider only three factors of production: land, capital, and labor. Under such an approach, the understanding of profit is changed, as is often mentioned in economic literature (e.g., Babeau, 1985). But it does not influence at all the understanding of the economic ability of a state as a separate factor of production and establishing state profit as a corresponding income.

6.2. THE CONCEPT OF DOMINANT FACTORS OF PRODUCTION

The factors of production theory have a long history and it has changed a great deal since the time of A. Smith and J.B. Say. The "Concept of Dominant Factors of Production" is one of its modern versions (Eilon, Gold, Soesan, 1976, Ch. 2).

According to this concept, even though all factors of production are used in the production of each concrete good, one of them will become the dominant source of increase in the efficiency of production. Based on the dominance of factors, authors of the concept distinguish among three types of production: capital-dominant, material-dominant, and labor-dominant.

According to this approach, production processes in which production workers control and secure the functioning of machines and other basic equipment and secure the technological process are capital-dominant (or machine-dominant, as they are also called). Material-dominant processes are production processes in which the production potential depends on raw materials and supplies, land, and other natural resources, while labor, buildings, machinery, and equipment simply promote the realization of existing production potential. Labor-dominant processes are production processes in which manual labor and the skill level of workers are of paramount importance, hence machine tools, equipment, and all other elements of fixed capital perform an auxiliary function for these works.

Authors of this conception list, for example, electric power plants, cement plants, and blast furnaces as capital-dominant types of production. They classify agriculture and fisheries as material-dominant, and define bricklaying, made-to-order clothing, and carpentry as labor-dominant. Citing examples of production in which one or another set of factors is dominant, the authors acknowledge that because reality is so varied, extreme variants with a clearly pronounced dominance of a given factor of production comprise a limited number of modern production processes. Nevertheless, this kind of classification of the latter has great significance for the goals of applied analysis.

Obviously, as an example, one could even consider a case in which the dominance of factors changes during the production process. Specific examples of such a case are air shipments in which the production process during takeoffs and landings is labor-dominant but becomes capital-dominant when the plane gains altitude (particularly when the automatic pilot is engaged).

Having briefly characterized the conception of dominant factors of production, it is possible to make certain generalizations with regard to other factors of production—entrepreneurial ability and the economic ability of the state.

Entrepreneur-dominant production processes should include those in which paramount importance is attached to innovations, the realization of which is, as is known, connected with the entrepreneur's initiative, while other factors of production perform an auxiliary function *vis-à-vis* the innovative activity of the entrepreneur. A competitive environment promotes the diffusion of a given concrete type of innovation, as a result of which its newness levels off and, in the absence of other significant innovations, the corresponding production process ceases to be entrepreneur-dominant; the dominant status of entrepreneurial activity is replaced by the dominant status of some other factor of production.

Production processes in which the state's economic ability will be dominant can be identified by analogy with other factors of production. A production process in which the economic ability of the state is of decisive importance and all other factors of production perform a subordinate function is state-dominant. The production of public and quasi-public goods is naturally classified among state-dominant production processes. In a communist-type economy the production of private goods is the state-dominant production processes and transition to market economy can be explained as a transition from state-dominant to entrepreneur-dominant production processes.

The dominance of a given factor in some production process determines the dominance of income produced by a given factor compared with other factors of production. In capital-dominant production, in particular, interest is the dominant income; in material-dominant production, it is rent; in labor-dominant production, wages; in entrepreneur-dominant production, entrepreneurial profit; in state-dominant production, state profit.

6.3. ON THE FULL MARKET CONCEPTION

It is necessary to note that it is wrong to equate the economic ability of the state with the public sector. The difference is the same as that between entrepreneurial ability and the private sector. It is also essential to emphasize that only the economic ability of state is the factor of production and not state itself, the analogy here being with entrepreneurial ability as the factor of production, but not the entrepreneur in question. The economic ability of the state is only one of the features of the state, just as entrepreneurial ability is only one of the features of an entrepreneur.

As is known, the entrepreneur is an owner of produced private goods who receives a corresponding income by selling these goods.

The situation is the same with public goods: they belong to the state, which sells them and receives the corresponding income.

There is a considerable difference between the selling of private and public goods. Obtaining the first is usually done individually, whereas the second is done by a group of people. In spite of this, the payment for the public goods obtained is also made individually in the same way as that for obtaining the private goods. Namely, direct taxes are the price for public goods and these taxes are paid individually by households' corporations.

To produce public goods, it is necessary to meet certain expenses. The public sector possesses three main sources of these expenses; taxes, state loans (e.g., state bonds), and money emission. In more or less normally functioning states, taxes are the most important among these three sources.

Thus, taxes, on the one hand, are used to cover expenses of production of public goods and, on the other hand, they constitute the price for the consumption of these goods.

It is noteworthy that if taxes were not levied, then it would be impossible to produce the public goods necessary for society.

Production of private goods is not the same as receiving benefits for a consumer; the benefits are obtained after buying the goods. In contrast to this it is sufficient only to produce public goods in order to obtain corresponding benefits. This can be explained by the absence of interdependence between consumption payment and the actual consumption of these goods. Nonexclusion and noncompetitiveness of public goods create a real possibility for their consumption by certain people without paying corresponding taxes. Special tax inspections exist to fight against this. As a result, levying taxes becomes an act of violence.

As for taxation, the system under which everybody is interested in paying taxes, rather than trying to dodge them, is considered to be the best (Adams, 1993, 1998). For this, taxpayers must see their economic interests in the payment of taxes.

If a model of such a market can be created in which there is no coercive taxation, and the functioning of a public sector closely approaches that of the private sector, the model can be called a *full market* (Papava, 1994, p. 46).

In contrast to free and regulated markets, the economic activity of a state is an internal part of a full market.

6.4. THE FUNCTIONING OF THE PUBLIC SECTOR IN THE SYSTEM OF THE FULL MARKET

As already mentioned, taxes fulfill two functions: the financing of expenses for the production of public goods and payment for their consumption. To understand how correct the merging of these two functions is, in the present system of taxation, let us consider how these functions are related in the production and consumption of private goods.

Let us say that a certain person, A, decides to produce some private goods but does not have enough money. In this case, he addresses a person, B, and borrows a certain amount of money to organize the production of these private goods. For the use of this money, A, during the whole period of the loan, has to pay B a certain amount of interest. When the loan period has expired, A will have returned the borrowed money to B.

If B has a certain demand for the goods produced by A, in order to buy them B will have to pay A the price for these goods.

Thus B lends money to A for the production of some private goods and receives interest for it; at the same time B, in buying the given private goods, pays their price to A. It is necessary to note that the given relation between those producing and consuming private goods is a multiple repetition of the simple action of a market system.

If the public sector wants to be a part of a market it needs to adopt the considered relationship between the producers and consumers of private goods in respect to the production and consumption of public goods.

Drawing a parallel with the previously mentioned example, the public sector should be considered as person A producing public goods, whereas the whole society should be considered as person B consuming public goods.

Money emission creates its own funds within the public sector. Besides, the funds of the public sector are also state profit (i.e., the indirect taxes), in the same way that undistributed profits are the funds of corporations.

High money emission can have well-known and grave consequences for an economy. Because of this, state profit and money emission in a normally functioning economy cannot provide for the necessary expenses of the public sector to produce public goods. That is why the public sector uses state loans (e.g., state bonds) and taxation. According to state loans, the public sector acts exactly the same way as person A in the above example, whereas levying direct taxes is nothing but a government racket (Papava, 1994, p. 46). As the public sector lacks its own funds to produce public goods, it should not expropriate, but borrow a part of the income from households and corporations following market laws; that is, a public sector should act as person A of the above example.

Thus, following market principles, the public sector has to borrow from households and corporations instead of levying direct taxes. As households and corporations are at the same time the consumers of public goods, they also have to pay for their consumption (i.e., act as person B). The public goods are also the result of economic production in the same way as private goods and they (public goods) have a corresponding price that the consumers pay through taxation and loans (Studenski, 1961, Ch. 10).

So direct taxes taken as debts and also as state loans simultaneously fulfill two functions: for financing expenses of the production of public goods and payment for their consumption. A merge of these functions is conditioned by the fact that finishing the production and starting the consumption of public goods coincides in time, it being different from private goods for which there is a time lag between the end of production and the start of consumption. In other words, the produced public goods are consumed immediately without being bought by consumers.

In spite of a great similarity between direct taxes taken as debts and state loans, there is a considerable difference between them. Public goods are consumed not only by the private but also by the public sector. Consequently, consumption of a part of public goods has to be paid for by the public sector. That is why state loans are the money borrowed by the public sector from the private sector to pay for consumption of public goods by the public sector. Thus, this money is to be returned to the private sector. Direct taxes, being the payment for consumption of public goods by the private sector, should not be returned. Nevertheless, interest has to be paid for these taxes because they are initially (before transformation of these taxes into payment for public goods consumption by the private sector) borrowed by the public sector to cover expenses for the production of public goods. The implication is that there is no room for coercive taxation in a full market system where the public sector is an internal part of this market. Direct taxes are replaced by state loans that are nonrepayable, but yield interest, or by irretrievable loans with computed interest in a full market system, and, together with state profit, are used to finance expenses of the production of public goods.

6.5. SIMPLE MODELS OF A BUDGET FOR AN ECONOMY WITH AND WITHOUT TAXES

Let us consider the main equations of an existing national budget system.

National budget expenditure includes government payments to purchase commodities and services (G), to cover the value of state bonds when payment becomes due ($\underline{B}$), to repay the interest (rB) on state bonds (B) (where r is the rate of interest on state bonds). Thus, national budget expenditure is equal to $G + \underline{B} + rB$.

National budget revenue is formed by total tax revenues (T).

Excess expenses of the national budget over revenues are covered by loans in the form of state bonds ($\bar{B}$), resulting in the following equation:

$$T + \bar{B} = G + \underline{B} + rB.$$ (6.5.1)

As a rule, in practice $\bar{B} > \underline{B}$, or $\Delta B = \bar{B} - \underline{B} > 0$. Consequently, (6.5.1) may be transformed as follows:

$$T + \Delta B = G + rB.$$ (6.5.2)

In (6.5.2) $B = B_0 + \Delta B$, where B_0 is the value of state bonds for the beginning of a fiscal year.

Total tax revenues, T, can be subdivided according to types of taxation: total revenues of individual income tax (T_h), total revenues from tax on corporation profits (T_p), total revenues from taxes and installments to social insurance funds (T_e) and total revenues from indirect taxes (T_b).

Consequently:

$$T = T_b + T_p + T_e + T_b.$$

Inserting (6.5.3) into (6.5.2) results in:

$$T_b + T_p + T_e + T_b + \Delta B = G + rB. \qquad (6.5.4)$$

Total tax revenues in the budget are formed of deductions from total factor incomes.

Thus, total tax revenues and contributions to social insurance funds are deducted from total wages (W) and total entrepreneurial profit (Π):

$$T_e = t_e W_e + t_\Pi \Pi, \qquad (6.5.5)$$

where t_e and t_Π are the tax rates paid, accordingly, by households and by corporations to social insurance funds.

In order to calculate the total tax revenues from a corporation's profit, first of all the taxable profit is determined. Here, in a simplified case, this value is $\Pi - t_\Pi \Pi$ (where t_Π is the tax rate paid by corporations to social insurance funds), because the firms can always transfer their share of social insurance into expenses. If t_p is the tax rate on a corporation's profit, the corresponding total tax revenues into budget will constitute:

$$T_p = t_p \Pi (1 - t_\Pi). \qquad (6.5.6)$$

Total revenues from individual income taxes are formed from all total factor incomes received by households, and in particular: total wages with the deduction of contributions into social security funds $W(1 - t_e)$, total interest (R), total rent (L) and total dividends ($q_h(1 - t_p)\Pi(1 - t_\Pi)$), where q_h is a dividend share paid to households in net profits (i.e., in profits after taxation of firms). If t_h is a rate of income tax, then:

$$T_h = t_h[W(1 - t_e) + R + L + q_h(1 - t_p)\Pi(1 - t_\Pi)]. \qquad (6.5.7)$$

In our case indirect taxes, without damaging common character, are limited by value-added tax (VAT), which consists of factor incomes and depreciation deductions (D). Let t_b be a VAT rate. Then:

$$T_b = t_b[D + W + R + L + \Pi(1-t_\Pi)]. \qquad (6.5.8)$$

The main correlations of the national budget constitute (6.5.4)–(6.5.8).

Of all state expenses used to purchase goods and services, the most notable are social security expenses (E) provided by installments to the budget from taxes and contributions to social insurance funds:

$$T_e = E. \qquad (6.5.9)$$

It is also necessary to mention that the revenue received from taxes and contributions into the social security fund cannot be spent for other purposes.

Let us consider the simplest model of an "economy without taxes" (Papava, 2000a), taking into account the main components of the aforementioned relation between persons A and B.

For simplification, let us assume that the public sector produces only one (aggregated) type of public good.

The public sector spends (G) of both its own and borrowed funds to produce the given public goods. The first is government profit (Π_{pg}) paid by corporations; the second is an increase in loans in the form of state bonds (ΔB) and irretrievable state loans with computed interest (C). All these funds are used to cover G and should provide interest payments on state bonds (rB) and on irretrievable state loans (R_c). Thus:

$$C + \Delta B + \Pi_{pg} = G + rB + R_c. \qquad (6.5.10)$$

It should be noted that (6.5.10)—in the conditions of an economy without taxes—has the same meaning as (6.5.4) in an economy with taxes.

The result of expenses (G) is the production of the public goods mentioned above, by a public sector. In contrast to the overwhelming majority of private goods, public goods cannot be measured in any way except in terms of value. Let $P(X_s)$ be the value of the public goods produced.

The value of the public goods will be:

$$P(X_s) = F_s + D_s + L_s + W_s + \Pi_s + rB + R_c + \Pi_{sg}, \qquad (6.5.11)$$

where: F_s is current expenses, D_s—depreciation deduction, L_s—rent, W_s—wages, Π_s—entrepreneurial profit, Π_{sg}—state profit (paid by public sector), are calculated in accordance with production of the given public goods.

It should also be noted that entrepreneurial profit is included, as a rule, in the value of public goods produced by utility plants.

It was mentioned earlier that completion of production and starting of consumption of public goods is a simultaneous process. In other words, incurrence of expenses on public goods production is almost simultaneous with their purchase. Because of this, expenses on production and the purchase of public goods generally coincide. In addition, to purchase public goods, the public sector has at its disposal state profits after production of these goods, which are paid by the public sector for the exploitation of the economic ability of the state as a factor of production.

Consequently:

$$C + \Delta B + \Pi_{pg} + \Pi_{sg} = P(X_s). \qquad (6.5.12)$$

Inserting (6.5.10) and (6.5.11) into (6.5.12) gives

$$C_l = F_s + D_s + L_s + W_s + \Pi_s. \qquad (6.5.13)$$

If one takes into consideration that

$$\Pi_{pg} = T_b,$$

and comparing (6.5.4) and (6.5.10) results in

$$C - R_e = T_h + T_p + T_e. \qquad (6.5.14)$$

Irretrievable loans with computed interest and corresponding interest incomes can be divided into three parts: loans and interest paid and received by households (C_h, and R_{ch}), corporations (C_p, and R_{cp}), and loans and interest paid jointly by both households and corporations with the aim of creation of egalitarian goods (C_e, and R_{ce}).
Then, if

$$C_h - R_{ch} = T_h, \qquad (6.5.15)$$

$$C_p - R_{cp} = T_p, \qquad (6.5.16)$$

$$C_e - R_{ce} = T_e, \qquad (6.5.17)$$

(6.5.14) will be fulfilled.
Taking (6.5.17) into consideration one will have

$$C_e - R_{ce} = E \qquad (6.5.18)$$

instead of (6.5.9).
If the main budget correlations in an economy with taxes are (6.5.4) and (6.5.9), then for an economy without taxes they are (6.5.10) and (6.5.18). The interdependence of these correlations is defined by equations (6.5.14) to (6.5.17).
The question of the mechanism of correlation between irretrievable loans with computed interest and these interest incomes is left open.

6.6. THE BORROWING MECHANISM OF AN IRRETRIEVABLE LOAN WITH COMPUTED INTEREST

The mechanism of borrowing irretrievable loans with computed interest does not depend on who (households or corporations) lends them or for what purposes (e.g., creation of egalitarian goods) they are lent. Our consideration can therefore be limited by a common case for C and R_e.

According to (6.5.14)–(6.5.17) irretrievable loans with computed interest include corresponding interest incomes, that is

$$C = C_r + R_c, \qquad (6.6.1)$$

where C_r is the computed part of interest on an irretrievable loan.

If r_c is a rate of interest on an irretrievable loan, and r—the number of years for the interest payment of the irretrievable loan, then using the well-known procedure of discounting gives

$$C_r = \frac{C}{(1 + r_c)^r} \qquad (6.6.2)$$

Interest computation on C_r is carried out according to a compound interest formula and as a result in r years

$$C_r(1 + r_c)^r = C.$$

Inserting (6.6.2) in (6.6.1) gives

$$R_c = \frac{C((1 + r_c)^r - 1)}{(1 + r_c)^r} \qquad (6.6.3)$$

Consider one of the possible variants of a mechanism of borrowing for an irretrievable loan with computed interest.

In order to economically stimulate households and corporations to give the irretrievable loans with computed interest, it seems expedient to adopt the principles of progressive taxation. In particular, I will consider the following system.

During a definite period of time, the amount of irretrievable loans with computed interest and the level of an interest rate should be constant. The period of interest payment should obviously equal the period of state bonds in the form of medium-term securities, that is, medium-term bills and bonds with a time of redemption from one to ten years. The possibility should not be excluded that the period of interest payments on irretrievable loans could be more, say thirty years—a period relevant to long-term obligations.

In each succeeding period, the amount of an irretrievable loan with computed interest should be correspondingly longer and the level of interest rate higher than the previous one. Every citizen getting income for the first time should pass through all these periods in turn, starting with the first, the shortest one. The same applies to newly created corporations, the difference being that in this case irretrievable loans with computed interest and the level of interest will be different, and also the number of years in the aforementioned periods of time.

If a person inherits a certain amount of irretrievable loans, this amount should be summed up (the procedure for this requires special elaboration) with the accumulated amount of the same loan.

The same approach is applied in the case of a merger between two or more corporations.

For clarity, let us consider the following conditional example (Table 6.6.1)

Let the conditional example in Table 6.6.1 concern a person. Let us assume that this person has not inherited irretrievable loans. Having received an income for the first time in life, the person has to provide to the public sector an irretrievable loan of $80 for the first year. The example assumes that the period of the loan is ten years, meaning that there will be service charges on the loan over ten years. These $80, as mentioned above, will give rise to service charges over ten years. At an annual interest rate of three percent, the interest calculation for every dollar, according to the compound interest formula, will amount to 1.344 over ten years, the inverse quantity of which is the coefficient of discounting. According to (6.6.2), if the $80 is multiplied by the given discount factor the part of the irretrievable loan (equal to $59.52) on which the service is charged is obtained. Thus, having given $80 to the public sector as an irretrievable loan, the person, according to (6.6.3), will get back $20.48 during ten years; $1.79 (59.52 × 0.03) during the first year, $1.84 ((59.52 + 1.79) × 0.03) during the second year, and so forth.

Table 6.6.1. Irretrievable Loan with Computed Interest (Conditional example)

	First period (two years)	Second period (three years)	Third period (four years)	Fourth period (five years)
Annual amount of irretrievable loan with computed interest (in dollars) (C)	80	96	129	160
Annual interest rate (r_c)	3	3.5	3.8	4
Compounded value of every dollar for a period of 10 years [$(1 + r_c)^t$]	1.344	1.411	1.452	1.480
Discounting coefficient ($1/(1 + r_c)^t$)	0.744	0.709	0.689	0.676
Part of irretrievable loan on which interest is computed (in dollars) (C_r)	59.52	69.06	82.68	108.16

In the second year the person has to give the public sector $80 in irretrievable loans on the same conditions. In the third year the person will have to pay $96; out of which the interest at the higher annual interest rate—3.5 percent—will be calculated on $68.06. It will last for three years. In the sixth year he will have to pay to the public sector $120 as an irretrievable loan, with the interest at 3.8 percent calculated on $82.68 over ten years. It will last for four years. Starting from the tenth year the individual will have to pay to the public sector $160 in irretrievable loan over five years, with the interest at 4 percent calculated on $108.16.

The foregoing example covers only four periods of time and fourteen years total, but it can be extended to subsequent periods, taking into consideration the increasing values of corresponding indices.

It should be stressed once more that interest is computed only on a part (though significant) of the irretrievable loan, after the whole annual amount is paid to the public sector.

It is expedient that the computed interest, say for ten years, be accumulated on specific fixed deposits so that the lender could draw money not earlier than in five (or more) years. Though interest on irretrievable loans is computed during a definite period of time (in this case during ten years) the interest on a sum of money accumulated on the aforementioned specific accounts is not time limited. If for any reason (not connected with natural disasters, wars, etc.) the lender is unable to pay the public sector its due money for a given year under the requirements for an irrecoverable loan (in full or in part), then the sum should be covered by percentage deductions from the mentioned fixed deposits. Besides, in order to overcome the economic interest in evasion of payments, under an irretrievable loan it is possible to introduce special penalties, by which interest income on the mentioned special fixed accounts calculated according to the compound interest formula will be reduced (written off) to the value of the sum of money unpaid to the public sector. If the accumulated interest deductions from the mentioned fixed accounts do not cover completely the annual sum of unpaid money under irretrievable loan requirements to the public sector, the money accumulated as loans up to a given moment should be written off (Papava, 1997). As a consequence, it will reduce the volume of future interest incomes.

The way the system is organized means that the lender will have a predisposition to pay the public sector the money due under irretrievable loan requirements completely and at the proper time. This is so because, first, he or she will want to receive rising interest payments, and second, the person will not want to lose the accumulated interest or the possibility of receiving other interest income in the future because of the writing off of a part of the irretrievable loan with computed interest, as a consequence of the mentioned penalties.

This system of financing public-sector expenditure differs greatly from the existing one, not least because the lender replaces the taxpayer.

If the level of taxes paid depends on annual income there is no relation between income and the sum of money paid to the public sector under an irretrievable loan. The public sector determines for lenders both the growing annual amount of irretrievable loans and interest rates. It should stimulate them indirectly to increase their income in order to receive even higher interest payments. Thus one can see that the state does not interfere with such an intimate sphere as the incomes of households and corporations.

Incentives for beginning lenders to pay a definite sum of money as an irretrievable loan are still very weak, because the interest rate is not high, and the level of possible penalties is not so significant either. That is why the activity of beginning lenders should be under supervision of a special financial inspection (just like today's tax inspection), though this inspection is considerably weaker than that of today's tax inspection. It is conditioned by the aforementioned difference between taxpayers and lenders.

Starting from the point when the interest rate of the irretrievable loans becomes higher, and especially when it exceeds the net rate of loan interest, the incentives to pay the public sector the money required under the irretrievable loans scheme completely and in due time become effective. By that time lenders must already have a significant amount of money both in irretrievable loans and corresponding fixed deposits on which increasing interest is compounding.

The effectiveness of the system of irretrievable loans will raise the interest rate on irretrievable loans, taking into consideration the inflation rate.

According to (6.6.13), irretrievable loans with computed interest include the interest in themselves; if at the same time one assumes that direct taxes are replaced by irretrievable loans with computed interest it can be concluded that the problem of state debt (Mankiw, 1992, Ch. 16) is considerably modified—the issue needs special study. It should also be noted that the Ricardian approach to budget deficits (Barro, 1989) does not have a direct relationship to the economy without taxes.

In conclusion, it is very important to stress that in this system of financing public sector expenditures the lender replaces the taxpayer.

7

The Laffer Effect in Post-Communist Economies

The power to tax involves the power to destroy.

John Marshall
(1755–1835; American jurist)

7.1. THEORETICAL ASPECTS OF THE LAFFER CURVE

One of the most disputed problems of modern economic theory is the tax burden's impact on economic activity as well as on national budgetary revenues.

More than four decades have elapsed since American economist Arthur Laffer proposed a curve (later named after him) that described the dependence of national budget tax revenues on an average aggregate tax (AAT), and according to which, initially, with an increase in the AAT, tax revenues grow, too; however, having reached a certain point (called a Laffer point) at which the tax revenues reach their maximum value, they start falling. Such dependence, also known as a Laffer effect, in some works is referred to as Laffer's law (Guesnerie, 1998).

The Laffer curve is the clearest illustration of the key postulations of supply-side economics (Canto, Joiness, Laffer, 1983). The "attractiveness" of the idea on which the Laffer curve was based, as well as its simplicity of presentation, influenced Ronald Reagan—who is said to have experienced the effects of the Laffer curve in real life (e.g., Mankiw, 1998, Ch. 8)—a candidate for the American presidency at the time, to the extent that it became the basis of the economic policy (later called Reaganomics) that the US administration pursued after Reagan was elected in 1980. Irrespective of the skeptical attitudes of many prominent economists of the time toward the Laffer curve itself, as well as the US position on it, the simple clarity of the graphically illustrated dependence of tax revenues on the AAT gradually gained popularity. Later, the theory of supply-side economics not only became a subject of research on the part of IMF experts (Gandhi, Ebrill, Mackenzie et al., 1987), but was at one time also recognized as apart of IMF programs (e.g., Moustapha, 1992).

Presently, almost all modern economics textbooks are critical of both the Laffer curve and the effects of Reaganomics (e.g., Dornbusch, Fischer, 1990, Ch. 16; Mankiw, 1998, Ch. 8; McConnell, Brue, 1990, Ch. 19; Samuelson, Nordhaus, 1995, Ch. 17). Despite this, a number of recent works focus on studying the mathematical (e.g., Guesnerie, 1998) and empirical (e.g., Slemrod, 1996) implications of the Laffer curve.

According to E. Balatskii, the works devoted to the research of the Laffer curve can be divided into two major groups that can be classified as theoretical and practical research groups (Balatskii, 2000B, p. 33). The first group consists of works aimed at modeling fiscal and production processes and providing theoretical reasoning for a parabolic curve and availability of the Laffer points (e.g., Sokolovskii, 1989; Movshovich, Sokolovskii, 1994; Kapitonenko, 1994; Arkin, Slastnikov, Shevtsova, 1999); the other group comprises reflections on the location of the Laffer points in different national contexts (e.g., Gusakov, Zhak, 1995; Balatskii, 1997b, 1997c, 1999, 2000B; Vishnevskii, Lipnitskii, 2000).

The idea underlying the Laffer curve is very simple: It is assumed that where the AAT amounts either to 0 percent ($t = 0$), or to 100 percent ($t = 1$), tax revenues of the national budget amount to zero; however, at a certain point between 0 percent and 100 percent, where the AAT, or t_{max} is located, the revenues reach their maximum value T_{max}. A graphical illustration of the Laffer curve is shown in Figure 7.1.1.

According to E. Balatskii, both the idea and the graphical presentation of the Laffer curve are based on the following purely artificial *postulations:*

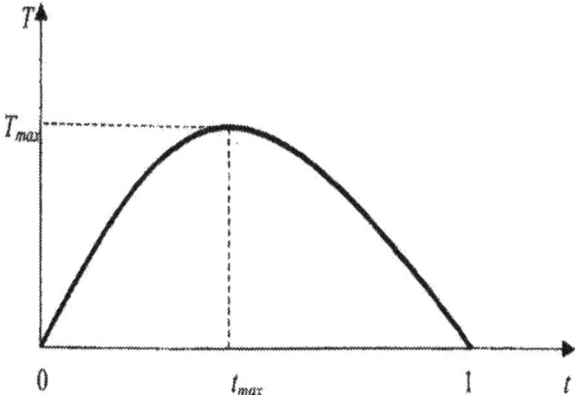

Figure 7.1.1. Laffer Curve

1. A dogmatic assertion (which, in fact, is just a logical supposition) that at a certain point between 0 percent and 100 percent, the AAT ensures a maximum amount of tax revenues (Balatskii, 1997A, p, 39); however, as is shown below, further research may shed more light on the correctness of this assertion;

2. A hypothetical reflection on certain marginal situations, as the immediate implication of zero-rate taxes is that there is no government at all (because there would be no funds to maintain the government); furthermore, a proposition that, as soon as the government succeeds in collecting all revenues in their entirety, production output will start falling and the government will no longer get anything may be disproved by the long experience of a command economy; from this point one can conclude that the Laffer curve does not cover the whole interval [0, 1], but rather a shorter section of it $(0, t_0)$, where $0.5 < t_0 < 1$ (Balatskii, 1997b, p. 93); with this correction the Laffer curve will look as it does in Figure 7.1.2;

3. A mechanical implication, stemming from an original macroeconomic statement of the problem, that all taxes are proportional (flat), as a result of which more sophisticated fiscal systems (of both progressive and regressive taxation) that are encountered quite often "cannot fit" the

aggregated framework of the Laffer curve in practice (Balatskii, 1997A, pp. 39–40);

4. A supposition that there is an economy without inflation, as the Laffer curve describes tax revenues in their nominal value; as a result, under the conditions of the Oliver-Tanzi effect, which causes the growth of tax revenues as well as the shrinking of tax base because of a relatively high inflation rate (i.e., in the environment of inflation), it becomes necessary to recalculate tax revenues in real terms; however, this may question the very existence of the Laffer curve, as such (Balatskii, 1997a, pp. 40–42).

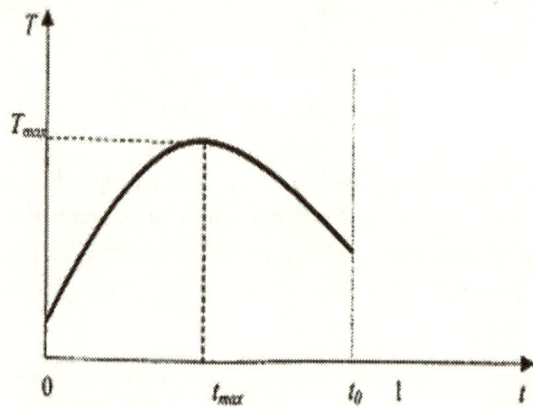

Figure 7.1.2. Laffer Curve under Undetermined Marginal Conditions

It is no surprise that in view of both the foregoing material and the results obtained by other researchers, Balatskii concludes that the Laffer curve is nothing but an unproved hypothesis (Balatskii, 2000a, p. 9). Despite this, many researchers presume the a priori existence of the Laffer curve (Aleksashenko, Kiselev, Teplukhin, Iasin, 1989; Dagaev, 2001; Papava, 1996a, 1999; Sokolovskii, 1992).

A number of works are designed to determine the level of dependence of specific taxes on the Laffer curve. Specifically, it has been demonstrated that what this curve describes best is the dependence of tax revenues on the valued-added tax (VAT) rate (Gusakov, Zhak, 1995; Movshovich, Sokolovskii, 1994); however, it should be noted that the applicability of the Laffer curve to some categories of taxes is questionable (Balatskii, 1997b, 1997c).

In fact, since the very introduction of the Laffer curve the question of using it with the purpose of setting an optimal profit tax rate (which was later replaced with total of all taxes withheld from profits) has been discussed continuously by researchers; however, the most recent theoretical studies have established that this curve is not usable for describing changes in the profit tax rate and that any rise in this rate will be followed by a rise in budgetary revenues as well (Movshovich, Sokolovskii, 1994, pp. 139–40).

It must be underlined that the Laffer curve was originally formulated in a macroeconomic context, which makes it applicable not to individual taxes, but rather to a certain AAT (Balatskii, 1997a, p. 39). Quite often, instead of the latter, the concept of tax burden is used, which is described as a ratio of actual tax revenues of the national budget to a country's GDP (Balatskii, 2000b, pp. 33–34).

I believe that this method of estimating the tax burden is debatable because it does not cover, on the one hand, all those potential tax revenues that, for a number of reasons, never go to the national budget, including the dead weight of the tax burden, and, on the other hand, the part of GDP that, for the same reasons, is produced by the shadow economy. In other words, this index, which is designed to measure the tax burden, does not cover the losses to both the national budget and the GDP because of its dead weight.

As was noted earlier, the Laffer curve is described graphically as the ratio of tax rate to tax revenues. As to the idea on which the curve is based, it covers not only fiscal but also production-related aspects of changes in the AAT. In particular, according to the proponents of supply-side economics, a decrease in the AAT from a relatively high point facilitates growth in the labor supply as well as in investments, which in turn, brings about the growth of GDP, and, in the long run, the expansion of the tax base. As Balatskii points out, the concept of the Laffer curve rests on the belief that there is a certain dependence of the tax base (i.e., of the GDP) on the AAT, analogous to the dependence of tax revenues on the same AAT; in other words, the Laffer curve makes it possible to simultaneously describe the fiscal and production-related aspects (effects) of any changes in the AAT (Balatskii, 1997a, p. 39).

On the basis of this assumption, Balatskii offers to split the entire concept of the Laffer point into two types. The first type encompasses cases where the GDP achieves its maximum value, and the second type in cases where the high point is reached by the national budget's tax revenues (Balatskii, 1997b). In addition, if we try to draw the Laffer curve on the basis of the aforementioned tax burden, we will see that the Laffer point of the first type will be shorter than that of the second type (it will be to the left side of the abscissa axis); in other words, the maximum amount of GDP can be reached at a lower value of tax burden that can enable maximum tax revenues to the national budget. This means that during the interval between the two Laffer points, an increase in tax revenues may be effected even under the conditions of a relative drop in production output (or reduction of GDP) (Balatskii, 2000b).

This result is in perfect accord with the works of A. Dagaev, who asserts that, whenever the Laffer curve is used to describe the dependence of investments on AAT, it is demonstrated that the value of the AAT at which the maximum amount of investments is reached is lower than the other that ensures the maximum amount of collected taxes (Dagaev, 1995, 2001); consequently, during the period between these two values of AAT, the decrease in investments will not disable increases in tax revenues.

As one can see, the Laffer curve is associated with a number of debatable questions involving conceptual and even graphical aspects. Irrespective of skepticism on the part of some prominent modern economists (e.g., Krugman, 1994, pp. 157–58; 1998, pp. 47–51) toward both the Laffer curve itself and its theoretical foundations, a number of applied developments, primarily regarding post-Communist economies, attest to the existence of Laffer effects in the real world (e.g., Balatskii, 2000b; Vishnevskii, Lipnitskii, 2000). Although this fact cannot be used as incontrovertible evidence of the verity of the whole curve, it does confirm that under certain circumstances there is an interdependence between the growths of both tax revenues of the national budget and the GDP, on the one hand, and the reduction of relatively high AAT, on the other hand.

7.2. THE LAFFER CURVE FOR ECONOMIES UNDERGOING POST-COMMUNIST TRANSFORMATION

As was noted above, the concept of the Laffer curve was born and fulfilled in the United States as a part of Reaganomics. One of its key goals was to reduce the existing national budget deficit. However, this goal was never reached; moreover, the effect was in fact just the opposite the—deficit grew (e.g., Krugman, 1994, pp. 157–58; 1998, p. 48; Slemrod, Bakija, 1996, p. 28; Steinmo, 1993, pp. 163–64). This had a very strong impact on the formation of a skeptical attitude toward the Laffer curve, which, as noted before, was also reflected in modern economics textbooks.

An empirical analysis of countries that are members of the Organization for Economic Cooperation and Development (OECD) significantly calls into question the existence of the Laffer curve, even in those countries (e.g., Leibfritz, Thornton, Bibbee, 1997, pp. 10–11). The most recent studies attest, however, that high marginal tax rates and their progressive nature are negatively correlated with sustainable economic growth (Padovano, Galli, 2001).

However, a logical question arises here: Are the facts that the Laffer curve was practically disproved by the US economy in the 1980s and that empirical studies have questioned its very existence in the context of the OECD countries, sufficient proof to assert that the Laffer Curve does not exist at all, even in countries that have a different economic background?

It is quite possible that the answer to this question will not be affirmative. At any rate, the question remains open in the case of post-Communist economies, because, as was noted above, some studies have shown that under certain circumstances Laffer effects do take place (Balatskii, 2000b; Vishnevskii, Lipnitskii, 2000). Of no less importance is the fact that some well-known economists (e.g., Prof. Gary S. Becker in relation to Georgia (Becker, 1998) and Prof. Jeffrey Sachs in relation to Ukraine (Mankiw, 1998, p. 169)) have advocated reducing the tax burden in such countries in order to encourage both economic activities and an increase in tax revenues to the national budgets. It is noteworthy that in the Georgian context, the reduction of some tax rates in 1996, accompanied by a reduction of AAT as well, actually resulted in the increase of national budgetary revenues. In 1997, as a result of reducing the payment rates for the Social Welfare and Medical Insurance Fund (SWMIF) from 37 percent to 27 percent, total payments made by legal entities for the benefit of the SWMIF increased to 41 percent; payments to the Employment Fund grew by 1 percent as a result of lowering the tax rate from 3 percent to 1 percent; budgetary revenues increased by 26.4 percent and 34.6 percent, respectively, as a result of reducing the excise rate on beer from 100 percent to 15 percent and import duties on certain goods from 12 percent to 5 percent. An counterexample of these was the government's decision—made under the IMF's pressure—to raise, as of January 1, 2000, the cigarette excise rates by 60 percent for filter cigarettes and by 110.5 percent for nonfilter cigarettes; as a result, tax revenues from the cigarette business dropped by 36.9 percent (Papava, 2003A, pp. 39–40).

An important feature typifies economies in post-Communist transformation and distinguishes them from other economies: A post-Communist economy is characterized by a free availability of idle production capacities, as a result of which real growth of production output can be attained without utilizing significant investments. This creates favorable grounds for the development of Laffer effects (Vishnevskii, Lipnitskii, 2000, pp. 110–11). However, here a very important remark must be made: Because of their inability to produce competitive goods, many enterprises in post-Communist countries are actually dead, which brings about what I call a necroeconomy (see, Ch. 3). Obviously, dead enterprises cannot have production capacities, as such.

During the transition from a command economy to a market economy, even if the reduced tax burden facilitates the growth of supply, to no less an extent, it will stimulate the growth of demand as well, which may be very important for post-Communist economies. Such a transition was formulated as a theoretical postulation called the Laffer-Keynesian synthesis, which forms a methodological base for a "tax therapy" whose goal is to stimulate the development of post-Communist economies (Papava, 1996a, pp. 263–67; 1999, pp. 285–91).

The Keynesian approach rests on the assumption that a decrease in tax rates causes an increase in consumption; in a short-term perspective, an increase in consumer spending results in the growth of demand for goods and services, in other words, of production output and employment; at the same time, a decrease in savings caused by the increase in consumption results in the intensification of competition between investors, which, in the long run, brings about an increase in interest rates; this, in turn, discourages local investors and produces incentives for foreign capital (e.g., Mankiw, 1992, Ch. 16). It has been argued that this effect has negative implications for countries with developed economies. However, as far as post-Communist economies are concerned, the following positive results can be expected: first, the reduction of tax burden may indirectly facilitate at least the partial utilization of the aforementioned idle production capacities, and, thereby, an expansion of production; second, the replacement of necroeconomy with competitive businesses can only be feasible via attracting modern foreign investments (Papava, 1996a, p. 264; 1999, p. 287).

As was noted above, in post-Communist economies, because of readily available production capacities, the likelihood that Laffer effects will show up grows. Nevertheless, as is shown hereafter, this does not necessarily mean that the Laffer curve itself exists. From now on, our attention will be focused on the disclosure of the Laffer effect relative to Laffer point 2, as this is exactly the foundation on which the very idea of the Laffer curve rests.

7.3. ALTERNATIVES TO THE LAFFER CURVE

Earlier, while reviewing the postulations on which the Laffer curve is based, it was pointed out that if such a curve really existed it would not cover the whole interval [0, 1], but rather a small section of it (0, t_0) (see Postulation 2).

Further corrections to the Laffer curve are based on a factor of time, in particular, of the time interval necessary for the Laffer effect to be disclosed.

Most recent studies have shown that whenever the time factor is taken into account, it is an equally important question in which direction the AAT is changing: upward (Balatskii, 2000A) or downward (Vishnevskii, Lipnitskii, 2000). Let us review each of these scenarios separately (Papava, 2002d, 2003a, pp. 59–73).

Balatskii proposes a concept of "post-effect," the key implication of which is that, at a certain point, a further increase in AAT brings about the cutting of the budget's tax revenues only after a couple of years (Balatskii, 2000a, p. 8). Dagaev, in turn, uses a concept of tax "hysteresis" ("deferment" in Greek) (Dagaev, 2001, p. 65). To the extent that the Laffer effect always appears a couple of years later, more precise phrasings would be "the Laffer effect with tax hysteresis" or "the Laffer effect with after-effects (post-effects)."

Because of a need to take into account the time factor, a so-called fiscal curve, in which this effect should be reflected, should not be expressed by "tax revenues and AAT" coordinates, as is the case in connection with the Laffer curve, but rather, as is proposed by Balatskii, by those of "tax revenues and time" (Balatskii, 2000A, p. 9). We believe, however, that the best option would be a three-dimensional fiscal curve presented by the following three coordinates: AAT (t), tax revenues (T), and time (τ).

Before we offer a graphical illustration of fiscal "hysteresis" on a fiscal curve, let us consider the scenario in which the AAT changes upward. Bearing this in mind, let us project the three-dimensional space (see Figure 7.3.1) (Papava, 2002d, p.76; 2003a, p. 70).

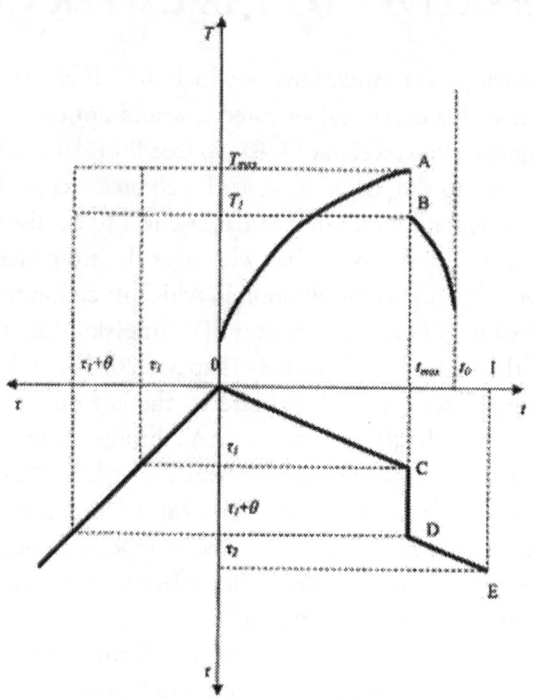

Figure 7.3.1. Balatskii-Papava Fiscal Curve

Let us consider the time interval $[0, \tau_2]$ during which AAT goes up from 0 to 1. As is shown in Figure 7.3.1, in the case of interval $[0, \tau_1]$, an increase in AAT (t) results in the growth of tax revenues, which reach their climax (T_{max}) at the point of t_{max}; A and C are relevant points on the fiscal and tax curves, respectively. It is during the transition from A to B on the fiscal curve that the Laffer effect with the tax hysteresis appears, provided the AAT is going upward; specifically, even at a very insignificant increase in t_{max} of AAT, the tax revenues will start falling only after θ years, that is, as of the year $(\tau_1 + \theta)$. In other words, A of the fiscal curve corresponds to C and D of the tax curve; at the same time, the latter (i.e., D) matches B of the fiscal curve.

Consequently, if AAT is equal to t_{max} in the year , tax revenues will reach their maximum value T_{max} whereas in the year $(\tau_1 + \theta)$ they will be reduced to T_1. The split of the fiscal curve at points A and B is the very reflection of the Laffer effect with the tax hysteresis. It is important to note that in case of a further increase in AAT, after it has passed the Laffer effect with tax hysteresis (which on the tax curve is illustrated by a move from D to E), during the interval (t_{max}, t_0), tax revenues will be dropping.

It is also noteworthy that on the fiscal curve we are considering here (Figure 7.3.1), the Laffer effect looks significantly modified, which, as was noted above, is a result of the effect of tax hysteresis. Furthermore, the Laffer point is missing and the fiscal curve itself, displayed in Figure 7.3.1, could hardly be referred to as the Laffer curve. To the extent that the fiscal curve in Figure 7.3.1 is a reflection of Balatskii's research efforts, it would be fairer to call it the "Fiscal Curve According to the Balatskii Version," or simply the "Balatskii-Papava Curve" and the t_{max} point (for the purposes of this curve) at which the effect of tax hysteresis appears, the "Balatskii-Papava Point" (Papava 2002e; 2003f).

The Laffer effect with tax hysteresis, as Vishnevskii and Lipnitskii show, reveals itself—albeit in a somewhat modified shape—in the case where the AAT is changing downward (Vishnevskii, Lipnitskii, 2000, pp. 113–14). As in the case of Figure 7.3.1, we draw a graph of the fiscal curve, where during the time interval $[0, \tau_2]$, the AAT goes down from 1 to 0 (see Figure 7.3.2) (Papava, 2002d, p.77; 2003a, p. 72).

According to Figure 7.3.2, during the time interval $[0, \tau_2]$, a reduced AAT rate (t) causes an increase in budgetary tax revenues up to t_{max}, which revenues, having approached the T_1 level (corresponding to A on the fiscal curve), drop immediately to the T_2 level (corresponding to B on the fiscal curve) and stay there for the subsequent years (θ). Consequently, A and B of the fiscal curve match D of the tax curve. In the year $(\tau_1 + \theta)$, however, provided the AAT rate is the same amounting to t_{max} because of the effects of tax hysteresis, tax revenues will jump to their maximum value, T_{max} (corresponding to C of the fiscal curve and E of the tax curve). On the fiscal curve, to the extent that the AAT rate is falling, the effect of tax hysteresis appears during the transition from A to C, through B. If that declining process continues, after the year $(\tau_1 + \theta)$, the tax revenues will start dropping as well.

As in the case of the Balatskii curve, again, because of tax hysteresis, the Laffer effect appears modified on this fiscal curve too (see Figure 7.3.2). Again, the Laffer point is missing, which is why one cannot call this a Laffer curve. To the extent that the fiscal curve on Figure 7.3.2 is a reflection of the research efforts of Vishnevskii and Lipnitskii, it would be fairer to call it the "Fiscal Curve According to the Vishnevskii-Lipnitskii Version," or simply the "Vishnevskii-Lipnitskii-Papava curve", and the t_{max} point (for the purposes of this curve) at which the effect of tax hysteresis appears, the "Vishnevskii-Lipnitskii-Papava Point" (Papava 2002e; 2003f).

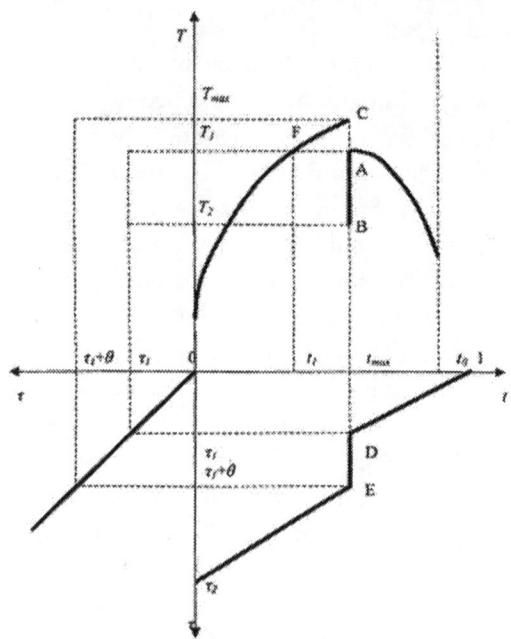

Figure 7.3.2. Vishnevskii-Lipnitskii-Papava Fiscal Curve

The fact that both the Laffer point and the Laffer curve are missing does not mean that in every event of a reduced AAT rate one has to expect that a tax hysteresis will show up; for example, if originally the AAT rate had been in the interval (t_{max}, t_0) and later it was cut to the extent that it was suddenly found in the interval (t_1, t_{max}), the tax revenues will grow almost immediately as they will be no less than T_1. That is exactly what happened in Georgia in 1996, when, as mentioned above, the cutting of certain tax rates, and thereby of the AAT rate, resulted in significant increases in the budgetary tax revenues.

The main problem related to the practical use of the Laffer effect is one of avoiding mistakes in identifying the economy's location along the Vishnevskii-Lipnitskii-Papava curve that corresponds to the interval (t_{max}, t_0). Likewise, it is difficult to identify the extent to which the AAT rate should be cut, in order to avoid an exit from the interval (t_1, t_{max}), which would be between C and F on the Vishnevskii-Lipnitskii-Papava curve (see Figure 7.3.2).

It happens quite often that discussions about selecting proper fiscal policies for specific countries become difficult because it is extremely hard to identify the exact location of an economy on the Balatskii-Papava and Vishnevskii-Lipnitskii-Papava curves.

8

Tax Federalism: Consensus Versus Separatism

Taxation and representation are inseparable...

Lord Camden
(1714–1794; British Whig politician; Lord Chancellor, 1766–1770)

8.1. THE PROBLEM OF FISCAL FEDERALISM

It is particularly important to choose such a pattern of regional arrangement of the fiscal system that can provide a maximum of budget receipts.

The tax system is an element of a fiscal system and is to a large extent defining an income item of the budget. In its turn, the territorial aspect of the fiscal system is predetermined by a territorial structure of the state. Economists usually use the term *fiscal federalism* regardless of whether it is a federal or a unitary state (Tanzi (ed.), 1993, Ch. 16). It is necessary to underline that jurisprudence does not give a full definition of a concept of "Federal State" while legal experts even altogether reject the possibility of defining it (e.g., Bothe, 1994, p.21).

The term "fiscal federalism" covers both sides of the state's tax and budgetary systems: On the one hand, it regulates tax incomes, and on the other, it deals with the distribution of expenditures to be financed by the government between the central ("Centre") and territorial ("Regions") government authorities. In the case of a federal state, by "Agents of a Federation" is meant regions hereinafter provisionally referred to as Federal Regions.

"Tax Federalism," (i.e., the separation of taxation power between the Centre and the Regions in a unitary state and between the Centre, Federal Regions, and Regions in a federal state) is the most complicated task for economics and one can say that no common and at the same time generally acceptable and hence a

114

faultless pattern is available (Tanzi (ed.), 1993, Ch. 16). Although modern economics does not possess any more or less cogent arguments concerning optimum ways of separating taxation powers, there is a smaller diversity of possible approaches to distribution of tax levying functions between Centre and Regions in unitary states than between the Centre, Federal Regions and Regions in the federal states (Tanzi (ed.), 1993, Ch. 16). This explains why fiscal federalism and, in particular, tax federalism are more interesting in the context of federal rather than unitary states.

The choice of this or that pattern of fiscal federalism depends on what functions the central government intends to perform itself and what functions are to be delegated to Federal Regions. To this end, the original problem is to define so-called "minimal functions" of the central government, which is a basic condition providing for the integrity of the state. These minimal functions include state defense, establishment of a common legal space, foreign relations, introduction of a common trade regime, emission of a common currency and control over its turnover, achievement of macroeconomic stability, and application of measures ensuring equalization of the social and economic development of regions. As international practice shows, any other functions could be, partially or fully, performed by the Federal Regions.

In any democratic (or claiming to be such) state, a central government usually declares its readiness to give as much freedom to regional authorities as possible. This means the delegation of more functions to them and exactly in the same way; these last very often publicly claim their loyalty to the central government and their endeavors toward strengthening the unity of the state. Despite this, the practical evidence is such that almost none of the federal states have succeeded in a perfect realization of these publicly made declarations. There are always a number of problems discussed between the Centre and the Regions (especially between Centre and Federal Regions) with more or less ardor in the course of discussions on the separation of state functions.

In federal states with a comparatively longer history of democratic development, the frame for discussion is comparatively narrow and the discussion itself is correspondingly less arduous.

As proved by international practice, the following principal approaches are used in the confrontation between the Centre and the Regions referred to earlier:

- The Centre is, as a rule, practically never content with implementation of just minimal functions (though, certainly it does not declare it) and seeks to maintain some extra instruments of state management. To this end, the Centre retains such mechanisms as transfers from the central budget intended for the regulation of problems both throughout the country and in separate regions. So, it is only natural that in many cases the Centre tries to extend the system of transfers;

- The Regions (especially federal regions) act through radically different mechanisms. They seek the growth of that part of tax revenues that is intended to remain in regions, at the expense of the coverage of the types of taxes and so through delay the process of tax incomes distribution to their benefit. This, in its turn, results in pulling over the functions to be performed by the government at a regional level. Apart from these legal methods, Regions in some cases also use illegal mechanisms. In some Federal States, where transfers of their shares by the Federal Regions to the central budget are made in conformity with relevant laws in a full amount and a due time frequently, there is one such Federal Region that, contrary to law, retains a part of income that belongs to the central budget; in such cases, the Centre cuts transfers for the offending Federal Region by a corresponding amount but a winner in this confrontation is still the Federal Region, as such action gives it a strong financial instrument empowering it to influence the policy pursued by the Centre. Consequently, the conclusion is that proceeding from common state interests, the Centre should be able to collect payments directly from those who participate in economic activities without consensus of the Federal Regions (Tanzi (ed.), 1993, Ch. 16).

8.2. THE HIERARCHICAL NATURE OF TAXES

Economics, as already mentioned, does not have any strict criteria on the basis that would clearly define whether this or that kind of tax is federal or local in nature. The only thing that could be said thereof is that a more-or-less precise theoretical statement as to their hierarchical nature could be found with regards to just two kinds of taxes: real estate tax (including land) and customs duty. The first one is considered local, for accumulation of property occurs on a certain territory and the second one is federal, for the customs belongs to the entire country and not to its separate regions. There have been frequent attempts to give a logical explanation as to why VAT and excise duty should also be regarded as federal. Theoretical grounds to this end are so artificial that they could by no means be considered satisfactory.

It should also be underlined that developed countries in which there is a federal structure use various schemes for the division of the taxation functions and there are no criteria for choosing the best among them (in terms of effectiveness). At the same time it is also remarkable that there is no explanation for proving why collection of several taxes by the Centre and the Regions at one and the same time is impossible.

It should also be noted that an approach suggesting a strict separation of taxes in accordance with the hierarchy is becoming more and popular with the Government of Georgia (and many other post-Communist countries), when, let us say, VAT shall be counted as a federal tax and recovered 100 percent in the central budget while, for example, an income tax shall be counted as a local tax and shall also be recovered 100 percent by the local budget, respectively. Within this context it is remarkable that as proved by the international practice, in more than one federal or unitary state an income tax is also federal (and not local) by 100 percent and in some of them it is divided between the Centre and the Regions (Table 8.2.1).

Such an approach, to my mind, is the main principle of the tax federalism pattern. At one glance it seems quite attractive, as the scheme of division of taxation powers is simplified, which to some extent gives grounds for an actual exclusion of objective possibilities to illegally retain or hide the tax income due to the central budget by a Federal Region. Under the aforementioned approach, the point at issue becomes irrelevant as the law states that the proceeds from this or that tax revenues should be transferred to the central budget either 100 percent or not transferred at all. The fact that in this case the subject for dispute disappears and the action of the Federal Region becomes rather transparent does not at all guarantee that, as proceeding from the aforementioned international experience, the Federal Region would not be left a chance to avoid the law in order to have a political impact on the Centre.

8.3. From Doctrine of Tax Separatism to Doctrine of Tax Consensus

The above approach, when the division of taxation power according to the types of taxes is made on the "all or nothing" principle ultimately lead us to *tax separatism,* when the interests of the Federal Regions are totally isolated from the national taxation interests with negative consequences for the integrity of the federal state. Proceeding from this, I call the application of the aforementioned approach in separation of taxation power the *Doctrine of Tax Separatism* (Papava, 2001b).

Table 8.2.1. Distribution of income taxes among various levels of government[1]

Countries	Upper Level Central Government	Medium Level (states, lands, etc.)	Lower Level (local authorities)
I. Unitary States			
Developed states			
Belgium	90.9	–	9.1
Great Britain	100.0	–	0.0
Netherlands	100.0	–	0.0
Norway	47.6	–	52.4
France	100.0	–	0.0
Sweden	24.7	–	75.3
Developing and post-Communist states			
Zimbabwe	100.0	–	0.0
Israel	100.0	–	0.0
Kenya	100.0	–	0.0
Poland	75.9	–	24.1
South Africa	100.0	–	0.0
Thailand	100.0	–	0.0
Hungary	71.9	–	28.1
Chile	100.0	–	0.0
II. Federal States			
Developed states			
Australia	100.0	0,0	0.0

---

1.   The table has been completed based on (Norregaard, 1995, p. 250).

USA	81.1	17,2	1.7
Germany	39.1	40,8	20.1
Spain	92.9	1,2	5.9
Canada	63.5	36,5	0.0
Developing states			
Argentina	34.2	65,8	0.0
Brazil	100.0	0,0	0.0
India	100.0	0,0	0.0
Mexico	98.1	1,3	0.6

In order to give a full description of this issue, it is also necessary to underline that, apart from the aforementioned defect, the doctrine of tax separatism—owing to its nature—is also practically unrealizable. The case is that the development in the regions of any state is marked by inequalities both from the social and economic viewpoint and because of this situation tax collection taxes varies between taxes and from region to region. Consequently, this means that there is a big possibility that while ascribing a regional title to the several types of taxes, an amount collected and retained in one of the regions might appear to be so small that it would need to be supplemented through transfers from the central budget, whereas in any other region tax collection according to the same types of taxes, makes up such a large amount that it would exceed the demand of this region for current budgetary expenditures and it would be reasonable to use it together with this surplus for the aforementioned central budget transfer. Thus, in practice, the principle of "all or nothing" might also come to an obvious disagreement with the maintenance/development of the country's state integrity.

Proceeding from all the above, it becomes apparent that the doctrine of tax separatism is generally unacceptable for any federal state, and for Georgia in particular.

In Georgia, at a contemporary stage of building up its statehood, when restoration of its territorial integrity is not yet covered by the question of its administrative-territorial system, great importance is attached to economic instruments creating incentives for regions to ascribe to a so-called "regional consensus" so as to, in the first place, make them economically interested in amplification of the state integrity of Georgia.

The concurrent mobilization of taxes both in central and local budgets could be used as such instruments.

Again, it should be stressed that there is no more or less cogent argument in economics that would at the least prove why it is impossible to recover this or that type of tax at one or another level of state hierarchy.

As mentioned above, the most impressive is the definition of real estate tax as local and of custom tax payment as federal. But, allow me to suggest that if a natural or legal entity owns real estate within (and not only within) various regions of the country, then it becomes difficult to decide unambiguously whether this payment should be paid to the local budget or to the central budget. According to the location of the real estate, it would be logical if the taxes were paid to local budgets, but insofar as the property belongs either to a natural entity that can without restriction move within the territory of its own country or to a legal entity, which might be functioning in several regions at one and the same time, the grounds for mobilizing this payment to the central budget should not be considered less justified. International practice proves that the real estate tax is regarded as entirely federal only in some unitary states; in other states (except Kenya, where it is regarded as entirely local) this payment is distributed between the various levels of government (Table 8.3.1).

Customs payment could also be made subject to similar considerations. Namely, as customs belongs to the state as a whole and not to any separate region, the idea of mobilization of customs payment solely to the central budget looks quite theoretically justified, though in practice customs-houses are located only in a few separate regions (e.g., at the country's borderlines, seaports, or airports), which creates some extra burden for these regions and therefore the reason for retaining at least a small portion of the revenues by a local budget of the region could be as successfully argued.

Therefore, a concurrent mobilization of all types of payments to the central and local budgets is a viable economic mechanism for attaining *regional consensus* in a federal state. To determine proportions for such distribution, it is first of all necessary to take in to consideration the statute of the Federal Region and at the same time the ratio of actual tax collection with regard to any type of taxes in each region to distribution of the budgetary expenses between the Centre and the Regions.

Table 8.3.1. Distribution of real estate taxes among various levels of government[2]

Countries	Upper Level (Central Government)	Medium Level (States, Lands, etc.)	Lower Level (Local Government)
I. Unitary States			
Developed states			
Belgium	100.0	–	0.0
Great Britain	99.2	–	0.8
Netherlands	65.1	–	34.9
Norway	37.9	–	62.1
France	100.0	–	0.0
Sweden	100.0	–	0.0
Developing and post-Communist states			
Zimbabwe	11.5	–	88.5
Israel	12.3	–	87.7
Kenya	0.0	–	100.0
Poland	48.3	–	51.7
South Africa	25.5	–	74.5
Thailand	81.9	–	18.1
Hungary	100.0	–	0.0
Chile	19.7	–	80.3
II. Federal States			
Developed states			
Australia	2.4	57.8	39.8
USA	6.0	6.7	87.3

---

2. The table has been completed based on (Norregaard, 1995, p. 250).

Germany	2.0	61.2	36.8
Spain	5.8	50.5	43.7
Canada	0.0	16.2	83.8
Developing states			
Argentina	49.2	50.8	0.0
Brazil	2.2	40.5	57.3
India	33.7	66.7	0.0
Mexico	1.2	0.0	98.8

Let me call the preceding approach, in which the distribution of recovered tax revenues between the Centre and the Regions is applicable to all types of taxes, a *Doctrine of Tax Consensus*. It can play a significant role in the formation of federal structure in Georgia and for reinforcement of its statehood. The importance of the tax consensus principles in the peaceful settlement of the problems concerning Abkhazia and South Ossetia (e.g., Chkhartishivili, Gotsiridze, Kitsmarishvili, 2004; Dzhikaev, Parastaev, 2004; Gumba, Ketsba, 2004) is also to be taken into account.

As noted above, none of the patterns of the fiscal federalism exclude a breach of the budget law on the part of any nonpayer region (first of all, Federal Region) when it illegally retains amounts due to the central budget, but the doctrine of tax consensus to a great extent serves to ease tension between the Centre and the Regions and, under other equal conditions, it might even minimize the afore-mentioned cases of nonpayment.

As a state today, Georgia is not institutionally ready to implement a complete pattern of the doctrine of tax consensus. To this end, the most important imped-ing factor is that the process of territorial arrangements is still underway in Geor-gia. Nevertheless, all elements of the doctrine of tax consensus are to be gradually realized with regard to all regions of Georgia, which in its turn shall make the prospects for territorial arrangement of Georgia clearer.

9

The Post-Communist Georgian Economy: Initial Results of Reforms

A party of order or stability, and a party of progress or reform, are both necessary elements of a healthy state of political life.

John Stuart Mill
(1806–1873; English philosopher and economist)

9.1. WHAT WAS BEFORE SHOCK THERAPY

The question is often posed asking when the economic reform started in Georgia. In my opinion the period from 1989, when the idea of national independence embraced the whole society, should be considered as its starting point (Suny, 1994, pp. 317–335). It became a turning point for both economists and those claiming to know economies, resulting in the creation of a number of interesting new concepts linked to the idea of economic independence (Papava, 1990). This first stage can conventionally be called *the stage of naive comprehension.*

The second stage of economic reform started after the election of the Supreme Council in the autumn of 1990. At that time, several very important laws on economic reform were issued, though they were unfortunately not implemented effectively. This stage of reform can therefore be considered *the stage of reform stagnation.*

After the coup d'état of December 1991–January 1992 there began *the stage of populist economic reform.* At that time the government transferred land and dwellings to people without compensation in order to enlist the easy support of the population. These redistributive policies caused substantial damage to the agricultural sector and house building. In particular, land privatization was carried out mechanically and it practically ruined the necessary infrastructure for agricultural production (the system of supply of machinery, fertilizers, and other resources); and without a legal basis for private ownership of land the efficiency of land tenure was very low. If differentiation of rental payments for dwellings had been made according to location and amenities, the money thus received could have been accumulated for further housing development. This became impossible because of the overly hasty, free distribution of dwellings (Papava, 1992, pp. 97–101).

During this populist stage of economic reform the method of Shock Therapy was used in Georgia at almost at the same time as in Russia, and in accordance with the Russian scenario. Was Georgia ready to apply this well-known approach to economic reform?

In order to answer this question, an important distinction of principle should be pointed out concerning the nature of the state. Thus, it turned out to matter a great deal whether countries were with or without their own independent statehood at the beginning of their reforms. To the first type belong the countries of Eastern Europe, such as Poland, Hungary, Bulgaria, and so on, and to the second—the newly created countries following the disintegration of the FSU, Yugoslavia, and Czechoslovakia). Among the latter countries, the legal successors of the original larger states are the only exceptions because they preserved almost all the attributes of statehood. Thus, after the disintegration of the USSR, Russia was recognized as the legal successor of the USSR, retained Moscow as its capital and preserved all the attributes of statehood, inheriting the institutions of the FSU. Hence, Russia can be classified with the group of post-Communist countries already possessing statehood. All other countries had to build up their own state institutions, often from almost nothing (to a certain extent, Ukraine and Belarus can be considered exceptions, since, although formally lacking independent statehood, they were already members of the United Nations). Georgia was one of the countries facing this situation. It therefore had to manage two major tasks simultaneously: the need to build up the institutions of a new state, and the process of transition from central planning to a market-type economy (see Ch.2, 2.1).

As is well known, the Shock Therapy method of economic reform was developed and used first in West Germany after the World War II. New life was breathed into it in post-Communist Poland with the introduction of the "Balcerowicz Plan" in 1990 (Balcerowicz, 1994; Schaffer, 1992). The implementation of this approach to macroeconomic stabilization requires the active involvement of several different governmental institutions. To successfully apply the method of Shock Therapy in the absence of these crucial institutions is impossible, and any attempt to do so is doomed to failure. The experience of Georgia also supports the validity of this view. It is not difficult to demonstrate this. It is enough to elaborate what Shock Therapy means according to the so-called Balcerowicz Plan (considered today as the modem and already classical scheme of Shock Therapy) and then to study defects in the implementation of Shock Therapy when it was applied in Georgia, blindly imitating the reflections in the Russian "mirror" (Papava, 1996a, 1996b, 1999, 2002a, pp. 6–16).

9.2. DEFECTIVE GEORGIAN MODIFICATION OF THE METHOD OF SHOCK THERAPY

The method of Shock Therapy generally assumes that a strict fiscal policy is being implemented. It entails the simultaneous adoption of measures concerned with price liberalization, a considerable reduction of the national budget deficit by canceling budgetary subsidies, and stringent control over the money supply and income of the population. The plan developed by the former Polish finance minister, Leszek Balcerowicz, is considered an excellent modern example of the method of Shock Therapy, and is frequently referred to favorably by other transition economies. According to this plan, the following measures were simultaneously implemented in Poland from the very start:

1. Multiple increases of all types of prices; a deliberate, though it is hoped temporary, increase in inflation aimed at ensuring and maintaining market equilibrium;

2. Tough restrictions on the (real) incomes of the population;

3. A substantial increase in (nominal) interest rates and restrictions of the money supply in circulation;

4. Increases in the interest rates on cash and other deposits, aimed at stimulating the population to save;

5. Sharp cuts in national budget expenses by reducing government investments and by refusing to subsidize unprofitable enterprises any longer;

6. Using issues of government bonds to help cover the national budget deficit;

7. Regulating the tax system and moving toward a more uniform, Western-type tax structure;

8. Introducing a common rate of exchange of the zloty to the dollar (involving a substantial initial devaluation) and ensuring zloty convertibility in the domestic market;

9. Introducing a common customs tariff in order to restrict imports and stimulate exports;

10. Providing social assistance to the population within the limits of government possibilities;

11. The elimination of monopoly positions and a substantial withdrawal of administrative intervention in enterprise activities.

The use of the Shock Therapy method began in Russia on January 2, 1992. A month later, it began in Georgia. To explain how the Shock Therapy approach used in Georgia deviated from the Polish approach, it is helpful to compare each step taken in Georgia with the corresponding item in the Balcerowicz Plan (which is a classical scheme of the Shock Therapy approach in post-Communist countries), as listed previously:

1. The reform of price formation started in Georgia as early as spring of 1991 when free prices on some types of goods were introduced. If in 1991 these changes were still of an exceptional character, by February 1992 (that is a month later than in Russia) there were radical changes in the price-formation system in Georgia. Thus, the prices of one group of goods and services were liberalized, while the regulated prices of another group increased considerably. All this was aimed at balancing the market. If in 1991 the consumer price index stood at 1.8, in 1992 it rose to 25. At the same time it is noteworthy that the regulated consumer prices increased sixty-eight times in 1992 in comparison with those of 1991 (for bread, the main food product in Georgia, 100 times). We can say that the first item of the Balcerowicz Plan was on the whole fulfilled in Georgia;

2. From 1992 indexation of minimum wages and social security benefits began to be used in Georgia. In 1991 this indexation was carried out only once, but in 1992, in the process of liberalizing price formation, income indexation was performed six times. In 1991 the minimum wage and the average wage of employees increased in comparison with the previous year by 1.85 times and 1.26 times, respectively, and in 1992 compared with 1991 by

13.14 times and 17.94 times, respectively. True, there were no strict regulatory measures in Georgia to control increases in the wage fund (as was done in Poland, when in the case of a 2 percent overspending of the wage fund the penalty imposed on an enterprise was equal to 200 percent of this sum; and if the overspending was more than 2 percent the penalty was 300–500 percent of the corresponding sum), but the increases in wages and social security benefits lagged behind price increases. Thus, it can be considered that item two of the Balcerowicz Plan was also, to a certain extent, more or less fulfilled in Georgia;

3 and 4. In 1992 in comparison with 1991, the interest rate on deposits increased from 2 percent to 5 percent per annum and for ten-year deposits the interest rate increased from 9 percent to 80 percent. Such an increase of the interest rate was still far from reflecting the actual inflation rate. It should also be noted that it was generally impossible to restrict the money supply in circulation in Georgia in those days by increasing the interest rate, because the country had no monetary system of its own; there were in circulation in Georgia only the ruble of the already disintegrated USSR, and the newly issued Russian ruble.

In summer 1992 it was decided to double cash deposits on a deferred withdrawal basis. In particular, on July 25 the decision was taken to double cash deposits devalued by inflation on August 1. The population immediately responded by depositing more money in cash deposits. On August 1, a new decision was made to prolong until August 10 the time available for placing money in cash deposits for doubling. After doubling the additional money could be withdrawn after only a year, unless the money was to be used in the process of privatization (which was, however, suspended at that period in Georgia). As it became rather difficult to receive the necessary quantity of bank notes from Russia in a timely way in the second half of 1992, the money accumulated in this way was paid out as wages and pensions, and this practically prevented the government from restricting the money supply. As a result, one can conclude that items three and four of the Balcerowicz Plan were not carried out in Georgia;

5. In 1992, the share of government investment in the total expenditure of the national budget was not reduced, and up to that year it varied in the range of 20–25 percent. The nominal amount of subsidies in 1992 compared with 1991 increased by about 5.1 times. However, in 1991 the share of subsidies in budget expenditure amounted to the remarkably high level of

47 percent, and in 1992 this was cut back to 30.1 percent. Even so, this does not enable us to suggest that item five of the Balcerowicz Plan was realized in Georgia;

6. Government internal bonds were formally issued in 1992. But they were offered for sale only in autumn 1993 and mainly in order to convert bonds of the FSU into new Georgian bonds. As for the use of government bonds to meet the national budget deficit, it should be noted that this has not yet proved feasible in Georgia. It is clear that item six of the Balcerowicz Plan was not implemented either;

7. Comprehensive reform of the tax system in accordance with the requirements of a market economy started as early as the spring of 1991. For this reason item seven of the Balcerowicz Plan should mainly be considered as fulfilled in Georgia at that time, although it should also be noted that further reform of the tax system is continuing constantly, as in many other countries of the world;

8. In 1992 there was no national currency in Georgia, and so it was practically impossible to fulfill item eight of the Balcerowicz Plan;

9. In 1992, general customs tariffs were introduced at rates of 2 percent on imports and 8 percent on exports. Obviously, this policy did not favor either import restrictions or export stimulation, so that item nine of the Balcerowicz Plan was clearly not fulfilled in Georgia either;

10. It was already mentioned that in 1992, as in 1991, there was income indexation, albeit imperfectly applied, and subject to lags. At that time any type of assistance to families with small incomes was disregarded. That is to say, the social protection system did not differentiate by income level in a way that supported those with low real incomes. As a result, the real minimum wage in 1992 amounted to only 86 percent of that of 1991. Since, despite the income indexation in 1992, targeted assistance to the families most in need was inadequate, item ten of the Balcerowicz Plan was unfortunately not fulfilled;

11. In 1992, for the first time in Georgia, legal and governmental resolutions and decrees restricting monopolistic institutions and practices and promoting competition were issued, although their effective implementation was significantly delayed. True, as early as 1991, the Soviet procedures for the centralized supply of resources to enterprises and final customers were dis-

rupted and gradually abandoned, but many elements of the system of state administrative interference in enterprise activity were still preserved. For instance, the mechanism of state orders continued to be widely used. Hence, item eleven of the Balcerowicz Plan was also not carried out at that time.

Thus, in 1992 in Georgia, eight out of eleven items of the Balcerowicz Plan (that is, all except items one, two, and seven) were not fulfilled.

Also neglected were such important measures as the canceling or at least serious restriction of budgetary subsidies and tough restriction of the money supply. Many of those items were actually doomed to failure, above all because there was no independent monetary system at that time in Georgia. In these conditions, implementing a defective variant of the Shock Therapy method based only on price liberalization could hardly be expected to succeed. In other words, in the absence of corresponding governmental institutions, the transition to a market economy using the Shock Therapy approach was practically impossible. In this situation it might have been much more effective to choose the step-by-step approach to the transition to a market economy, which could have been based on the successive creation of the various institutions necessary both for pursuing reforms and for constructing the Georgian state.

The populist stage of economic reform ended with the inevitable failure of the defective Georgian modification of the Shock Therapy approach, and this then gave rise to serious delays in the economic reform process.

9.3. DELAYED ECONOMIC REFORM

The stage of delayed economic reform includes 1993 and the first half of 1994 (Georgia, 1995). One factor resulting in delayed reforms was outside the economic sphere, while another factor explained delays in terms of basic mistakes of economic policy. The economy of Georgia (and not only the economy) was neither prepared for the full-scale military operations that started in Abkhazia in summer 1992, nor for the civil war that intensified in autumn 1993. These events seriously strained the national budget, and in 1993–94 it proved impossible to get the budget approved in advance in the normal manner. To cover the resulting deficits, the only possible source was money emissions. The gap between state expenditures and revenues was 1.118 billion coupons in 1993, and in 1994 the corresponding deficit amounted to 28.293 billion coupons.

Both in consequence of a general amnesty announced in the winter of 1992, and later on through its participation in military operations (as a country without an army), the crime situation in Georgia worsened so much that it became too dangerous to conduct most economic activity. As a result, many businessmen left their native land, and this accelerated the outflow of capital. At the same time, undisguised robbery was replaced by racketeering, which is also not conducive to successful business development. These criminal elements could not usually manage to accumulate wealth (had they done so, it might in the future have put them in a position where they needed a stable situation to protect their new wealth). The reason for this is that the overwhelming majority of these people were drug addicts or had links with the drug trade, and so there was substantial leakage of stolen property to the neighboring countries from where the drugs illegally penetrated into Georgia.

In late 1992 and early 1993 the most important policy mistake occurred. The government, for some reason, did not expect that it would receive additional banknotes from Moscow, and it therefore brought into circulation the temporary banknotes of Georgia—the coupon of the National Bank of Georgia (NBG). Unfortunately, representatives of the different levels of authority in Georgia were unable to take the new currency seriously, sometimes revealing contemptuous attitudes toward it. This had a decisive impact on the already serious devaluation process under way. Basically, the nature of the mistake was the illusion that it was economically expedient for Georgia to remain temporarily or even permanently within the proposed "ruble zone." As a result of this unfortunate illusion, the coupon became the sole legal tender of payment only in July–August 1993, when Russia carried out a partial currency reform of its own and withdrew the ruble of the FSU from circulation. This act made it clear that Georgia would be obliged to introduce its own currency.

Uncontrolled credit emissions were the foundation of the inflationary process in Georgia. Attempts to solve agricultural problems (e.g., the procurement of agricultural products in autumn 1993 and carrying out essential agricultural work in spring 1994) from a budget that had been practically nonexistent since the autumn of 1993 resulted in initially unreported budgetary emissions that finally ruined the financial system of the country. Georgia developed a hyperinflationary spiral, with the inflation rate from 1993 until autumn 1994 proceeding at some 60–70 percent per month. In the long run, this money was not, unfortunately, used for agricultural purposes. In conditions of such high inflation, the coupon could not perform the normal function of sustaining commercial turnover, because the real value of the coupon supply was constantly falling. Other things being equal, this promoted wider use of the ruble instead of the coupon as means of payment (Gurgenidze, Lobzhanidze, Onoprishvili, 1994).

In 1991–92 the foundations of the system of informal relations, which is characteristic of low-income countries (Adams and Fitchett, 1992), were laid down in Georgia.

The incorrect policy of the NBG toward restricting cash circulation (which gave rise, contrary to common sense, to restrictions on the withdrawal of coupons from the banking system) resulted in substantial discrepancies between cash and noncash monetary values. This further restricted the circulation of the coupon. Also, state commercial banks tolerated excessive overdrafts, which promoted hidden credit emission. Subsidized prices on bread, gas, electricity, and transport gave the budget an additional loading and also promoted budgetary emissions.

A serious error was perpetrated in Georgia's foreign trade policy, which allowed the "unique Georgian" clearing system to be consolidated. Barter was considered the only way to receive gas from Turkmenistan. The prices of both Turkmen gas and a lot of poor-quality goods produced in Georgia were artificially overcharged. According to the "innovators" of such an approach, this would result in the creation of an environment for Georgian enterprises that stimulated their activity. It should be mentioned that such an environment for producing goods of poor quality has really been created. At the same time this production had to be purchased by government. In the absence of a proper budget, however, this operation could be only partially carried out, and even then only by means of money emission (which also promoted inflation). Most of this production was taken from enterprises by the government using a form of the state order system, with guarantees to pay the corresponding price in the future. Using the system of state orders required a complicated system of quotas and licensing. When receiving debts from different foreign countries and international organizations, in some cases the interest rates and prices on goods bought with the help of credits were artificially increased, and the credits received were partly used in less important directions. Needless to say, this put these enterprises in a difficult financial situation and resulted in the formation of a nonpayment network within the country, which was difficult to stop. For the government it became impossible to collect the full volume of goods within the country to fulfill the barter commodity exchange agreed with Turkmenistan. In recent years the existing difficulties with the Azerbaijan transport route, first the blocking of the railway line passing through Abkhazia and then through Chechnya, at first complicated and then made impossible the normal transportation of goods, assembled by the government, to Turkmenistan. As a result of these difficulties and mistakes, Georgia's debt to Turkmenistan amounted to about half a billion US dollars over two years. The country's total external debt rose to one billion US dollars.

Ignoring the interests of enterprise workers and employees effectively impeded the privatization process in 1992–93 and held up the restructuring of enterprises into joint-stock companies.

Much of this lay behind the energy crisis, associated with the use of credits for purposes other than the intended ones; non-payment of the real cost of power resources (in other words, absurdly low domestic prices); chronic irresponsibility in regard to technical norms that made it impossible to carry out not only capital renewal, but even routine repairs and maintenance; and constant theft of power equipment containing copper (including wire) to sell in Turkey. All the afore-mentioned factors, including the energy crisis, gave rise to an unprecedented collapse of production.

Moreover, given the general state of disarray in both national and enterprise-level accounting, it became impossible to obtain full information on firms and their activities. This, in its turn, artificially exaggerated the already apparent decline in the major macroeconomic indicators and, at enterprise level, facilitated firms' efforts to hide their tax liabilities.

This stage of economic reform was characterized by extremely imperfect recording of foreign economic activities, inefficient customs procedures, extensive waste of commodity stocks, uncontrolled transfers of state property to foreign countries, a decline in the economic role of normal wages, unrecorded expansion of the shadow economy, and uses of humanitarian aid for purposes other than those intended. Overall, the picture of the Georgian economy was exceedingly bleak.

9.4. THE GEORGIAN APPROACH: "MINIMAL SHOCK WITH MAXIMUM THERAPY"

At the beginning of 1994 the head of state of Georgia, Eduard Shevardnadze, initiated the preparation of an anti-crisis program of macro-economic stabilization and systemic change. In spring 1994 the program was initiated, and this made a good start to *the stage of correction of errors* committed during the earlier stages of the process of economic reforms.

This new stage of economic reform was also characterized by problems of a noneconomic nature. By spring 1994 the hostilities in Abkhazia had already come to an end. True, this fact had a positive influence on the economy as a whole, but it also gave rise to a new problem: social protection of refugees and displaced people, which was a heavy burden on the government budget. Until the refugees and displaced people return to their homes these social (but not only social) problems will not be solved.

Law-enforcement institutions intensified the fight against criminals in order to improve the situation. Definite positive results were achieved, but the country still had a long way to go to solve the problem. Many enterprises, for instance, were afraid to undertake high levels of production for fear of being robbed by organized (including semi-official) and other criminal elements.

From spring 1994 the government gradually changed its attitude toward the coupon. According to the standard policy of the IMF, it is ready to assist any country that has its own currency and whose government does its best to strengthen it. If Georgia stayed within the ruble zone the IMF would undoubtedly prefer to work with Russia—the country issuing the ruble. This fact undermined the positions of those in power supporting the ruble zone, since they would have had to openly advocate the requirement to regard the Russian ruble as the sole legal tender. Conversely, it assisted those in power who, from the very beginning, realized that the Georgian economy had no prospects without its own national currency. Interestingly, in 1994 a noble but perhaps hopeless experiment was already going on in Kutaisi, where the city authorities were supporting the coupon—the one region of Georgia to do so. All this, together with the relative stabilization of the Georgian coupon and worsening depreciation of the ruble, encouraged the population to take the coupon more seriously.

Uncontrolled monetary emissions became impossible owing to the increasing firmness of the authorities of the NBG. In autumn 1994 the Bank cancelled the prevailing restrictions on the withdrawal of cash from the banks, under obvious pressure of the IMF. As a result cash and noncash money values drew considerably closer to each other.

From late 1994, on the advice of the IMF, the NBG started regulating the banking system using the classical methods widely used elsewhere in the world. Apart from solving other problems, this prevented the state-commercial banks from continuing to work in overdraft conditions. Also, from the second half of 1994 the process of corporatization of the state-commercial banks started.

According to the program worked out with the IMF in September 1994, the prices of gas and electricity were raised to world levels, the price of bread increased 285 times(!), metro fares increased greatly, and so did tariffs on other municipal services. There was a wage increase for those employed in activities financed by the budget, and pensions and social welfare payments were also increased, but these increases lagged considerably behind the price rise. This enabled a great reduction in the budgetary subsidies needed to cover the discrepancies between consumer and producer prices or between producer prices and actual costs. A substantial strengthening of the rate of the Georgian coupon followed it. Whereas before the price rise on bread one dollar was worth 5.3 million coupons, after the price rise one dollar was already valued at 2.4 million coupons. This process continued; at the end of 1994 the price of bread increased again by 40 percent and as a result a stable coupon exchange rate was established (at one dollar = 1.3 million coupons) (Wang, 1998; Wellisz, 1996).

Unfortunately, Georgia could not manage a full recovery of money neither for gas nor electricity. However, if enterprises and the population did not pay for their gas and electricity supplies, or paid only negligible sums, the price of bread was almost fully paid by the population. Delays in enforcing these payments encouraged a more skeptical attitude to the coupon by economic agents: trade organizations, enterprises, and banks delayed corresponding money transfers and conducted speculative operations in the currency market, sustaining significant losses in the process. Starting from 1995, when the coupon rate became stable, timely withdrawal of these sums was prevented not only by the sluggishness of the banks, but also by some local authorities using these sums temporarily in order to settle the problems of their local budgets.

Also, the pseudo-protection of enterprises by some representatives of government, and the often groundless fears of the population about interruptions of supply, meant that enforcement of payments by cessation of deliveries—the normal method in market-type economies—was not achieved. Gas supply to the population of Tbilisi stopped only in January 1995. Carrying out a stricter policy to recover the cost of bread was achieved step by step in the first and second quarters of 1995.

The impossibility of collecting the full cost of gas and electricity also meant that the government could not revise the corresponding prices, because of the general commitments on reform. The dollar prices of gas and electricity increased every month as a result of the strengthening of the coupon. This led to an artificial increase in the product cost, having an adverse affect, first of all, on industrial enterprises. Following a review of its commitments to the IMF, the Georgian government revised coupon prices downward. In particular, since April 1995 the cost of gas has been reduced by 35 percent and the cost of electricity by 25 percent. At the same time, the government of Georgia refused to purchase gas after June 1995. Instead, purchases had to be undertaken by the immediate consumers, namely by Sakenergo (Georgian state energy company), big industrial enterprises, and municipalities. To enable these direct purchases of gas by consumers to take place, the aforementioned Georgian clearing system was, in effect, annulled.

All this put on the agenda the requirement to terminate quotas and simplify licensing. This process soon started. The system of quotas was completely annulled with effect from June 1, 1995, and licensing was preserved for only a limited list of goods. Order was also reestablished in borrowing and using debts, building on the practices established in connection with Georgia's first loans from the IMF and the World Bank. In December 1994, Georgia received the first tranche of a Systemic Transformation Facility (STF) (approximately 39 million US dollars) from the IMF.

Approval of the national budget by Pparliament at the beginning of 1995, after a two-year interval, can be considered a very important step toward establishing order in the financial system of Georgia. The real significance of this budget is that emissions of credit and monetary emissions themselves were not used to balance budgetary income and expenditure. In 1995, only 47 percent of the expenditures of the national budget were covered by taxes and the remaining 53 percent had to be covered through the monetization of wheat and flour received as humanitarian aid (mobilizing proceeds of sales in the national budget). In that way, an unbalanced budget could be balanced without monetary emission. It was achieved through the help of donor countries and organizations promoting reforms in Georgia. Unfortunately, the planned financial indicators for the first two quarters were not achieved, though the actual results were improving considerably month by month.

With the support and efforts of the IMF, the majority of the countries to which Georgia's debt of approximately one billion US dollars was owed agreed to debt rescheduling. This allowed the IMF to allocate the second credit tranche of the STF at the end of June 1995 (approximately 44 million US dollars) and the stand-by credit (approximately 113 million US dollars). All this was expected to create the conditions for Georgia to preserve financial stability, to carry out currency reform, and to place the *lari* (national currency) into circulation, avoiding the errors previously committed by the government in connection with the coupon (Wang, 1998; Wellisz, 1996).

The exchange rate of the national currency was expected to remain unaltered until the end of 1995. After July 1995 the price of bread increased by 7 percent on average, while the wages of budget sector employees increased by 50 percent on average. In autumn 1995 the liberalization of bread prices was planned. This was expected to become possible as a result of the planned dissolution of the government monopoly in this sphere.

From July 1, 1995, the minimum monthly wage of those employed in the budget sector was just US$2.69 and the maximum US$12.69. These figures are, of course, very low, though one should recall that at the beginning of September 1994 the minimum wage was less than ten cents, and the maximum a little more than a dollar (all evaluated using the then prevailing exchange rate, without adjustment for purchasing power parity).

From the point of view of sectoral development, the reforms in Georgia are being implemented most vigorously in the healthcare system, where the project for reform was elaborated in close cooperation with experts of the World Bank. In the healthcare sphere a gradual transition to paid medical service and establishing a system of medical insurance was started.

In May 1994 the head of state issued a decree according to which enterprise personnel were given precedence in the process of corporatization. This speeded up the process. At the same time, the process of privatization, by means of direct purchases, was also encouraged. In 1995 in Georgia, as in many other former Communist countries, the process of using vouchers in privatization began: Part of the social property is distributed to people free of charge. The approach is justified by the necessity to give everyone a fair chance to acquire assets in the course of privatization (Papava, 1992, pp. 92–7).

The success of the Shock Therapy in 1994–1995 rests on the paradox: "The Worse, the Better." Therefore such a situation might be classified as "Minimal Shock with Maximum Therapy" (see Ch. 2, 2.3).

10

Involvement of the International Monetary Fund in the Transformation of Georgian Economy from 1991–2003

It's only those who do nothing that make no mistakes, I suppose.

Joseph Conrad (Teodor Josef Konrad Korzeniowski)
(*1857–1924; Polish-born English novelist*)

10.1. POST-COMMUNIST GEORGIA BEFORE STARTING REFORMS WITH SUPPORT OF THE IMF

After the regaining of independence by Georgia, perhaps of greatest importance was whether or not the coming to power of healthy and truly professional people who would be able to push economic reforms in the right direction was possible. To be victorious, any good idea needs serious political and financial support. However, for a country like Georgia, which was so weakened by exhausting military actions, the mobilization of domestic financial resources turned out to be a very hard—if not practically unsolvable—problem. A great role in addressing this issue has been played by international financial and other institutions such as the IMF, the World Bank, the EU, and others. Obviously, of these institutions, particular stress should be placed on the IMF, owing to coordinating functions that the international financial system has conferred on it.

Naturally, it is economic science that has to answer the question of what changes should be made in the economic basis of society in the course of post-Communist transformation, and especially how these changes should be made. Unluckily, it turned out that economists had not been prepared to ensure scientific support of the process of transformation: There was no universal economic theory on the basis of which an essentially right economic policy for all post-Communist states could have been developed (Stiglitz 1996, p. 3). Under such circumstances, in view of, at best, sound professional intuition of an economist giving advice, any economist who makes judgments on the basis of general principles of economic theory and the experience of market-oriented reforms implemented in other countries in transition can be regarded as optimally close to what is desired (see Ch. 2).

In the early phases of transition to a market economy, the government of Georgia was tempted to solve the hardest problems of transition on its own. In a number of instances members of the government would seek "free advice" of either their compatriots who had temporarily returned to their homelands, or foreign charlatans "transiting" through the country. Very often, these latter, ostensibly with the purpose of pushing economic reforms and improving the hard social conditions of the people, would attempt to import into the country billions of dollars earned by drug trafficking, illegal manufacturing of or trade in weapons, and so on—in other words, "dirty" money. In that case, the mechanism of laundering such money is to compel the government to issue financial guarantees for borrowing huge credit resources (tens and hundreds of millions, even billions of dollars). As a rule, such transactions are implemented through obviously suspicious mediators.

Given the ways by which dirty money is generally made and, more importantly, the sort of people who are usually involved in making such money, a natural question arises: If dirty money can only be made by cheating and robbing people, how can it be expected that, in the course of "laundering" such dirty money, the magnates who make that money will become honest overnight? Undoubtedly, I believe a crook is not likely to ever give up wrongdoing, whatever the circumstances may be.

It must be noted that in the early 1990s, Georgia did have some attempts to use financial guarantees in order to attract some dirty money. The NBG and the Ministry of Finance (MoF) issued many of letters of guarantee for many billions of dollars. Further developments showed that this was a wrong way to get credits. Furthermore, the guarantees themselves became the subject of international speculation. If the IMF had not interfered, Georgia's financial situation could have been even more difficult.

At the time when Georgia joined the IMF and the World Bank, the number of their members equaled 170. A quota (or vote) of Georgia in these institutions amounts to 0.08 percent.

As was noted above, at the time of Georgia's joining the IMF and the World Bank, the world nations had already maintained financial order, which actually was the only lawful way to receive monetary support in the shape of "clean" money. Maintenance of such an order is the only choice for any country, including Georgia, which has opted for civilized forms of economic development.

The first IMF mission arrived in Georgia in November 1991. The objective of this first visit was to get familiar with local circumstances. After that, during each successive visit, the IMF mission would leave the Georgian government with their recommendations on how to accomplish macroeconomic stability in the country. Unfortunately, governmental officials in charge at the time (with rare exceptions) paid little attention both to those recommendations and their authors (Gotsiridze, Kandelaki, 2001; Papava, 1995a). As a result, the country's financial system came to the state of complete disorder. In 1993 and 1994 Georgia did not have any parliament-adopted national budget; the constitutional and legislative process was practically nonexistent; poor quality of adopted laws and, what really matters, extensive tax privileges to a wide range of organizations (such as churches, theaters, etc.) made it impossible to raise fiscal revenues even to a minimum level; government officials' attitude toward a temporary national currency—coupon—was that of sustainable nihilism; the NBG's self-indulgent monetary policy and repeated issue of huge amounts of Georgian currency (aimed, for example, at covering agricultural production costs) caused hyperinflation; in consequence, in 1993 and 1994 the rate of inflation reached 50–70 percent a month (Gurgenidze, Lobzhanidze M., Onoprishvili, 1994) (see. Ch. 9).

10.2. MAIN POSITIVE RESULTS

In 1994, President Eduard Shevardnadze initiated an "anti-crisis program," one of the key premises of which was to advance relationships with the IMF to an essentially new level; specifically, the status of IMF recommendations was upgraded from "desirable" to "mandatory." This fact was to bear very positive economic consequences.

Given this, for the facilitation of analysis, the IMF activities in Georgia can be split into two phases.

During *phase one,* that is, in 1991–1994, the IMF would provide the Georgian government with important recommendations, although this "naughty child" would take no notice of those; during *phase two,* that is, since 1994 to the present time, the IMF recommendations have been considered mandatory, although very often it has been hard to implement those recommendations and, above all, they have not always been commensurate with the true aspirations of some governmental officials.

The most important consequences of IMF activities in Georgia are that the country has succeeded in building up its own financial system and achieving macroeconomic stability.

More specifically, one has to place stress on the following achievements (Papava, 1995a; 1996a; 1999, 2003a, pp. 9–12, 2003c, p.7–9; Wang, 1998; Wellisz, 1996):

1. The legal framework of the country's financial system regulating market-based budgetary and monetary processes has been developed and adopted;

2. As a result of "hard" monetary policy, the NBG's hyperinflation was curbed; this made possible the successful implementation of the currency reform (the Russian ruble was removed from circulation and a newly introduced stable national currency, lari, was granted the status of legal tender);

3. The process of liberalization of prices has practically been completed (the hardest part of which was a release of bread prices);

4. As of 1995, parliament would adopt national budgets practically in the beginning of each successive year;

5. A two-tier banking system was formed by which functions of the NBG and commercial banks have been delineated; in addition, the NBG has adopted a regulatory framework for commercial banks on the basis of which the government controls the banking system;

6. The process of privatization of all former government-owned banks has been completed;

7. Full liberalization of external trade has been achieved (inclusive of the encouraging of exports via lifting VAT and customs duties, as well as

releasing external trade from all nontariff regulating mechanisms) (Papava, Beridze, 1996/1997);

8. Foreign debts have been restructured, and conditions for the servicing of those debts have been established; Georgia has acquired the image of a country that is able to pay back its debts.

It must also be noted that the IMF took an active position with respect to the support from the World Bank, one of the key requirements of which was to give priority to the budgetary spending for education and health care. It is also noteworthy that the IMF has provided sustainable support of the World Bank programs in Georgia, the primary objective of which was to implement structural reforms of the Georgian economy.

In 1996 and 1997, as a result of the IMF operations in Georgia, both a high rate of economic growth and a very moderate rate of inflation were observed. Macroeconomic stability, in the meantime, is the most important condition without which it is impossible to implement any more-or-less significant investment project in a country. Aggressive measures recommended by the IMF for forming a favorable environment for investments, under other equal conditions, are of great importance for the realization of the Silk Road reinstating plan as well (Shevardnadze, 1999).

Of course, this list could be extended, but perhaps the most important outcome of cooperation between Georgia and the IMF is the fact that, at least, there has been a reduction of "popular amateurishness," a phenomenon that unluckily could repeatedly be observed in the government's actions (e.g., "swelling" foreign debts by using artificially increased clearing prices; imposing special taxes on local producers and importers of grains and flour, and official attempts to get the IMF's authorization for that; announcing that the government was going to tax amnesty to tax evaders and presenting a relevant program of actions to the IMF; "distorting" the country's financial system by establishing a Ministry of Tax Revenues and weakening the MoF "for the benefit" of certain governmental officials; utilizing commercial bank loans with the purpose of implementing the national budgetary plans and thereby interfering with the process of forming a stock market; direct distribution of different food products or rendering certain services instead of paying unpaid pensions, etc.). Without insistent pressure on the part of the IMF, for example, distribution of flour in place of paying pensions (and other similar actions) in some parts of Georgia would have become a general rule rather than a single fact, which sooner or later would have brought down the national economy and finance. The key "achievement" of such "popular amateurishness" consisted in the gradual worsening of relationships between Georgia and the IMF.

10.3. MAIN MISTAKES

One of the leading economists of our time, former vice president and former senior economist of the World Bank, Joseph Stiglitz, wrote that during the sessions devoted to the fiftieth anniversary of the Bretton Woods institutions (the World Bank and the IMF), one could repeatedly hear remarks such as: "Fifty years is enough" (Stiglitz, 1999b, p. F577).

Naturally, everyone makes mistakes, and the IMF is not an exception—it makes mistakes too, both in general (e.g., De Gregorio, Eichengreen, Ito, Wyplosz, 1999) and with respect to particular countries (e.g., Gomulka, 1995, pp. 14–19). Unfortunately, Georgia could not escape the IMF's mistakes as well (Papava, 2003a, pp. 27–47, 2003c, pp. 9–24).

Mistakes made by the IMF in Georgia vary both by their nature and implication. One has to note, however, that some of those mistakes have a very general character; in other words, they have been made by the Fund not only while working in Georgia, but also in a broader context, in other countries as well.

One has to also note that the Georgian governmental team, which had to negotiate with the IMF in the earliest phase of relationships, practically had neither any experience with conducting such talks nor a good understanding of IMF procedures, a situation the members of the IMF missions would take advantage of either consciously (perhaps to simplify a task) or unintentionally (which is more probable), but in all cases, quite skillfully (at any rate, as it seems from the present angle). In each particular case, in order to get each successive tranche, the Georgian party had to assume such commitments, the implementation of which in given time limits (actually, as a rule, in a very short period of time) would be very difficult; at the moments of accepting such commitments, the government was not always confident about how difficult the task of implementing those commitments could have been. Reformers, repeatedly resorting to unpopular measures while dealing with certain problems, as a rule, would point at the recommendations of the IMF and other financial institutions, for which reason, the public in general, and businesspeople in particular, started strongly disapproving of those institutions.

At the same time, it must be noted that all requirements of the IMF have officially been fixed as statements of the government (rather than the IMF requirements). As a result, in each disputable situation, the IMF experts, as a rule, would remind the government that these have been the commitments taken on by the government; that is, it has been the government's position, rather than that of the IMF. Also, one has to take into account the fact that in all cases, in order to carry out agreements reached between the Georgian government and the IMF, it was the governmental team conducting the negotiations that would assume a full and exclusive responsibility for the measures to be carried out. Furthermore, not all members of such teams (first of all, those responsible for fiscal and budgetary issues) would agree to assume such a responsibility; some members of the government (and Parliament too) at best never understood (and perhaps even never wanted to understand) what it meant to carry out commitments to the IMF.

Moreover, one has to take into account circumstances such as inclusion in the negotiating teams of certain governmental officials (at their request) who had a very poor reputation among the IMF staff. Ultimately, this would bring about a rejection of issues raised by such people, however justified from the standpoint of reforms they could be. (However, this would happen quite seldom, because more often during such meetings they would raise obviously erroneous and even completely unacceptable questions, which would negatively affect the reputation of the person representing the government, as well as that of the governmental agency, which was directly represented by such a person.) In all such instances, the negative reputation of such persons would have a negative impact on public opinion in regard to the IMF-supported programs as well. Furthermore, individual politicians, officials, and ordinary citizens would get a false impression that the members of the governmental team involved in the official negotiations with the Fund lacked competence and consistency and that they were not able to find the right arguments during their discussions with the IMF; however, if they could have taken over, the success would have been very quick and definite. Under such circumstances, without a firm reform-oriented attitude of both the president and the parliament leadership, Georgia would never achieve those results that we discussed above and that were achieved owing to the IMF's extensive support.

In the context of such an experience of cooperation with the IMF, perhaps it is easier to understand which mistakes could have been avoided in the very beginning and which mistakes were completely unavoidable.

Before starting to review those mistakes, it is essential to give some explanations that may facilitate our understanding of the substance of most of them. Specifically, because the majority of mistakes made by the IMF in Georgia are related to taxation, we must formulate those criteria, or more specifically, we must give those characteristics of the taxation system on the basis of which the nature and the meaning of each mistake can be evaluated.

An ideal taxation system should be built on the following key principles (Chappell, 1990, pp. 41–44):

1. *Simplicity:* The primary goal of the system must be that each individual could understand independently, that is, without any assistance of tax experts, all issues related to taxes;

2. *Plainness:* Taxation should be based on a single flat rate;

3. *Rate:* A tax rate should depend on a required amount of receivable incomes; at the same time, the rate should be high enough to discourage taxpayers from tax evasion;

4. *Universality:* Taxes and tax rates should be universal throughout the country, and no exemptions and privileges should be allowed. At the same time, certain governmental support may be provided, for example, to the disabled. However, such support should be in the form of special social programs and grants, rather than tax exemptions;

5. *Comprehensiveness:* Taxes should be imposed on both incomes and expenses;

6. *Evenhandedness:* Taxes should not distort different forms of saving and ideally should not make any distinction between spending and saving.

Naturally, there is no ideal taxation system in the real world, however, its significance for the estimation of strengths and weaknesses of existing taxation systems is obvious.

Political Mistakes. While reviewing the criticism of the IMF activities, we noted that the Fund often disregards the history, cultural traditions, and national peculiarities of the countries in which it operates. The same mistake could be observed from the very beginning of the IMF operations in Georgia. In particular, we are referring to the Fund's advice to the Georgian government to stay in the "ruble zone" and not to introduce a national currency. This advice was given to the Georgian government in February 1992.

It would hardly be possible to completely understand the motives that drove the Fund to give such advice. At best, we have to presume that it wanted to be cautious about irritating certain still influential and imperialistically ambitious forces in Russia. Perhaps it was for this reason that the IMF was not hurrying to make a violent intrusion into a monetary domain of the disintegrating empire.

But if we remember that this advice was applicable to the rest of the former Soviet republics too, except for the Baltic states (Estonia, Latvia, and Lithuania), we may presume that the Fund would have preferred to work with one single issuer of the national currency, rather than with twelve issuers, which would enable the Fund to establish one mission instead of twelve, and thereby save some money. It is noteworthy, in this regard, that only those countries that have introduced their own currencies are eligible for the IMF credits (e.g., Lavigne 1995, p. 207).

Anders Åslund tried to explain the IMF's desire to preserve the ruble zone by the fact that the IMF was skeptical about the technical abilities of the newly independent states that emerged after the disintegration of the FSU to introduce their own currencies and believed that a good currency reform should have been preceded by a country's preparation for genuine macroeconomic stabilization (which, we believe, is completely impossible if the country is out of its own monetary mechanisms of macroeconomic regulation). As a result, the IMF was afraid of being blamed for possible failures of the newly introduced national currencies (Åslund 1995, Ch. 4).

Opponents who were radically critical about the IMF considered that this mistake was a result of the fact that the IMF and the governments of the donor countries—members of the IMF—had failed to understand (or even had never tried to understand) the political situation that had emerged after the disintegration of the USSR; that they had failed to analyze (or even had never wanted to) the history of that imperialistic nation; that they had failed to realize national and cultural features of the countries such as Georgia, which had driven Georgia and other former Soviet republics to strive after real national independence. We believe that such a judgment is obviously exaggerated and the reason for the IMF's behaving in the above-described manner was that the IMF had been cautious about Russia.

One must presume that without stringent steps taken by Russia itself, as a result of which it ceased providing Georgia and other former Soviet republics with the Russian rubles, the IMF would never have hurried to change its attitude toward the ruble zone. Here we must remember that the NBG raised a question of introducing a national currency at the very first meeting with the IMF mission (in November 1991), having presented all necessary calculations and samples of national currency bills and coins. The NBG requested the IMF to help Georgia prepare for currency reform. Unfortunately, this request was not taken into consideration. One has to presume that the Fund's refusal, in addition to what was stated above, was motivated by the outburst of military actions in Georgia in the winter of 1991–1992.

In 1993, Georgia was practically unprepared to introduce its own currency. To a certain extent, this was prompted by the actions on the part of the IMF. However, it would be unfair to put the blame completely on the IMF, because at the time, first, the Georgian government had never paid any attention to the IMF recommendation and, second, it had been under an illusion that it would have been possible to stay within the ruble zone for a certain period of time. Such an attitude, under other equal conditions, was clearly reflected in the government's extremely nihilistic position on the temporary Georgian currency—coupon.

The IMF corrected (if we are allowed to use this word) this mistake in the fall of 1995, when in line with a plan coordinated with the IMF and owing to its financial support a currency reform was implemented. In other words, a new Georgian currency—the lari—was introduced.

Another big mistake in relation to Georgia was made by the IMF while dealing with a problem of identifying the successors of foreign debts and assets of the FSU.

In 1993, Russia and Georgia signed an agreement (known as a "Zero Scenario") according to which Russia would become a successor of all foreign debts and assets of the FSU. For some reason, the text of the signed agreement did not contain provisions (more precisely, they were "dropped" from it) about the fate of both the Diamond Stocks of the FSU and the deposits of the Georgian individuals and entities in the Vnesheconombank of the USSR, which had been included in the original, initialed version of the agreement.

Unfortunately, during the subsequent seven years, the IMF constantly refrained from intervening in this disputable question, although because of the aforementioned difference between the signed and the initialed versions, Georgia would refuse to ratify the agreement; meanwhile, according to the IMF procedures, this might have become a serious impediment to the IMF's extending credits to Russia because of the failure of Russia to settle its foreign debts.

After the end of this seven-year period, however, when the question of restructuring Georgia's debts to Russia (accumulated after the disintegration of the USSR) was put on the agenda, under the pressure of the Russian government and with the silent consent of the IMF, Georgia had to ratify the agreement, thereby putting a question mark over the possibility of serving justice and reinstating in the agreement the aforementioned provisions that had been "dropped" from the initialed text of the agreement.

Methodic Mistakes. Immediately after gaining independence, Georgia faced the problem of establishing numerous governmental institutions. A taxation system was one of those institutions: There was a need to adopt a new tax law, establish tax and customs offices, and ensure the staffing of these latter in spite of the scarcity of qualified human resources. One has to remember that, by then, the people of Georgia and particularly its developing businesses had no experience and tradition of paying taxes under the conditions of market economy, and a sense of responsibility in this regard had been practically nonexistent. In other words, neither taxpayers accurately knew what and how they should pay, nor the government knew what and how it should collect. Naturally, under such circumstances, the taxation system could not avoid certain shortcomings and mistakes and, as an immediate effect of it, corruption as well (it is noteworthy that at the time corruption was based on the traditions and experience accumulated during the Soviet period).

Elementary logic requires that at the initial stage of transition to a market economy, the taxation system should be as simple as possible. On the whole, the IMF shares such a belief, too. Specifically, one of the IMF experts, Leif Muten, notes that in the course of transition to a market economy the taxation system must be simple enough (Tanzi (ed.), 1993, Ch. 8).

The improvement of the taxation system must be carried out gradually, in line with the improvement of tax education and the development of taxpayer habits.

In view of this logic, it was a complete mistake to replace the turnover tax with the VAT from the very beginning, when the financial system of independent Georgia was still in its embryonic state. The point is that in Communist-type economies, the turnover tax by its nature is not a tax at all; instead, it is a government-established difference between a unit cost and a producer's price (or wholesale price) (e.g., Tanzi (ed.), 1993, Ch. 7, 1994, Ch. 6). As to the VAT, its economic contents, calculating methodologies, and mechanisms of collection are too complicated for mass application (e.g., Ebrill, Keen, Bodin, Summers, 2001). By far more justified would be to impose any other indirect tax, the administration of which would be much simpler. The sales tax (or the turnover tax based on a value-added rate) is a good example, because it has to be paid at the final stage of procurement; for this reason, the mechanism of imposing this tax is quite transparent to a taxpayer and, at the same time, it is quite easy for a tax collector to administrate it. This practice was applied, for example, in Romania (Tanzi (ed.), 1994, Ch. 6).

One has to admit, though, that, owing to its economic nature, the VAT is more acceptable than the sales tax because, in the case of the former, subject to taxation are all phases of business and, therefore, a burden of taxation lies on all such phases. Despite this, in the United States, a country with long and rich tax traditions, the sales tax is still in effect and discussions on the topic of whether or not the VAT should be introduced seem practically endless (e.g., Slemrod, Bakija, 1996, pp. 209–215).

In the countries of West Europe, the VAT was introduced after quite a long period when market traditions had finally been established. For example, in the United Kingdom and other European countries the VAT was introduced as late as 1973, although by then the country had had a centuries-old(!) tradition of market relationships. Besides, a long period had elapsed from the time when this tax was developed to the moment when it was finally recognized and established. Specifically, EU member countries introduced the VAT after about twenty years had passed since 1954 when it was invented in France.

Today, the VAT is one of the key conditions precedent to a country joining the EU (for example, in order to become an EU member state, Finland introduced the VAT as late as July 1994). Desire to become members of the EU is exactly the key motive for which the post-Communist countries have adopted the VAT (Tanzi, (ed.), 1993, Ch. 9).

It must be noted that the IMF has developed an eighteen-month schedule for the adoption of the VAT (Tanzi (ed.), 1993, Ch. 9). For the benefit of some countries, this schedule can even be extended; for example, in Romania, two and a half years passed in order for the VAT to be established (Tanzi (ed.), 1994, Ch. 6). According to the leading specialist of the IMF in fiscal issues, Vito Tanzi, if there is no uniform sales tax in a country, a two-year period is required for the introduction of the VAT; this period can be reduced to a year though, if transition to the VAT is to take place from the existing sales tax (Tanzi 1992, p. 49). If you add to this a period of five to ten years, which, according to the IMF experts, is necessary for ensuring computer and telecommunications support of the VAT administration (IMF, 1991, Ch. V.4), there will be no doubt how long and difficult the process of introducing and establishing the VAT can be.

To this extent, one has to admit that it was a big mistake on the part of the Georgian government to make an overnight shift from a Communist-style turnover tax to the VAT. By doing this, it disregarded the first principle of the ideal taxation system previously described—*simplicity*. As a result, Georgia lost huge tax revenues, the public got a very negative attitude toward the VAT, and favorable conditions for the booming of corruption were created.

The IMF's mistake was that, unlike the Georgian government, it knew what negative consequences could come up after instituting the VAT. Therefore, the right action on its part would be if it recommended the Georgian government to adopt the sales tax on a temporary basis and in parallel to take preparatory steps to ensure a smooth transition to the VAT. The IMF never did that. Whether or not our remark is correct can be verified by the Tax Policy Guidelines developed by the IMF experts primarily for the benefit of economists working with the IMF missions, in which it is clearly and directly stated that the introduction of the VAT should be preceded by broad taxpayer education and tax officer training campaigns. It is for this reason that, in some cases, the Fund recommends that before the VAT is introduced certain steps should be taken for the improvement of the sales tax collection practices (Shome (ed.), 1995, p. 280). Unfortunately, the IMF gave no such recommendation to the Georgian government.

As far as the VAT is concerned, a bigger mistake was that it was imposed on agricultural produce as well, although there had been no objective conditions for administering this tax in rural areas.

There is an assumption that has been shared by everyone in the IMF that, as a general rule, agricultural sectors of the countries in post-Communist transformation are represented mainly by the big government-owned and cooperative companies, which can be made accountable for the VAT, and in relation to which appropriate VAT-collecting practices could be developed. Small farmer businesses are exempted from the VAT, and they are responsible for paying it only in the case that their annual turnovers reach a certain upper limit (Tanzi (ed.), 1993, Ch. 9). It was due to this general assumption that the Georgian government, at the IMF's insistence, imposed the VAT on agricultural production. Originally, the upper limit of annual turnover, above which all agricultural businesses should be liable for the VAT, was set at $2,300; later it was raised, first to $10,000, then up to $17,500. Finally, however, it was lowered to $12,000, which became applicable to all sectors of the economy.

Here we have to stress the fact that, as is stated in the aforementioned Guidelines, the Fund usually identifies those sectors in which, because of certain difficulties connected with the VAT administration, it should not be applied; for example, it is recognized that agriculture should not be subject to the VAT. However, as a matter of fact, the IMF restrained itself from applying this general rule to the post-Communist countries, and the reason for doing this was that those countries had preserved big agricultural enterprises (Shome (ed.), 1995, p. 280).

While applying this scheme to Georgia, the IMF failed to take into account the fact that, almost immediately after the reestablishment of national independence, all big agricultural enterprises (both government-owned and cooperative enterprises) had broken up and that by the time of making that recommendation the Georgian agricultural sector had been represented mainly by small farmer businesses. Naturally, under such circumstances, first, the whole sector had been left without indirect taxation, and second, a strong disincentive discouraging the enlargement of agricultural companies and, therefore, the growth of economic efficiency of agriculture had come up. From the perspective of the ideal taxation system, both the first principle—*simplicity*—and the fourth one—*universality*—were broken.

The Georgian government's suggestion about a potential replacement of the VAT with an increased land tax (administration of which is obviously simpler and which is practically safe from corrupted practices) was completely rejected by the IMF experts. As they explained, the reasons for their negative attitude toward this question were twofold: First, all sectors should have been subject to the VAT, as this tax had been the most developed among all other indirect taxes (IBRD, 1991, p. 31); second, the IMF experts recognized that in case of raising the land tax rate by the level of the VAT rate, they would have been unable to develop a mechanism of recalculating it at the later stages of VAT having been paid by producers at preceding stages.

Another methodic mistake of the IMF existed in its recommendation—which later became its requirement—that the Georgian government lift the exemptions from VAT from such parts of corporate profits that should have been used for reinvestments. By doing this, the Georgian businesses, which had actually suffered from a big deficit of investments, would face a problem of losing all incentives to save some funds for the business development. To do justice, one has to note that in 1995, when the IMF demanded that the said exemption be abolished because of the significant drop of production output over the preceding period, the factual extent of its applicability was very little. However, the very fact of abolishing this exemption "washed away" from entrepreneurs' horizon even distant hopes for getting financial incentives from the government to use their own funds for reinvestments. What should also be underlined in this respect is that, by exempting the reinvested sections of profits from any taxes—inclusive of the VAT, one may contribute to the smoothening of the profit accounting system too, which ultimately may result in the growth of tax revenues. Unfortunately, the abolition of the said exemption caused negative effects to the tax accounting system in general.

Also evident is the IMF's mistake with respect to the income tax, that is, its progressive nature. To shed light on this problem we must bear in mind that under the Communist rule all employees used to work for state-owned companies and agencies and, accordingly, only staff salaries could be subject to the income tax. Under such circumstances, instead of charging tax on each individual separately, it would suffice to withhold the income tax from a company's payroll. Under the market economy, however, where, on one hand, people are involved not only in the public sector but also (and even to a greater extent) in the private sector, and on the other hand, where, in addition to salaries, they get some other income too, such as interest, rent, dividends, and so on, the government has to deal with a problem of taxing the incomes of each individual separately.

The administering of the progressive tax requires a quite sophisticated mechanism that should be based on a taxable earnings declaration scheme. Under this scheme every individual, at the end of each calendar year, should sum up his or her earnings for the year that he or she received from all sources and, accordingly, earned a taxable income; after that, on the basis of a progressive schedule, he or she should calculate a taxable amount and pay it. To the extent that tax payment practices among the population are either completely nonexistent or, at best, very poorly developed, it is no surprise that very few follow such a procedure. In addition, even tax offices are not prepared to carry it out properly. For this reason, the progressive income tax only facilitates the growth of a tax-evader mentality in each taxpayer and prompts him or her to break the tax law. Thus, in this case, out of the above six principles of an ideal taxation system, the first two were disregarded—*simplicity* and *plainness.*

From the perspective of administration, by far simpler and, accordingly, more transparent is a flat income tax scheme, where all individual earnings are charged a uniform tax rate and nobody has to make any additional recalculations (Hall, Rabushka, 1995).

Given all that was stated above, it must be clear what a big mistake was made by the IMF in Georgia when it demanded establishment of the progressive income tax scheme. The reason for such behavior of the IMF seems especially obscure in the context of what the IMF's experts say in this regard. For example, Ved P. Gandhi and Dubravko Mihaljek believe that in the initial phase, it is more reasonable to apply a flat income tax scheme (Tanzi, (ed.), 1993, Ch. 7). Leif Muten, in turn, points out that the progressive income tax scheme may create disincentives to work and risk and discourage people from observing the tax law (Tanzi, (ed.), 1993, Ch. 8).

Whatever the case may be, there is nothing to be done with regard to the first of the above three problems, that is, the potential replacement of the VAT with the sales tax. The point is that the Georgian government has already received from the IMF quite a bit of technical assistance for improving VAT collecting practices, owing to which certain positive results have already been achieved. More importantly, for the reasons described above, it does not make sense that Georgia, a country that has already expressed its aspirations to join the EU (in a long-term perspective), gives up the VAT at the present stage.

Also, the possibility that the IMF will change its mind in respect of charging agriculture by the VAT seems quite dubious.

As per the exempting of reinvested profits from the VAT, this issue has to be discussed with the IMF, especially as, according to an expert of the IMF, Krister Andersson, one of the most important steps toward improving the efficiency of tax policy is to extend investment credits (Tanzi (ed.), 1993, Ch. 5).

Although the asserted need for transition from the progressive income tax scheme to the flat income tax scheme seems obvious to me (to which assumption, as was noted above, even agrees with some IMF experts), odds are that no official agreement will be reached with the Fund on this issue.

Mistake Resulting from Confusion. In 1995–96, the government would almost permanently raise the question of excise stamps. The IMF's position would remain categorically negative, as the IMF experts believed that the government would not be able to avoid the forgery of those marks. In 1998, however, the IMF started insisting on the opposite: It demanded in a most categorical manner that the government institute excise stamps on cigarettes and alcoholic beverages. In 1999, after the introduction of excise marks, average monthly revenues from imported cigarettes grew by 3.2 times and from locally produced cigarettes by 19.2 times. This enables us to conclude that over the preceding years the country's budget must have lost huge amounts of income.

Mistake Resulting from a Stereotyped Approach. One of the most manifest mistakes of the IMF resulting from its stereotyped approach is the Tax Code of Georgia, which was drafted by the Finance Ministry under pressure of the IMF experts and which was adopted by Parliament in late 1997. Of course, the very fact of adopting a new tax law can only be welcomed. However, the Code was written in such awkward language (perhaps because of the stereotyped translation of an English sample) that sometimes it is hardly comprehensible not only to an average taxpayer, but also to specialists. In addition, some procedures described in the Code are so sophisticated that businesspeople would rather pay bribes to avoid certain confusions. It is worth noting that even the IMF has recognized that one of the reasons for inadequate tax collections may be that procedures are too complicated (IMF, 1997).

If we approach the Georgia Tax Code from the perspective of the previously described ideal taxation system, we can easily notice that it has failed to meet all of its six principles altogether. But the most disappointing thing, in our opinion, is that the Code disregards the most important of those principles—*simplicity.*

Many government officials, researchers, businesspeople, and media people consider that one of the key reasons for the burst of "budgetary crisis" in Georgia in 1998 is the new Tax Code, which contains numerous mistakes and obscurities and, therefore, is hardly understandable.

Despite the repeated attempts of some Georgian governmental officials to persuade the IMF to allow the government to reconsider the existing Tax Code, the Fund's stance has been unchangeable: *Institutional patriotism* prevents its experts from admitting their own mistakes.

Tactical mistake. The adverse impact of Russia's financial crisis of August 1998—which the IMF had failed to predict (Zevin, 2001, pp. 17–18)—was first felt by Georgia as early as the beginning of September. A sensitive shortage of US dollars in the Russian domestic market caused a dramatic increase in the need of US dollars in the Commonwealth of Independent States (CIS) countries. Especially sensitive to such a need were those countries for which Russia has been the most important trade partner.

In the Georgian context, the situation was aggravated by the fact that the Russian military bases existing in the Georgian territory were used as a facility for uncontrolled imports into the country of devalued Russian ruble bills with the purpose of buying and carrying US dollars to Russia. In the meantime, the Tskhinvali corridor (in South Ossetia), which has practically been beyond the Georgian government's control, was used for the intensification of smuggling cheap Russian goods and for carrying huge amounts of US dollars out of the country to Russia. This negatively affected the exchange rate of the national currency—lari—that had been adjusted by the NBG via implementing dollar interventions in the interbank currency exchange. Under such circumstances, the NBG had no choice but to release dollar stocks it had kept so strictly by then. Obviously, this could not last for a long time, as the amount of such stocks was limited and could be exhausted shortly.

Under such circumstances, the IMF's recommendation was that the NGB stop implementing currency interventions and give up lari exchange rate adjustments, which would enable it to preserve the NBG dollar stocks. Had the government followed this recommendation, it would inevitably have done irremediable harm to the country: The released exchange rate would have dropped immediately, provoking panic at the currency market, which, in turn, would have contributed to a further decrease in the lari exchange rate. Such circumstances would have prompted people to rush to commercial banks to carry away their savings, which ultimately would have resulted in the bankruptcy of most commercial banks and, thereafter, the impoverishment of all those individuals and companies that had kept their money with such banks.

One has to admit that the reaction of both the NBG and the government to the situation was highly commendable. They never agreed to the above—obviously wrong in terms of tactics—advice of the IMF and by manipulating the lari exchange rate through a gradual devaluation alerted commercial banks and the public, in general, to the need of converting their lari stocks into dollars. Although this maneuver cost the NBG tens of millions of dollars, by the time it stopped its currency interventions into the currency market, the lari exchange rate had been as low as necessary to prevent, in commercial banks (because they had already disposed of most of their lari reserves), immediate and harmful devaluation of the Georgian currency. The immediate effect of such tactical steps was that irrespective of the destructive impact of the Russian financial crisis, no single commercial bank of Georgia went bankrupt for the reasons described above.

Unfortunately, the IMF experts disregarded such a successful—in general terms—performance of the Georgian government, having focused their attention on the fact that the NBG had spent a considerable part of its hard currency reserves.

Mistakes Resulting from the Abuse of Powers. The functions of the IMF and the World Bank had been delineated from each other. The IMF has repeatedly confirmed that there are certain areas, such as reformation of government-owned enterprises and public service, ensuring the right to ownership, ensuring that agreements be observed and public procurements be implemented, and so forth, with respect to which the Fund must be guided by more competent institutions and, basically, by the World Bank (IMF, 1997).

From this perspective, very strange seems the IMF's categorical statement made in September 1999, that in the very near future the Georgian government would have to establish a new governmental institution—an independent anticorruption service endowed with broad responsibilities.

Meanwhile, a memorandum of the IMF Executive Board dated July 25, 1997, says that all issues related to governance, inclusive of corruption, should be considered by the Fund exclusively from the economic standpoint and within the limits of the IMF's mandate (IMF, 1997).

The fact is that in this particular case the IMF obviously abused its powers. Only after the World Bank had stepped in and—having been based on both international experience and institutional underdevelopment of Georgia—had expressed its disagreement to the establishment of an independent anticorruption department, the IMF "softened" its tone and shifted its focus to a possibility of applying predominantly economic mechanisms of struggle against corrupt practices existing in the financial system.

Another mistake related to the IMF's abuse of powers was made in the fall of 2000, when the IMF insisted that the government commit itself to raising an electricity tariff in order to address a problem of outstanding debts of the energy sector.

Meanwhile, in 1997, under the pressure of the World Bank and with the support of the IMF, Georgia established and has since operated a National Energy Regulating Committee (NERC), which was designed to be a self-governing agency, totally independent from the government. One of the key functions of the NERC was to pursue an independent tariff policy of the energy sector and to harmonize its decisions only with the principles of market economy. Accordingly, the government had no right (and, of course, the IMF was aware of this fact) to commit itself to effecting any changes to the existing electricity tariffs. Unfortunately, the independent (from the government)—by virtue of law—NERC actually became dependent on the will of the government and, ultimately, of the IMF.

10.4. THE IMF—A STRATEGIC PARTNER OF GEORGIA

Georgia has already made an exclusively right choice—to tie up its future with Europe, with the West (Rondeli, 2001). This is both a very difficult and long way to go, and success in it is achievable only by the gradual adoption of the European system of values. Indeed, such an approach concerns all spheres of life, inclusive of the financial and economic arrangement of the country.

Today the IMF has no alternative, and the existing global financial order requires that Georgia perform the role of recipient country defined by that order itself. Otherwise, Georgia may be deprived of the right to receive the comprehensive assistance that is so important for accomplishing a genuine national independence. Again, without the financial and political assistance of the West it will be practically impossible for Georgia to preserve its national independence, especially bearing in mind the hardships of economic transition and temporarily lost territories.

Irrespective of some mistakes as described above, the IMF remains a reliable financial guarantor and a real supporter of the Georgian government in its striving to establish a sound and healthy financial and economic system for Georgia. If one keeps in mind the fact that the IMF is changing its programs and tactics, the key objective of which is to alleviate poverty and ensure economic growth (GG, 2003), one may see that the intensification of cooperation with the IMF is a need that is beyond all doubts.

Indeed, the IMF is a strategic partner of Georgia, and it has to remain such even after Georgia overcomes its current position of recipient country. This is true because there is no alternative for Georgia other than to become an integrated part of the civilized world.

11

The Pre- and Post-Revolutionary State of Georgia's Economy

America's present need is not heroics, but healing;
not nostrums but normalcy; not revolution, but restoration.

Warren G. Harding
(1865–1923; American Republican statesman; 29th President of the United States, 1921–1923)

11.1. ECONOMIC COMPONENTS OF THE ROSE REVOLUTION

The fall of 2003 appeared to be a turning point in the history of independent Georgia; over the course of two days, November 22 to 23, Georgia witnessed the so-called Rose Revolution (e.g., Ascherson, 2004; Baran, 2004; CSCE, 2004; Radon, Onoprishvili, 2003; Welt, 2004; Zhvania, 2004). There were a number of negative factors, including economic ones, having very harmful social consequences, which made this event happen.

To describe the overall economic situation in pre-revolutionary Georgia, it is important to note that the monetary system was the only sphere where macroeconomic indicators pointed to any degree of stability (Beridze, Papava, 2003). Over the last couple of years, as a result of the NBG tight monetary policy, the exchange rate of the Georgian national currency (the lari) remained stable and the inflation rate was fairly moderate (e.g., Kakulia 2001; Papava, Chocheli, 2003, pp. 10–17). The only significant devaluation of the lari (by 70%) took place in late 1998, and that devaluation was due not to internal but to external factors (i.e., the Russian default in August 1998). As to the inflation rate, for the whole period from 1996 onward, only in 1998–1999 was it slightly higher than 11 percent (yet another negative effect of the aforementioned Russian default), whereas in all other years since 1996, it has never exceeded 7 percent a year. (For comparison it must be noted that in 1993–1994 the inflation rate reached 50–70 percent a month; in 1995, however, the situation started changing and the rate dropped to 57 percent a year.) (Gurgenidze, Lobzhanidze, Onoprishvili, 1994; Papava, 1995a, 1996a, 1999; Wang, 1998; Wellisz, 1996) (See Table 11.1)

Table 11.1.1. Annual Growth of GDP and Inflation Rate in Georgia, 1995-2003 (in percent)

	1995	1996	1997	1998	1999	2000	2001	2002	2003
Annual growth rate of GDP	3.1	10.5	11.2	2.9	1.8	4.8	4.8	5.5	11.1
Consumer price index (December over December of the previous year)	57.4	13.8	7.3	10.7	10.9	4.6	3.4	5.4	7.0

In addition to the relative stability of the monetary system, another positive trend could be observed over the recent years, namely that of consistent economic growth. In contrast to an almost threefold economic decline in 1989–1994, the highest GDP growth rate was reached in 1996–1997 (11.2 percent and 10.5 percent respectively) (e.g., Papava, 1998). Although GDP growth rate was relatively modest in 1998–2000 (3.1 percent, 2.9 percent and 1.8 percent respectively), in 2001–2002 it grew again (to 4.8 percent and 5.5 percent).

A special emphasis should be placed on the year 2003, when, because of the commencement of the Baku-Tbilisi-Ceyhan oil pipeline, the GDP growth rate reached the considerable level of 11.1 percent. It must also be noted that growth in almost all sectors of the Georgian economy was conditioned by shadow activities. During 2003, for example, the share of the *untaxed economy* in Georgia's GDP reached 65–70 percent (e.g., Chocheli, 2003).

It is important to note that GDP growth for the first half of 2003, compared to the analogous period of 2002, also made up 9.5 percent. In other words, in the first half of 2003 GDP growth equaled the growth rate of the entire previous year, which suggests that the Rose Revolution had no impact from economic growth.

Also the so-called inflationary component of the Rose Revolution was not as serious as it could have been. According to the Indicative Plan of Georgia's Economic and Social Development (IPGESD) for 2003, the annual inflation rate was expected to be around 5–7 percent, whereas from January to October 2003, the actual rate was very low, 1.9 percent. In November, in the period of one month, under the conditions of a revolutionary situation, the inflation rate grew to 4.8 percent. This was a direct result not only of the political instability, but also of provocative statements made by government officials about the diminished supply in the Georgian market and the inevitable growth in prices of consumer goods because of the approaching revolution. No doubt, such statements intensified people's anticipation of inflation.

Even in spite of these statements and the volatile political situation, the actual inflation rate for 2003 was never higher than 7 percent (i.e., it never exceeded the expected upper threshold projected in the 2003 IPGESD). This was largely because the new post-revolutionary government under the leadership of Mr. Mikhail Saakashvili had the full confidence of the Georgian people and because the NGB continued to pursue its tight monetary policy.

To sum up what was stated above about the inflationary component of the Rose Revolution, the revolution actually managed, in a sense, to squeeze itself into the projected limits of inflation rate and, therefore, the Rose Revolution did not "cost" the Georgian people too much.

Now the question that arises is this: If the economic growth rate in 2003 was satisfactory and the inflation rate was moderate, what was the macroeconomic component of the Rose Revolution?

11.2. THE GEORGIAN PHENOMENON OF BUDGETARY CRISIS

Many economists and politicians in Georgia believe the alleged *economic crisis* (e.g., Gotsiridze, Kandelaki, 2001) in Georgia to be one of the key reasons of the Rose Revolution. Although this explanation may seem quite attractive at first glance because of its simplicity, it does not accurately describe the pre-revolutionary situation in Georgia's economy.

Indeed, the fact that there was no economic crisis before the Rose Revolution will look quite logical if one recalls that economic theory knows just two types of economic crises—those of *overproduction* and those of *underproduction*.

As we know, when crisis is due to overproduction, supply by far exceeds demand and the amount of unsold products keeps mounting, whereas prices are drastically dropping. As a result, companies go out of business one after another and the unemployment rate keeps growing.

As to the crisis of underproduction, in this case demand is much larger than supply, as a result of which prices go up, stimulating the growth of supply in the long run.

As was noted above, recent years saw relatively stable economic growth and moderate inflation, which are clear indications that there were no symptoms of an economic crisis in Georgia for whatever cause—overproduction or underproduction.

In order to properly understand the macroeconomic preconditions of the Rose Revolution, it is necessary to draw attention to the country's budgetary problems. Specifically, focus should be placed on the year 1998, which was marked by both a devaluation of the national currency (which, as was noted earlier, was an immediate effect of the Russian default in August 1998) and the emergence of major gaps in the national budget which ultimately led to actual revenues considerably below projected ones. The most stark example of this phenomenon was the year 1999, when the budget deficit reached US $150 million, or about 30 percent of projected total tax revenues.

We believe that *budgetary crisis* would be the most accurate description of this long, drawn-out process that stretched into late 2003. Specific elements of the government's overall failure to fully collect projected revenues were:

1.   Failure to fully collect projected tax revenues;

2.   Failure to fully collect projected nontax revenues, such as those resulting from the privatization of state-owned property;

3.   Failure to receive all available loans and grants from international financial institutions and donor countries.

Each of the elements had a number of specific causes. With that in mind, it must be stressed that the first of those elements (i.e., the failure to collect in full projected tax revenues) had an immense influence on the two other ones.

As described above, in practically all years since 1998 onward, major gaps in the national budget appeared between projected tax revenues and actual revenues. Moreover, the Tax Code of Georgia was adopted by the Georgian Parliament in late 1997, which led many politicians and economists in Georgia to quite rightly believe that the new tax legislation was the immediate cause prompting a budgetary crisis to emerge (see Ch. 10, 10.3).

IMF experts proposed the draft tax code to the government of Georgia. It was based on a model tax code that IMF specialists had developed taking into account both theory and international practice of taxation. As a matter of fact, however, the "ideal" tax law was based on the assumption that all national borders were under the control of national border and customs authorities. Yet this by no means reflected Georgian reality. Unfortunately, the territories of Abkhazia and South Ossetia, major channels of smuggled goods coming from Russia to Georgia, were then and continue to be beyond the Georgian government's control.

The government, in turn, contributed significantly toward worsening an already bad tax code. In a few years it made thousands of amendments and additions to the tax code that ultimately led to its transformation into a totally confusing document that simply paved the way for uncurbed corruption in the taxation system.

Personal interests of corrupted government officials and numerous lacunae in the tax code that are quite easy to conceal, making the existing gap between actual and projected tax revenues even bigger.

A remarkable peculiarity of the Georgian phenomenon of budgetary crisis was the so-called "war of budgets" that has been waged for about a decade between the national budget and that of the Autonomous Republic of Ajara. It consists in the refusal by the leadership of the autonomous republic to fill the central budget with legitimately established portions of fiscal revenues raised within their jurisdiction (Papava, 2001b). According to the Ajarian leaders, the reason they refused to contribute to the central budget was that the central government was allegedly failing to provide them with funds from the national budget. Whatever the reason they were not contributing funds, the fact remains that the central budget and ultimately all other regions of Georgia have been short of receivable budgetary transfers. Such circumstances further aggravated the budgetary crisis that already existed in the country.

In addition to the previously described problems, corrupt government officials resorted to various fraudulent machinations to achieve fictitious implementation of the *national* budget revenues. Specifically, the practices of compelling companies to pay taxes in advance, returning collected taxes to taxpayers by means of forged documents, filing fictitious offsets, and artificially raising the prices of public procurements so that they could pocket the difference between the official and the actual prices were widespread.

To compensate for the gap between actual and projected tax revenues, the government of Georgia invented fictitious increases in planned nontax revenues of the *national* budget. For example, in the *national* budget revenues, they often artificially raised the earnings from the privatization of state-owned property. In practice, however, these earnings were significantly smaller than they were represented to be and, as a result, the actual budget fell even further behind the official projections.

As to the failures to receive all available loans and grants from international financial institutions and donor countries, they were caused primarily by the government's inability from 1999 onward to implement the IMF programs without any delay. This problem became especially painful in 2002 when the IMF suspended its programs in Georgia. Moreover, this led to the blocking of all financial assistance to Georgia from other international financial institutions and, in addition, aggravated the problem of foreign debt, which by then made up about 50 percent of GDP. Without debt restructuring in the Paris Club, Georgia would have been unable to manage this huge debt.

The suspension of the IMF program was an immediate result of both the government's inability to adopt and implement a realistic *national* budget and the deferment of almost all reforms oriented toward democratization and a free market system.

In June of 2003, Georgian President Eduard Shevardnadze issued an ordinance by which he approved the Economic Development and Poverty Reduction Program of Georgia (EDPRP) for 2003–2015 (GG, 2003). This program was developed in close cooperation between the public authorities, on the one hand, and NGOs and academic experts, on the other hand. At a later stage, experts from international financial institutions and donor governments joined them. Unfortunately, because of its usual lack of political will, the Shevardnadze government never even attempted to embark on the implementation of this program. Indeed, the Shevardnadze government's apathetic attitude toward the program resulted in the extreme deterioration of Georgia's relationship with the IMF and other international donors.

In 2003, as a result of the government's numerous failures in all aspects related to the budgeting process, the *national* budget deficit reached US $90 million, i.e., 15 percent of projected budget revenues. By the end of 2003, the aggregate internal debt accumulated as the government consistently failed to pay salaries and pensions to public sector employees and pensioners. During the years of budget crisis, internal debt reached around US $120 million, of which unpaid pensions totaled US $70 million (even though monthly pensions in Georgia are as low as US $7 per month).

Unsurprisingly, with such financial problems in place, the poverty rate in Georgia reached 52 percent at the time. Deteriorating social problems and the overall dissatisfaction with the Shevardnadze regime in Georgian society created an unsustainable budget crisis, the logical consequence of which was the Rose Revolution.

11.3. KEY MACROECONOMIC DEVELOPMENTS IN THE POST-REVOLUTIONARY PERIOD

As the initial post-revolutionary months have shown, in early 2004, all key positive macroeconomic trends were still there. For example, GDP growth for the first quarter of 2004, compared to the analogous period of the last year, was 9.5 percent, whereas the inflation rate stayed at 1 percent.

As early as February 2004, the Parliament of Georgia supported the President's initiative to change the country's constitutional model, including the creation of a cabinet of ministers. (The constitutional amendments also curtailed the rights of the Parliament and shifted the balance between the legislature and the executive power in favor of the latter.) Indeed, during the first couple months of the post-revolutionary period, the government of Georgia was engaged in purely organizational matters. In spite of this fact, based on the extensive efforts of the MoF, the government of Georgia made its first important steps toward establishing financial order in the country. Almost all mechanisms that could be used for the aforementioned manipulations of the *national* budget revenues were abolished.

It is important to note that, immediately after the Rose Revolution, members of government and civil society wrongly believed that the relationship between the government of Georgia and the Ajarian leadership could be improved and that the aforementioned war of budgets would come to end. Later developments proved that expectations of closer cooperation were illusory, and not only in the arena of budgets (Gegeshidze, 2004; Tsereteli, 2004). However, after the revolution of May 6, 2004, in the Autonomous Republic of Ajara (e.g., ICG, 2004), there have emerged new opportunities for arranging normal budgeting processes between the central government and this region of Georgia. As a result of the changes that took place in Ajara, tax revenues of the national budget during 2004 significantly increased for the first time since Georgia's independence in 1991. The new government succeeded in overcoming the budgetary crisis and covering all old liabilities in the budgetary sector, including paying pensions and salaries in arrears.

While working on the draft *national* budget for 2004, the new government targeted a 6 percent GDP growth rate and a 5 percent inflation rate as a basis for its forecasts. It should be noted that the targeted GDP growth rate for 2004 was lower than the one anticipated for 2003 in the optimistic scenario of the EDPRP (8 percent). In the end, GDP growth rate for 2004 was 8.4 percent and the inflation rate was 7.5 percent.

As far as the goal of overcoming the long, drawn-out budgetary crisis is concerned, it was particularly important to adopt a new tax code that would be based on generally accepted principles of making the tax burden lighter and the taxation system simpler (Chappell, 1990). That is what many international experts suggested immediately after the Rose Revolution (e.g., Phillips, 2004). Remarkably, President Saakashvili was one of the early advocates of such changes, long before the revolution. Soon after the Rose Revolution, a special governmental commission of experts was established that started working on a draft of the new tax legislation, and the Parliament adopted that new legislation at the end of 2004. In the new tax code, VAT decreased from 20 percent to 18 percent, the payroll tax decreased from 32 percent to 20 percent, and a flat income tax of 12 percent replaced the old progressive income tax.

In summer 2004, the government managed to facilitate the renewal of the IMF program. The renewed program reopened the Paris Club door for Georgia and enabled the government to start negotiations on restructuring the country's foreign debt.

One extremely important task for the government is to re-embark on the implementation of the EDPRP. Implementing this program will enable the government to seek more extensive international financial assistance for strengthening Georgia's economic reforms. Adopted in 2003 the EDPRP needs significant changes, but the post-revolutionary government has unfortunately lost much of the program-creative skills because many professionals from different ministries were discharged on the grounds of staff reduction.

One of the visible results of the post-revolutionary period in Georgia is a marked decrease in the role of international financial institutions (the IMF and the World Bank) in the reform of Georgia's economy. Because these institutions are less involved in guiding the government, many unsuitable changes have been made in governmental agencies. In particular, the State Department of Statistics suffered most of all, since it was subordinated to the Ministry of Economy and, later, all branch offices of the Department (outside Georgia's capital—Tbilisi) were cancelled.

The post-revolutionary period is particularly remarkable because of the initiation by the government of an effective battle against corruption. Criminal charges were filed against numerous former high-ranking government officials and their relatives suspected of having been involved in corrupt practices. Many of them have already returned some of the money that they obtained by illegal means to the state. These additional funds have enhanced the government's capacity to pay off some of its debts owed to the people of Georgia. Of course, this kind of income is of a temporary nature and the government will not be able to rely on such returns in the future (Papava, 2000c). It is very important to stress that not all of the aforementioned government incomes are directed to the national budget. A significant part of them are controlled by the so-called power agencies (Office of Public Prosecutor, Ministry of Defense, Ministry of Internal Affairs, Ministry of State Security). In the commercial banks of Georgia, these agencies have created special off-budget accounts that are not overseen by Parliament or any other government organs. This practice has provoked suspicion that we are currently facing a *civilized corruption*, with the use of banking system, which had served as an "anticorruption" phenomenon in post-revolutionary Georgia.

In 2004, the government of Georgia started the implementation of ambitious plans to privatize large companies in manufacturing, energy, seaports, ocean shipping, railways, and other industries. So far, it has been mostly Russian companies, many of which are Russian state-owned or unofficially state-controlled, that have been interested in acquiring the privatized companies. The heavy involvement of Russian companies creates a distinct risk for Georgia of being "occupied economically" by Russia, a fact that Russian officials do not bother to hide (e.g., *Torbakov, 2003*). The Georgian government has so far continued aggressively with this process, which has put Georgia's economic and energy independence at serious risk. The increasing influence of Russia's government in the Georgian economy, in turn, endangers Georgia's European orientation.

Ultimately, the government of Georgia faces a post-revolutionary temptation to extend the Rose Revolution to the economic sphere. Such a course could be very dangerous for the country's development because revolutionary decisions are often hastily made and have drastic consequences, all of which may have a harsh effect on the economy (not to mention other spheres of Georgian society). That is why the main task of the government is the transition from a revolutionary approach to one that works within the regular channels of government to reform the economy and accelerate the ongoing process of democratization.

References

Abalkin L. I., 1996. Economic Realities and Abstract Schemes (Concerning a Conceptual Basis of the Monetarist Financial Stabilization Program). *Voprosy ekonomiki,* No. 12. (In Russian).

Abalkin L. I (ed.), 1997. *A Course on Transitional Economy.* Moscow, Finstatinform. (In Russian).

Abalkin L. I., 2000. Looking for Self-Determination. The Russian Economic Thought at the Turn of the 20th Century. *NG-Politekonomia, An Addition,* Vol. 15, No. 56. (In Russian).

Abalkin L. I., 2001. *Challenges of a New Century.* Moscow, IE RAN. (In Russian).

Acconcia A., D'Amato M., Martina R., 2003. Corruption and Tax Evasion with Competitive Bribes. *CSEF (Centre for Studies in Economics and Finance) Working Papers,* No. 112. Fisciano, University of Salerno.

Adams C., 1993. *For Good and Evil. The Impact of Taxes on the Course of Civilization.* Lanham, Madison Books.

Adams C., 1998. *Those Dirty Rotten Taxes. The Tax Revolts that Built America.* New York, The Free Press.

Adams D. W., Fitchett D. A. (eds.), 1992. *Informal Finance in Low-Income Countries.* Boulder, Westview Press.

Adams W., Brock J. W., 1993. *Adam Smith Goes to Moscow. A Dialogue on Radical Reform.* Princeton, Princeton University Press.

Akhvlediani A., 2001. International Trade and Economic Growth in Post-Communist Georgia. *Proceedings of the Georgian Academy of Sciences—Economic Series,* Vol. 9, No. 3.

Akubardia T., 2000. Business Development in Georgia. In *VI World Congress for Central and East European Studies.* 29 July–3 August 2000 Tampere, Finland. Helsinki, ICCEES.

Aleksashenko S., 1990. Economic Reform: A Polish Path. *Mirovaja ekonomika i mezhdunarodnye otnoshenija,* No. 7. (In Russian).

Aleksashenko S. V., Kiselev D. A., Teplukhin P. M., Iasin E. G., 1989. Tax Scales: Functions, Properties and Management Methods. *Ekonomika i matematicheskie metody,* Vol. 25, No. 3. (In Russian).

Alekseev A. M., Volkov N. V. et al., 1995. *Modern Civilized Market. International Experience and Its Application in CIS.* Moscow, EA. (In Russian).

Allen M., 1992. IMF—Supported Adjustment Programs in Central and Eastern Europe. In *Central and Eastern Europe Roads to Growth.* Papers Presented at a Seminar Held in Baden, Austria, April 15–18, 1991. Mod. by G. Winckler. Washington, IMF.

Andor L., Summers M., 1998. *Market Failure. Eastern Europe's "Economic Miracle."* London, Pluto Press.

Antachak R., Guzhinski M., Kozarzhevski P., 2001. *Economy of Belarus from Market to Planning.* Vol. 2, Warsaw, CASE. (In Russian).

Apostolou A., 1997. Is the Uzbek Model Working? No: Political Repression Thwarts Economic Growth. *Transitions,* Vol. 4, No. 2.

Arkin V., Slastnikov A., Shevtsova E., 1999. *Tax Stimulation of Investment Processes.* Moscow, RPEI / Eurasian Foundation. (In Russian).

Ascherson N., 2004. After the Revolution. *London Review of Books,* Vol. 26, No. 5, http://lrb.veriovps.co.uk/v26/n05/asch01_.html.

Åslund A., 1995. *How Russia Became a Market Economy.* Washington, The Brookings Institution.

Åslund A., 1996. "Rent-Seeking Behavior" in the Russian Transition Economy. *Voprosy ekonomiki,* No. 8. (In Russian).

Åslund, A., 2001. The Myth of Output Collapse after Communism. *Voprosy ekonomiki,* No. 7. (In Russian).

Åslund A., 2002. Building Capitalism. The Transformation of the Former Soviet Block. Cambridge, Cambridge University Press.

Atkinson A. B., Stiglitz J. E, 1980. *Lectures on Public Economics.* London, McGraw-Hill.

Aukutsionek C., 1996. Theory of Transitional Economy and Its Place in a System of Economic Science. *Mirovaja ekonomika i mezhdunarodnye otnoshenija,* No. 10. (In Russian).

Avtonomov V. S., 1996. Political Economy of Transitional Period. *Mirovaya ekonomika i mezhdunarodnye otnoshenija,* No. 9. (In Russian).

Avtonomov V. S., 1997. "Market Behavior": Rational and Ethical Aspects. *Mirovaya ekonomika i mezhdunarodnye otnoshenija,* No. 12. (In Russian).

Avtonomov V. S., 1998. *The Model of Man in Economic Science.* St. Petersburg, Ekonomicheskaia Shkola. (In Russian).

Babeau A., 1985. *Le Profit.* Paris, Presses Universites de France.

Balatskii E. V., 1997a. Fiscal Regulation in an Inflationary Environment. *Mirovaia ekonomika i mezhdunarodnye otnosheniia,* No. 1. (In Russian).

Balatskii E. V., 1997b. Laffer Effects and Financial Criteria of Economic Activity. *Mirovaia ekonomika i mezhdunarodnye otnosheniia,* No. 11. (In Russian).

Balatskii E. V., 1997c. Laffer Points and Quantitative Assessment of Them. *Mirovaia ekonomika i mezhdunarodnye otnosheniia,* No. 12. (In Russian).

Balatskii E. V., 1999. Corporate Property Tax and Accumulation of Fixed Assets. *Mirovaia ekonomika i mezhdunarodnye otnosheniia,* No. 3. (In Russian).

Balatskii E. V., 2000a. The Reproduction Cycle and the Tax Burden. *Ekonomika i matematicheskie metody,* Vol. 36, No. 1. (In Russian).

Balatskii E. V., 2000b. Effectiveness of Government Fiscal Policy. *Problemy prognozirovaniia,* No. 5. (In Russian).

Balcerowicz L., 1994. Poland, 1989–92. In: *Political Economy of Economic Reform.* Ed. by J. Williamson. Washington, Institute for International Economics.

Balcerowicz L., 1995. *Socialism, Capitalism, Transformation.* Budapest, CEU.

Baran Z., 2004. Removing the Thorn in Georgia's Rose Revolution. *Georgia in US Media.* Embassy of Georgia to the USA, Canada and Mexico. 2004, 24, March, http://www.georgiaemb.org/DisplayMedia.asp?id=325&from=media.

Barr N. (ed.), 1994. *Labor Markets and Social Policy in Central and Eastern Europe. The Transition and Beyond.* Washington, The World Bank.

Barro R.J., 1989. The Ricardian Approach to Budget Deficits. *Journal of Economic Perspectives,* Vol. 3, No. 2.

Basilia T., Silagadze A., Chikvaidze T., 2001. *Post-Socialist Transformation: Georgian Economy at the Turn of the 21st Century.* Tbilisi. (In Georgian).

Becker G. S., 1971. *The Economics of Discrimination.* Chicago, The University of Chicago Press.

Becker G. S., 1976. *The Economic Approach to Human Behavior.* Chicago, The University of Chicago Press.

Becker G. S., 1998. A Free-Market Winner vs. a Soviet-Style Loser. *Business Week,* August 3.

Becker G. S., Becker G. N., 1997. *The Economics of Life. From Baseball to Affirmative Action to Immigration, How Real World Issues Affect Our Everyday Life.* New York, McGraw-Hill.

Bell D., 1973. *The Coming of Post-Industrial Society.* New York, Basic Books.

Berend I. T., 1994. End of Century Global Transition to a Market Economy: Laissez-Faire on the Peripheries? In *Transition to a Market Economy at the End of the 20th Century.* Eleventh International Economic History Congress, session A-3, September 12–17, 1994, Milan, Italy. Ed. by I. T. Berend. München, Sutdeseuropa-Ges.

Berend I. T., 1995. Alternatives of Transformation: Choices and Determinants—East-Central Europe in the 1990s. In *Markets, States, and Democracy: the Political Economy of Post-Communist Transformation.* Ed. by B. Crawford. Boulder, Westview Press.

Berezin I., 1999. *The Short History of Economic Development.* Moscow, Russian Business Literature. (In Russian).

Beridze T., 1996a. Economic Sovereignty: New Aspects of Introduction between Economics and Politics. In *Government Structures in the U.S.A. and Sovereign States of the Former U.S.S.R. Power Allocation among Central, Regional, and Local Governments.* Ed. by J. E. Hickey Jr., A. Ugrinsky. Westport, Greenwood Press.

Beridze T., 1996b. The Republic of Georgia: Problems of Transition to a Market Economy. *CIBER, Occasional Paper,* No 83.

Beridze T., 2000. Employment and Unemployment during the Transition Period in Georgia. In *VI World Congress for Central and East European Studies.* 29 July–3 August 2000 Tampere, Finland. Helsinki, ICCEES.

Beridze T., Papava V., 2003. The Main Macroeconomic Tendencies of Georgia in 1995–2002. In *Central Asia and South Caucasus Affairs: 2003.* Ed. by: B. Rumer, Lau S. Y. Tokyo, The Sasakawa Peace Foundation.

Bertenev S. A., 1996. *Economic Theories and Schools (History and Modern Time).* Moscow: BEK. (In Russian).

Bhattacharya D. K., 1999. On the Economic Rationale of Estimating the Hidden Economy. *The Economic Journal,* Vol. 109, No. 456.

Birman I., 1996. *I'm an Economist (About Myself and What I Love).* Novosibirsk, EKOR. (In Russian).

Blanchard O., 1997. *The Economics of Post Communist Transformation.* Oxford, Calderon Press.

Blanchard O., Dornbush R., Krugman P., Layard R., Summers L., 1994. *Reform in Eastern Europe.* Cambridge, The MIT Press.

Boaz D., 1998. *Libertarianism: a Primer.* New York, The Free Press.

Boettke P. J., 1998. Promises Made and Promises Broken in the Russian Transition. *Constitutional Political Economy,* Vol. 9, No. 2.

Bogomolov O. T., 1998. *Reforms in a Mirror of International Comparisons.* Moscow, Ekonomika. (In Russian).

Boone P., Gomulka S., Layard R. (eds.), 1998. *Emerging from Communism. Lessons from Russia, China, and Europe.* Cambridge, The MIT Press.

Bothe M., 1994. Föderalismus—Ein Konzept im Geschichtlichen Wandel. In *Chancen des Föderalismus in Deutschland und Europa.* Hrsg. T. Evers. Baden-Baden., Nomos.

Bożyk P., 1999. Gradualism versus Shock Therapy. In *Systemic Change in Post-Communist Economies.* Selected Papers from the Fifth World Congress of Central and East European Studies, Warsaw, 1995. Ed. by P. G. Hare. London, Macmillan Press.

Brezinski H., Frirsh M., 1996. Bottom Up Transformation: Prerequisites, Scope and Impediments. *International Journal of Social Economics,* Vol. 23, No. 10–11.

Brown M. B., 1995. *Models in Political Economy. A Guide to the Arguments.* London, Penguin Books.

Buchanan J. M., 1992. Economics in the Post-Socialist Century. In *The Future of Economics.* Ed. by J. D. Hey. Oxford, Blackwell.

Buchanan J. M., Tollison R. (eds.), 1972. Theory of Public Choice: Political Applications of Economics. Ann Arbor, University of Michigan Press.

Buchanan J. M., Tullock G., 1962. *The Calculus of Consent: Logical Foundations of Constitutional Democracy.* Ann Arbor, University of Michigan Press.

Bukharin N. I., 1990. Economy of Transitional Period. In: *N.I. Bukharin. Collected Works.* Moscow, Ekonomika. (In Russian).

Buzgalin A. V., 1994. *Economy in Transition: A Course of Lectures in Political Economy.* Moscow, Taurus. (In Russian).

Calkins P., Vezina M., 1996. Transitional Paradigms to a New World Economic Order. *International Journal of Social Economics,* Vol. 23, No. 10–11.

Campbell R. W., 1991. *The Socialist Economies in Transition: A Primer on Semi-Reformed Systems.* Bloomington, Indiana University Press.

Canto V. A., Joines D. H., Laffer A. B., 1983. *Foundations of Supply-Side Economics: Theory and Evidence.* New York, Academic Press.

Carrier J. G., Miller D. (eds.), 1998. *Virtualism. A New Political Economy.* Oxford, Berg.

Chand S. K., Verhoeven M., Korczyk S., Vroman W., 1997. *Georgia: Restructuring Social Support Systems for Sustained Adjustment.* Washington, IMF.

Chander P., Wilde L., 1992. Corruption in Tax Administration. Journal of Public Economics, Vol. 39, No. 3.

Chappell P., 1990. The Assault on Fiscal Privilege: A Simpler System with Lower Tax Rates. In *P. Chappell, J. Kay, B. Robinson. Which Road to Fiscal Neutrality?* London, IEA.

Cheung S. N. S., 1998. Den Xiaoping's Great Transformation. *Contemporary Economic Policy,* Vol. XVI, No. 2.

Chkhartishivili D., Gotsiridze R., Kitsmarishvili B., 2004. Georgia: Conflict Regions and Economies. In *From War Economies to Peace Economies in the South Caucasus.* Ed. by Ph. Champain, D. Klein, N. Mirimanova. London, International Alert.

Chocheli V., 2003. "Syndrome of Shadow Economy": Low Tax Burden—Low Rate of Economic Growth," *Proceedings of the Georgian Academy of Sciences—Economic Series,* Vol. 11, No. 1–2. (In Georgian).

Claessens S., Glaessner T., 1997. *Are Financial Sector Weaknesses Undermining the East Asian Miracle?* Washington, The World Bank.

Cornes R., Sandler T., 1996. *The Theory of Externalities, Public Goods and Club Goods.* Cambridge, Cambridge University Press.

Crawford B., 1995. Post-Communist Political Economy: A Framework for the Analysis of Reform. In *Markets, States, and Democracy: The Political Economy of Post-Communist Transformation.* Ed. by B. Crawford. Boulder, Westview Press.

CSCE (Commission on Security and Cooperation in Europe), 2004. Georgia's "Rose Revolution." *A Report Prepared by the Staff of the Commission on Security and Cooperation in Europe.* Commission on Security and Cooperation in Europe, 108th Congress, 2nd Session, http://files.csce.gov/Georgia_Revolution.pdf.

Cukrowski J., 2000. Financing the Deficit of the State Budget by National Bank of Georgia (1996–1999). *Studies & Analyses, Working Papers,* No. 215. Warsaw, CASE.

Cukrowski J., Kavelashvili G., 2001. Determinants of Foreign Direct Investment in Georgia. *CASE-CEU Working Papers Series,* No. 39. Warsaw, CASE.

Dagaev A. A., 1995. Investments and Tax Policy (Outlines of a Reviving Paradigm). *Economist,* No. 10. (In Russian).

Dagaev A. A., 2001. Will a Tax Cut Lead to Increased Investment? *Mirovaia ekonomika i mezhdunarodnye otnosheniia,* No. 1. (In Russian).

Dang T. K. L., 1999. *Vietnam: Transition to Market.* Moscow, IE RAN. (In Russian).

Davidson J. D., Rees-Mogg W., 1998. *The Sovereign Individual. The Coming Economic Revolution. How to Survive and Prosper in It.* London, Pan Books.

De Gregorio J., Eichengreen B., Ito T., Wyplosz C., 1999. *An Independent and Accountable IMF.* Geneva Reports on the World Economy 1. Geneva, ICMB.

De Melo M., Denizer C., Gelb A., 1997. From Plan to Market: Patterns of Transition. In: *Macroeconomic Stabilization in Transition Economies.* Ed. by M. I. Blejer, M. Škreb. Cambridge, Cambridge University Press.

Derlien H.-U., 1999. The Triple Revolution: Administrative Transformation in the Former GDR. In *Nunberg B. The State after Communism: Administrative Transition in Central and Eastern Europe.* Washington, The World Bank.

De Soto H., 1989. *The Other Path: The Invisible Revolution in the Third World.* New York, Harper & Row.

Diykanbayeva G., 2001. Some Aspects of the Reform of Financial Sector in Kyrgyzstan and the Experience of the Countries of South-East Asia. In *Experience in Developing Financial and Fiscal Systems and Attracting Direct Investments in East Asia: Lessons and Recommendations.* Almaty. (In Russian).

Dornbusch R., Fischer S., 1990. *Macroeconomics.* New York, McGraw-Hill.

Drucker P. P. 1986. *Innovation and Entrepreneurship: Practice and Principles.* New York, Harper Business.

Drucker P. F., 1993. *Post-Capitalist Society.* New York, Harper Business.

Dzhikaev V., Parastaev A., 2004. Economy and Conflict in South Ossetia. In *From War Economies to Peace Economies in the South Caucasus.* Ed. by Ph. Champain, D. Klein, N. Mirimanova. London, International Alert.

Ebrill L., Keen M., Bodin J. P., Summers V., 2001. *The Modern VAT.* Washington, IMF.

Ehrenberg R. G., Smith R. S., 1994. *Modern Labor Economics: Theory and Public Policy.* New York, Harper Collins.

Eichengreen B., 2000. *Can the Moral Hazard Caused by IMF Bailouts be Reduced?* Geneva Reports on the World Economy Special Report 1. Geneva, ICMB, CEPR.

Eilon S., Gold B., Soesan J., 1976. *Applied Productivity Analysis for Industry.* Oxford, Pergamon Press.

Ékes I., 1994. The Hidden Economy and Income: The Hungarian Experience. *Economic Systems,* Vol. 18, No. 4.

Elliott K. A. (ed.), 1997. *Corruption and the Global Economy.* Washington, Institute for International Economics.

Ericson R. E., 2000. The Post-Soviet Russian Economic System: An Industrial Feudalism? In *Russian Crisis and its Effects.* Ed. by T. Komulainen, L. Korhonen. Helsinki, Kikimora Publications.

Esping-Andersen G. (ed.), 1997. *Welfare States in Transition. National Adaptations in Global Economies.* London, SAGE Publications.

Fedorenko N. P., 2001. *Russia: Lessons of the Past and Outlines of the Future.* Moscow, Ekonomika. (In Russian).

Feldstein M. (ed.), 1980. *The American Economy in Transition.* Chicago, The University Press.

Feyerabend J., 1985. *Fluchtburgen des Geldes, Wo die Reichen sich verstecken.* Düsseldorf-Wien, Econ Verlag.

Fischer S., Dornbusch R., Schmalensee R., 1988. *Economics.* New York, McGraw-Hill Publishing Company.

Fischer S., Sahay R., 2000. The Transition Economies after Ten Years. *NBER Working Paper Series,* No. 7664. http://papers.nber.org/papers/w7664.pdf.

Friedman M., 1982. *Capitalism and Freedom.* New York, Chalidze Publications.

Friedman M., Friedman R., 1990. *Free to Choose. A Personal Statement.* San Diego, A Harvest Book.

Gachechiladze R., 1995. *The New Georgia. Space, Society, Politics.* London, UCL Press.

Gaddy C., Ickes B. W., 1998. Russia's Virtual Economy. *Foreign Affairs,* Vol. 77, No. 5.

Gaddy C., Ickes B. W., 2002. *Russia's Virtual Economy.* Washington, Brookings Institution Press.

Gaidar E., 1997. *Anomaly of Economic Growth.* Moscow, Eurasia. (In Russian).

Galbraith J. K., 1973. *Economics and the Public Purpose.* New York, Houghton Mifflin Company.

Galbraith J. K., 1992. Economics in the Century Ahead. In *The Future of Economics.* Ed. by J. D. Hey. Oxford, Blackwell.

Galbraith J. K., 1996. *The Good Society. The Humane Agenda.* Boston, Houghton Mifflin Company.

Galbraith J. K., 1998. *The Affluent Society.* Fortieth Anniversary Edition. Boston, A Mariner Book.

Gandhi V. P., Ebrill L. R., Mackenzie G. A. et al, 1987. *Supply-Side Tax Policy. Its Relevance to Developing Countries.* Washington, IMF.

Gegeshidze A., 2004. Georgia's Regional Vulnerabilities and the Ajaria Crisis. *Insight Turkey,* Vol. 6, No. 2.

Geiger L. T., 1992. *Macroeconomic Analysis and Transitional Economy.* St. Davids, Eastern College.

GG (Government of Georgia), 2003. *Economic Development and Poverty Reduction Program of Georgia.* Tbilisi.

Georgia, 1995. *IMF Economic Reviews,* 1994, No. 15 (March). Washington, IMF.

Gogishvili T., Gogodze J., Tsakadze A., 1996. The Transition in Georgia: From Collapse to Optimism. *Innocenti Occasional Papers, Economic Policy Series,* No. 55. Florence, UNICEF.

Goldstone J., 2001. Theories of Revolution, the Revolutions of 1989–1991 and the Trajectory of the "New" Russia. *Voprosy ekonomiki,* No. 1. (In Russian).

Gomulka S., 1995. The IMF-Supported Programs of Poland and Russia, 1990–1994: Principles, Errors and Results. *Studies & Analyses, Working Papers,* No. 36. Warsaw, CASE.

Gordon R., 1983. AN Optimal Taxation Approach to Fiscal Federation. *Quarterly Journal of Economics,* Vol. 98, Issue 4.

Gotsiridze R., Kandelaki O., 2001. Georgia: Halfway Reforms as a Factor of the Economic Crisis. *Central Asia and the Caucasus,* No. 6.

Griffiths A., Wall S. (ed.), 1995. *Applied Economics. An Introductory Course.* Sixth edition. London, Longman.

Griffiths A., Wall S. (ed.), 1997. *Applied Economics. An Introductory Course.* Seventh edition. London, Longman.

Guesnerie R., 1998. *A Contribution to the Pure Theory of Taxation.* Cambridge, Cambridge University Press.

Gumba Y., Ketsba T., 2004. Economic Development Prospects in Abkhazia and the Concept and Regional Cooperation. In *From War Economies to Peace Economies in the South Caucasus.* Ed. by Ph. Champain, D. Klein, N. Mirimanova. London, International Alert.

Gurgenidze L., Lobzhanidze M., Onoprishvili D., 1994. Georgia: From Planning to Hyperinflation. *Communist Economies & Economic Transformation,* Vol. 6, No. 2.

Gusakov S. V., Zhak S. V., 1995. Optimum Equilibrium Prices and the Laffer Point. *Ekonomika i matematicheskie metody,* Vol. 31, No. 4. (In Russian).

Gwynne R. N., Klak T., Shaw D. J. B., 2003. *Alternative Capitalisms. Geographies of Emerging Regions.* London, Arnold.

Hall R. E., Rabushka A., 1995. *The Flat Tax.* Stanford, Hoover Institution Press.

Havrylyshyn O., Nsouli S. M. (eds.), 2001. *A Decade of Transition: Achievements and Challenges.* Washington, IMF.

Hayek F. A., 1976. *Denationalisation of Money—The Argument Refined. An Analysis of the Theory and Practice of Concurrent Currencies.* London, Institute of Economic Affairs.

Hayek F. A., 1988. *The Fatal Conceit. The Errors of Socialism.* Chicago, The University of Chicago Press.

Heilbroner R., Milberg W., 1996. *The Crisis of Vision in Modern Economic Thought.* Cambridge, Cambridge University Press.

Hinshaw R. (ed.), 1996. *The World Economy in Transition. What Leading Economists Think.* Cheltenham, Edward Elgar.

Hoen H. W., 1999. "Shock versus Gradualism:" The Inappropriateness of the Labels Applied to the Strategies in Central Europe. In *Systemic Change in Post-Communist Economies.* Selected Papers from the Fifth World Congress of Central and East European Studies, Warsaw, 1995. Ed. by P. G. Hare. London, Macmillan Press.

Ibadoglu G., 2002. The Question of Privatization in Azerbaijan and Georgia. In *Central Asia and South Caucasus Affairs: 2002.* Ed. by B. Rumer and Lau S. Y. Tokyo, The Sasakawa Peace Foundation.

IBRD (International Bank for Reconstruction and Development), 1991. *Lessons of Tax Reform.* Washington, The World Bank.

ICG (International Crisis Group), 2004. Saakashvili's Ajara Success: Repeatable Elsewhere in Georgia? *Europe Briefing,* Tbilisi/Brussels, 2004, August 18, http://unpan1.un.org/intradoc/groups/public/documents/UNTC/UNPAN018787.pdf.

Ignatenko A. A., 1988. *Caliphs without Caliphate. Islamic Non-governmental Religious/Political Organizations in the Middle East: History, Ideology, Activities.* Moscow, Nauka. (In Russian).

Illarionov A., 1996. Models of Economic Development in Russia. *Voprosy ekonomiki,* No. 7. (In Russian).

IMF, 1991. A *Study of the Soviet Economy.* Vol. 3. Paris, OECD.

IMF, 1997. *Reliable Governance: The Role of IMF.* Washington, IMF.

Inozemtsev V. L., 1995. *Contribution to the Theory of Post-Economic Formation of Society.* Moscow, Taurus. (In Russian).

Inozemtsev V. L., 1998. Rethinking of the Future. Most Prominent American Economists and Sociologists about the Perspectives and Contradictions of

Modern Development. *Mirovaya ekonomika i mezhdunarodnye otnoshenija,* No. 11. (In Russian).

Intriligator M. D., Braguinsky S., Bowen II J. R., Tullock G., Root H. L., 1999. Role of Market Institutions in Pacific Rim Development and Transition. *Contemporary Economic Policy,* Vol., XVII, No. 1.

Jochem A., 1999. Monetary Stabilization in Countries in Transition. *International Advances in Economic Research,* Vol., 5, No. 1.

Johnson S., Kowalska M., 1994. Poland: The Political Economy of Shock Therapy. In *Voting for Reform. Democracy, Political Liberalization, and Economic Adjustment.* Ed. by S. Haggard, S. B. Webb. Oxford, Oxford University Press.

Kakulia M., *Problems of Currency System Development in Georgia.* Tbilisi, SESPSKI, 2001. (In Georgian).

Kanth R. K., 1997. *Against Economics. Rethinking Political Economy.* Aldershot, Ashgate.

Kapitonenko V. V., 1994. Inflation Shift of the Tax Rate on the Laffer Curve. In *The Economy and Technology.* Moscow, REA. (In Russian).

Kasenov U., 1998. Post-Soviet Modernization in Central Asia: Realities and Prospects. In *Central Asia: The Challenges of Independence.* Ed. by B. Rumer, S. Zhukov. Armonk, M. E. Sharpe.

Kazmer D. R., Konrad M., 2004. Economic Lessons from the Transition. The Basic Theory Re-Examined. Armonk, M. E. Sharpe.

Khikmetov A.K. (ed.), 2001. *Uzbekistan: Ten Years in the Way to Market Economy.* Tashkent, Uzbekiston. (In Russian).

Kiseliova E. A., 1996. Macroeconomic Stabilization: The Orthodox and Heterodox Scenarios. In *Elements of the Theory of Transitional Economy.* Ed. by E. A. Kiseliova, M. N. Chepurin. Kirov, KOT. (In Russian).

Klaus V., 1997. Promoting Financial Stability in the Transition Economies of Central and Eastern Europe. In *Maintaining Financial Stability in a Global*

Economy. A Symposium Sponsored by The Federal Reserve of Kansas City. Jackson Hole, Wyoming, August 28–30, 1997.

Klitgaard R., 1998. *Controlling Corruption.* Berkley, University of California Press.

Koichuev T., 2001. *The Economy of Kyrgyz Republic on the Way of Reforms.* Bishkek, Reform.

Kolodko G. V., 1999. Lessons of 10 Years of Post-Communist Transformation. *Voprosy ekonomiki,* No. 9. (In Russian).

Kolodko G. V., 2000. *From Shock to Therapy. Political Economy of Post-Socialist Transformations.* Moscow, Zhurnal Ekspert. (In Russian).

Konings J., Walsh P. P., 1998. Disorganization in the Transition Process: Firm Level Evidence from Ukraine. *Center for Transition Economies, LICOS Discussion Paper,* No. 71/1998. Leuven, Katholieke Universiteit Leuven.

Kornai J., 1992. *The Socialist System. The Political Economy of Communism.* Princeton, Princeton University Press.

Kornai J., 1993. Transformational Recession: A General Phenomenon Examined through the Example of Hungary's Development. *Institute for Advanced Study, Discussion Paper,* No. 1. Budapest, IAS.

Kowalik T., 1994. The "Big Bang" as a Political and Historical Phenomenon: A Case Study on Poland. In *Transition to a Market Economy at the End of the 20th Century.* Eleventh International Economic History Congress, session A-3, September 12–17, 1994, Milan, Italy. Ed. by I. T. Berend. München, Sutdeseuropa-Ges.

Krogel J., Mazner E., Grabcher G., 1992. *The Market Shock.* Vienna. (In Russian).

Krugman P., 1994. *Peddling Prosperity: Economic Sense and Nonsense in the Age of Diminished Expectations.* New York, Norton.

Krugman P., 1998. *The Accidental Theorist: and Other Dispatches from the Dismal Science.* New York, Norton.

Kuzin D. V. (ed.), 1994. *"Economic Miracles": Lessons for Russia.* Moscow, OLMA-PRESS. (In Russian).

Kuznetsov V., 1994. Towards the Theory of Transitional Economy. *Mirovaya ekonomika i mezhdunarodnye otnoshenija,* No. 12. (In Russian).

Lapachi K., 2001. Anti-Monopoly Regulation in a Transition Country: The Example of Georgia. *European Competition Law Review,* Vol. 22, Issue 9.

Lavigne M., 1995. *The Economics of Transition. From Socialist Economy to Market Economy.* New York, St. Martin's Press.

Leibfritz W., Thornton J., Bibbee A., 1997. Taxation and Economic Performance. *OECD Economic Department Working Papers,* No. 176.

Lipowski A., 1998. *Towards Normality. Overcoming the Heritage of Central Planning Economy in Poland in 1990–1994.* Warsaw, Adam Smith Research Center, Center for Social and Economic Research.

Lipton D., Sachs J., 1990. Creating a Market Economy in Eastern Europe: the Case of Poland. *Brookings Papers on Economic Activity,* No. 1.

MacPhee C. R., 2001. Economic Education and Government Reform in the Republic of Georgia. *The Journal of Economic Education,* Vol. 32, No. 1.

Mankiw N. G., 1992. *Macroeconomics.* New York, Worth Publishers.

Mankiw N. G., 1998. *Principles of Economics.* Fort Worth, The Dryden Press.

Mau V., 1999. Russian Economic Reforms from the Viewpoint of International Critics. *Voprosy ekonomiki,* No. 11. (In Russian).

Mauro P., 1997a. The Effects of Corruption on Growth, Investment, and Government Expenditure: A Cross-Country Analysis. In *Corruption and the Global Economy.* Ed. by K. A. Elliott. Washington, Institute for International Economics.

Mauro P., 1997b. *Why Worry About Corruption?* Economic Issues, 6. Washington, IMF.

McConnell C. R., Brue S. L., 1990. *Economics. Principles, Problems, and Policies.* New York, McGraw-Hill Publishing Company.

McKinnon R. I., 1993. *The Order of Economic Liberalization. Financial Control in the Transition to a Market Economy.* Baltimore, The Johns Hopkins University Press.

McMillan J., 2002. *Reinventing the Bazaar. A Natural History of Markets.* New York, W. W. Norton & Company.

Men'shikov S. M., 1996. *Russian Economy: Practical and Theoretical Aspects of Transition to Market.* Moscow, Mezhdunarodnye otnoshenia. (In Russian).

Metreveli R., 1995. *Georgia.* Nashville, Publisher's International.

Meurs M., 1998. Imagined and Imagining Equality in East Central Europe: Gender and Ethnic Differences in the Economic Transformation of Bulgaria. In *Theorising Transition. The Political Economy of Post-Communist Transformations.* Ed. by J. Pickles, A. Smith. London, Routledge.

Mikulskiy K. I., 1999. Concerning the Modern Phase and Mechanisms of Overcoming of System Crisis of Post-Socialist Society. *Obschestvo i ekonomika,* No. 10–11. (In Russian).

Milanovic B., 1998. *Income, Inequality and Poverty during the Transition from Planned to Market Economy.* Washington, The World Bank.

Mill J. S., 1976. *Principles of Political Economy.* Book 5. Fairfield, Augustus M. Kelley Publishers.

von Mises L., 1947. *Planned Chaos.* Irvington-on-Hudson, Foundation for Economic Education.

von Mises L., 1981. *Socialism. An Economic and Sociological Analysis.* Indianapolis, Liberty Classics.

von Mises L., 1996. *Human Action. A Treatise on Economics.* Chicago, Contemporary Books.

Moustapha A. F., 1992. Supply-Oriented Adjustment Policies. In: *Macroeco-nomic Adjustment: Policy Instruments and Issues.* Ed. by J. M. Davis. Wash-ington, IMF.

Movshovich S., Sokolovskii L., 1994. Output, Taxes, and the Laffer Curve. *Ekonomika i matematicheskie metody,* Vol. 30, No. 3. (In Russian).

Murrel P., 1992. Evolution in Economics and in the Economic Reform of the Centrally Planned Economies. In *The Emergence of Market Economies in Eastern Europe.* Cambridge, Basil Blackwell.

Nafziger E. W., 1997. *The Economics of Developing Countries.* Upper Saddle River, Prentice-Hall.

Naím M., 1995. Latin America: The Second Stage of Reform. In *Economic Reform and Democracy.* Ed. by L. Diamond, M. F. Plattner. Baltimore, The Johns Hopkins University Press.

Narinskiy R., 1990. Economic Program of the Mazovetsky Government. *Voprosy ekonomiki,* No. 4. (In Russian).

Negru I., Ungurean S., 2001. Corruption and Transition Economics. *Proceed-ings of the Georgian Academy of Sciences—Economic Series,* Vol. 9, No. 1–2.

Nelson R. R., Winter S. G., 1982. *An Evolutionary Theory of Economic Change.* Cambridge, The Belknap Press of Harvard University Press.

Nikipelov A. D., 1996. *Essays on Post-Communist Economies.* Moscow, CISN. (In Russian).

Nolan P., 1995. Politics, Planning, and the Transition from Stalinism: the Case of China. In *The Role of the State in Economic Change.* Ed. by H.-J. Chang, R. Rowthorn. Oxford, Clarendon Press.

Norregaard J., 1995. Intergovernmental Fiscal Relations. In *Tax Policy Hand-book.* Ed. by P. Shome. Washington, IMF.

North D., 1997. Institutional Changes: Limits of Analysis. *Voprosy ekonomiki,* No. 3. (In Russian).

Nove A., 1993. Economics of the Transitional Period—a Critical Review. *Revue europienne des sciences sociales,* Vol. XXXI, No. 96.

Nove A., 1995. Economics of Transition: Some Gaps and Illusions. In *Markets, States, and Democracy: the Political Economy of Post-Communist Transformation.* Ed. by B. Crawford. Boulder, Westview Press.

Nunberg B., 1999. *The State after Communism: Administrative Transitions in Central and Eastern Europe.* Washington, The World Bank.

O'Brien J. C., 1989. *The Communist Credo: Man is the Measure of All Things.* Allied Social Sciences Association. Annual Conference, Atlanta, Georgia, December 28–30, 1989. Fresno, California State University.

Olson M., 1995. Devolution of Power and Society in a Transitional Period. Remedies to Corruption, Economic Decline and Deceleration of Economic Growth. *Ekonomika i matematicheskie metody,* Vol. 31, Issue 4. (In Russian).

Olson M., 2000. *Power and Prosperity: Outgrowing Communist and Capitalist Dictatorships.* New York, Basic Books.

Ol'sevich Y., 1997a. *Towards the Theory of Economic Transformations.* Moscow, IE RAN. (In Russian).

Ol'sevich Y., 1997b. Monetarism and Russia: The Problem of Compatibility. *Voprosy ekonomiki,* No. 8. (In Russian).

Padovano F., Galli E., 2001. Tax Rates and Economic Growth in the OECD Countries (1950–1990). *Economic Inquiry,* Vol. 39, No. 1.

Pankow W., 1993. *Work Institutions in Transformation. The Case of Poland 1990–1992.* Warsaw, Friedrich Ebert Stiftung.

Papava V., 1990. On the Concepts of Economic Reform in the USSR. *Ekonomika i matamaticheskie metody,* Vol. 26, No. 6. (In Russian).

Papava V., 1992. Privatization of Major Production Factors. *Fair Play, Problems of Management,* No. 3. (In Russian).

Papava V., 1993. A New View of the Economic Ability of the Government, Egalitarian Goods and GNP. *International Journal of Social Economics,* Vol. 20, No. 8.

Papava V., 1994. The Role of the State in the Modern Economic System. *Problems of Economic Transition,* Vol. 37, No. 5.

Papava V., 1995a. "The Georgian Economy: Problems of Reform." *Eurasian Studies* Vol. 2, No. 2.

Papava V., 1995b. Marxist Points of View on the Soviet Communist Economic System and the Manifestation of Egalitarianism in Post-Communist Economic Reform. *International Journal of Social Economics,* Vol. 22, No. 6.

Papava V., 1996a. The Georgian Economy: From "Shock Therapy" to "Social Promotion." *Communist Economies & Economic Transformation,* Vol. 8, No. 8.

Papava V., 1996b. "Social Promotion" of Economic Reform in Georgia. *Economic Systems,* Vol. 20, No.4.

Papava V., 1997. On the Possible Functioning of the Social Sector According to the Principles of the Private Sector (Taxation Aspect). *Problems of Economic Transition,* Vol. 40, No. 2.

Papava V., 1998. Toward the Progress of Reform and Prospects of Economic Growth. *Obscestvo i ekonomika,* No. 2. (In Russian).

Papava V., 1999. The Georgian Economy: Main Directions and Initial Results of Reforms. In *Systemic Change in Post-Communist Economies.* Ed. by P. G. Hare. London, Macmillan Press.

Papava V., 2000a. State, Public sector and Theoretical Prerequisites to a Model of an "Economy without Taxes." *International Journal of Social Economics,* 2000, Vol. 27, No. 1–2.

Papava V., 2000b. On the Theory of Post-Communist Transformation of Economy. *Obschestvo i ekonomika,* No. 7. (In Russian).

Papava V., 2000c. Economic Approach to the Restriction of Corruption in Georgia. *Georgian Economic Trends,* No. 3–4.

Papava V., 2001a. *Necroeconomics and Post-Communist Transformation of Economy.* Tbilisi, Company Imperial.

Papava V., 2001b. Tax Federalism Concept: Consensus versus Separatism. *Georgian Economic Trends,* No. 3–4.

Papava V., 2001c. Necroeconomics—A Phenomenon of the Post-Communist Transition Period. *Problems of Economic Transition,* Vol. 44, No. 8.

Papava V., 2001d. Indexes of Tax Corruption. In *Bulletin of the International Statistical Institute. 53 Session. Contributed Papers. Tome LIX. Book 3.* 22–29 August 2001, Seoul, Republic of Korea. Seoul, ISI.

Papava V., 2001e. What Will the Tax Relief Give? *Macro Micro Economics,* No. 4. (In Georgian).

Papava V., 2001f. The Laffer Effect and Its After-Effect. *Mirovaia ekonomika i mezhdunarodnye otnosheniia,* No. 7. (In Russian).

Papava V., 2002a. *Leszek Balcerowicz and Georgia.* Tbilisi, GFSIS.

Papava V., 2002b. *Political Economy of the Post-Communist Capitalism and Its Application for Georgian Economy.* Tbilisi, PDP. (In Georgian).

Papava V., 2002c. Necroeconomics—the Theory of Post-Communist Transformation of an Economy. *International Journal of Social Economics,* Vol. 29, No. 9/10.

Papava V., 2002d. On the Laffer Effect in Post-Communist Economies (On the Bases of the Observation of Russian Literature). *Problems of Economic Transition,* Vol. 45, No. 7.

Papava V., 2003a. *Splendours and Miseries of the IMF in Post-Communist Georgia.* Laredo, We-publish.com.

Papava V., 2003b. The Basic Causes of "Dragging Out" the Transition Period. In *Central Asia and South Caucasus Affairs: 2003.* Ed. By B. Rumer and Lau S. Y.. Tokyo, The Sasakawa Peace Foundation.

Papava V., 2003c. On the Role of the International Monetary Fund in the Post-Communist Transformation of Georgia. *Emerging Markets Finance & Trade,* 2003, Vol. 39, No. 5.

Papava V., 2004. The Doctrine of Market Equality: Questions of Theory and Its Application to the Process of Post-Communist Transformation. *Problems of Economic Transition,* Vol. 47, No. 8.

Papava V., 2005. On the Theory of Post-Communist Economic Transition to Market. *International Journal of Social Economics,* Vol. 32, No. 1/2.

Papava V., Beridze T., 1996/1997. Industrial Policy and Trade Regime in Georgia. *Eurasian Studies,* 1996/1997 Vol., 3, No. 4.

Papava V., Chocheli V., 2003. *Financial Globalization and Post-Communist Georgia. Global Exchange Rate Instability and its Implications for Georgia.* New York, iUniverse.

Papava V., Khaduri N., 1997. On the Shadow Political Economy of the Post-Communist Transformation. An Institutional Analysis. *Problems of Economic Transition,* Vol. 40, No. 6.

Petrakov N. Y., 1998. *The Russian Roulette: An Economic Experiment Costing 150 Million Lives.* Moscow, Ekonomika. (In Russian).

Petukhov S., 1999. The Georgian Economic Miracle Is Already on the Way! *Ogoniok,* No. 30. (In Russian).

Phillips D. L., 2004. *Stability, Security, and Sovereignty in the Republic of Georgia.* New York, The Council on Foreign Relations.

Popov V., 2000. The Shock Therapy vs. Gradualism: Ten Years Later. In *G.V. Kolodko. From Shock to Therapy. Political Economy of Post-Socialist Transformations.* Moscow, Zhurnal Ekspert. (In Russian).

Potemkin A., 2000. *A Virtual Economy and Surrealistic Existence. Russia. Threshold of the XXI Century. Economy.* Moscow, INFRA-M. (In Russian).

Radon J., Onoprishvili D., 2003. Rescuing Georgia. *Commentary.* Project Syndicate. An Association of Newspapers around the World, 2003, December, http://www.project-syndicate. org/commentaries/commentary_text.php4? id=1414&lang=1&m=contributor.

Rakitskaya G., 1996. Social/Economic Strategies in Modern Russia. *Voprosy ekonomiki,* No. 8. (In Russian).

Roemer J. E., 1996. *Egalitarian Perspectives. Essays in Philosophical Economics.* Cambridge, Cambridge University Press.

Rondeli A., 2001. The Choice of Independent Georgia. In *The Security of the Caspian Sea Region.* Ed. by G. Chufrin. New York, Oxford University Press.

Rose-Ackerman S., 1999. *Corruption and Government. Causes, Consequences, and Reform.* Cambridge, Cambridge University Press.

Rosser J. R., Rosser M. V., 1997. Schumpeterian Evolutionary Dynamics and the Collapse of Soviet-Bloc Socialism. *Review of Political Economy,* Vol. 9, No. 2.

Rostovskij I., 1997. *Macroeconomic Instability in Post-Communist Countries.* Moscow, Ekonomika. (In Russian).

Rumer B., 2000. Economic Crisis and Growing Intraregional Tensions. In *Central Asia and the New Global Economy.* Ed. by B. Rumer. Armonk, M. E. Sharpe.

Sachs J., 1993. *Poland's Jump to the Market Economy.* Cambridge, The MIT Press.

Sachs J., 1994. *Market Reforms and Russia.* London, BBC MPM.

Safaev S., 1997. Is the Uzbek Model Working? Yes: A Triumph of Gradualism. *Transitions,* Vol. 4, No. 2.

Samuelson P. S., 2002. Free Market Key to Prosperity. *The Daily Yomiuri,* June 24.

Samuelson P. S., Nordhaus W. D., 1995. *Economics.* New York, McGraw-Hill Publishing Company.

Sanyal A., 2000. Audit Hierarchy in a Corrupt Tax Administration. *Journal of Comparative Economics,* Vol. 28 No. 2.

Sanyal A., Gang I. N., Goswami O., 2000. Corruption, Tax Evasion and the Laffer Curve. *Public Choice,* Vol. 105, Issue 1–2.

Schaffer M., 1992. The Economy of Poland. *Center for Economic Performance, Discussion Paper,* No. 67. London, LSE.

Schumpeter J. A., [1943] 1976. *Capitalism, Socialism and Democracy.* London, George Allen & Unwin.

Segvari I., 1999. Seven Different Assumptions on Russian Reforms: Are they Right? *Voprosy ekonomiki,* No. 9. (In Russian).

Shavans B., Manyan E., 1999. The Post-Socialist Trajectories and the Western Capitalism. *Mirovaja ekonomika i mezhdunarodnye otnoshenja,* No. 12. (In Russian).

Shevardnadze E., 1999. *Great Silk Route. TRACECA-PETrA. Transport Corridor Europe-Caucasus-Asia. The Eurasian Common Market. Political and Economic Aspects.* Tbilisi, Georgia: Georgian Transport System.

Shevardnadze K., Chechelashvili R., Chocheli V., Khaduri N., 2000. *Papava Indexes of Tax Corruption.* Tbilisi, Company Imperial.

Shokhin A. N., 1989. *Social Problems of Perestroika.* Moscow, Ekonomika. (In Russian).

Shome P. (ed.), 1995. *Tax Policy Handbook.* Washington, IMF.

Shurgalina I. N., 1997. *Reforming the Russian Economy. An Experiment of Analysis in Light of the Catastrophe Theory.* Moscow, ROSSPEN. (In Russian).

Simonia N., 1999. Methodological Problems of the Analysis of Social/Economic Development Models. *Obschestvo i ekonomika,* No. 10–11. (In Russian).

Sirkin G., 1968. *The Visible Hand: The Fundamentals off Economic Planning.* New York, McGraw-Hill.

Slemrod J., 1996. On the High-Income Laffer Curve. In *Tax Progressivity and Income Inequality.* Ed. by J. Slemrod. Cambridge: Cambridge University Press.

Slemrod J., Bakija J., 1996. *Taxing Ourselves: A Citizen's Guide to the Great Debate over Tax Reform.* Cambridge, MIT Press.

Sokolovskii L. E., 1989. Income Tax and Economic Behavior (Introduction to the Literature). *Ekonomika i matematicheskie metody,* Vol. 25, No. 4. (In Russian).

Sokolovskii L. E., 1992. Value-Added Tax and the Profit-Maximizing Enterprise. *Ekonomika i matematicheskie metody,* Vol. 28, No. 4.

Sorokin P.A., 1959. *Social and Cultural Mobility.* New York, The Free Press.

Standing G., 1997. Social Protection in Central and Eastern Europe: A Tale of Slipping Anchors and Torn Safety Nets. In *Welfare States in Transition. National Adaptations in Global Economies.* Ed. by G. Esping-Andersen. London, SAGE Publications.

Steinmo S., 1993. *Taxation and Democracy. Swedish, British, and American Approaches to Financing the Modern State.* New Haven, Yale University Press.

Stiglitz J. E., 1986. *Economics of the Public Sector.* New York, W.W. Norton & Company.

Stiglitz J. E., 1992. Another Century of Economic Science. In *The Future of Economics.* Ed. by J.D. Hey. Oxford, Blackwell.

Stiglitz J. E., 1996. *Whither Socialism?* Cambridge, The MIT Press.

Stiglitz J., 1998. *More Instruments and Broader Goals: Moving Toward the Post-Washington Consensus.* WIDER Annual Lectures 2. Helsinki, UNU/WIDER.

Stiglitz J. E., 1999a. *Whither Reform? Ten Years of the Transition.* Annual Bank Conference on Development Economics, April 28–30, 1999. Washington, The World Bank.

Stiglitz J. E., 1999b. The World Bank at the Millennium. *Economic Journal,* Vol. 109, No. 459.

Stiglitz J. E., 2002. *Globalization and its Discontents.* New York, W.W. Norton & Company.

Stroev E. S., Bliakhman L. S., Krotov M. I., 1999. *Russia and Eurasia at the Crossroads. Experience and Problems of Economic Reforms in the Commonwealth of Independent States.* Berlin, Springer.

Studenski P., 1961. *The Income of Nations, Theory, Measurement and Analysis: Past and Present.* New York, New York University Press.

Suny R. G., 1994. *The Making of the Georgian Nation.* Bloomington, Indiana University Press.

Sušjan A., Lah M., 1997. Inflation in the Transition Economies: the Post-Keynesian View. *Review of Political Economy,* Vol. 9, No. 4.

Svensson B., 1983. *Ekonomisk kriminalitet.* Göteborg, Tholin/Larsson/Gruppen förlag.

Torbakov I., 2003. Russian Policymakers Air Notion of "Liberal Empire" in Caucasus, Central Asia. *Eurasia Insight.* Eurasianet, 2003, October 27, http://www.eurasianet.org/ departments/insight/articles/eav102703.shtml.

Tanzi V., 1992. Fiscal Restructuring and the Tax System. In *Structural Adjustment and Macroeconomic Policy Issues.* Ed. by V. A. Jafarey. Washington, IMF.

Tanzi V., 1995. Corruption: Arm's-Length Relationships and Markets. In *The Economics of Organized Crime.* Ed. by G. Fiorentini, S. Peltzman. Cambridge, Cambridge University Press.

Tanzi V., 1997. Economic Transformation and the Policies for Long-Term Growth. In *Macroeconomic Stabilization in Transition Economies.* Ed. by M. I. Blejer, M. Škreb. Cambridge, Cambridge University Press.

Tanzi V., 1999. Uses and Abuses of Estimates of the Underground Economy. *The Economic Journal,* Vol. 109, No. 456.

Tanzi V. (ed.), 1993. *Fiscal Policies in Economies in Transition.* Washington, IMF.

Tanzi V. (ed.), 1994. *Transition to Market: Studies in Fiscal Reform.* Washington, IMF.

Taylor M. L., 1988. *Divesting Business Units.* Lexington, Lexington Books.

Thomas J., 1999. Quantifying the Black Economy: 'Measurement without Theory' Yet Again? *The Economic Journal,* Vol. 109, No. 456.

Thurow L. C., 1996. *The Future of Capitalism. How Today's Economic Forces Shape Tomorrow's World.* New York, Penguin Books.

Tiebout C. M., 1956. A pure Theory of Local Government Expenditures. *Journal of Political Economy,* Vol. 64, Issue 5.

Tirole J., 2002. *Financial Crises, Liquidity, and the International Monetary System.* Princeton, Princeton University Press.

Todaro M. P., 1994. *Economic Development.* New York, Longman.

Trushin Esh., 1998. Uzbekistan: Foreign Economic Activity. In *Central Asia: The Challenges of Independence.* Ed. by B. Rumer, S. Zhukov. Armonk, M. E. Sharpe.

Trushin Esk., 1998. Uzbekistan: Problems of Development and Reform in the Agrarian Sector. In *Central Asia: The Challenges of Independence.* Ed. by B. Rumer, S. Zhukov. Armonk, M. E. Sharpe.

Tsereteli M., 2004. The Political Economy of the Ajarian Crisis. *Central Asia-Caucasus Analyst.* Central Asia- Caucasus Institute. 2004, April 21, http://www.cacianalyst.org/ view_article.php?articleid=2297.

Tullock G., 1996. Corruption Theory and Practice. *Contemporary Economic Policy,* Vol. 14, No. 3.

UNICEF, 2001. *A Decade of Transition. The MONEE Project CEE/CIS/Baltics.* Regional Monitoring Report No. 8–2001. Florence, United Nations Children's Fund Innocenti Research Centre.

Veduta E. N., 1998. *Government's Economic Strategies.* Moscow, Delovaya Kniga. (In Russian).

Vishnevskii V., Lipnitskii D., 2000. Assessment of the Possibilities for Reducing the Tax Burden in a Transitional Economy. *Voprosy ekonomiki,* No. 2.

Vreeland J. R., 2003. *The IMF and Economic Development.* Cambridge, Cambridge University Press.

Waller C. J., Verdier T., Gardner R., 2002. Corruption: Top Down or Bottom Up? *Economic Inquiry,* Vol. 40, No. 4.

Wane W., 1999. Tax Evasion, Corruption, and the Remuneration of Heterogeneous Inspectors. *Policy Research Working Paper Series,* No. 2394. Washington, The World Bank.

Wang J.-Y., 1998. From Coupon to Lari: Hyperinflation and Stabilization in Georgia. *Caucasica. The Journal of Caucasian Studies,* Vol. 1.

WB (World Bank), 1993. *The East Asian Miracle. Economic Growth and Public Policy.* New York, Oxford University Press.

WB (World Bank), 1996. *From Planning to Market. A Report on International Development—1996.* Oxford, Oxford University Press.

WB (World Bank), 1999. *Global Economic Prospects and the Developing Countries. Beyond Financial Crisis.* Washington, The World Bank.

WB (World Bank), 2000. *Anticorruption in Transition. A Contribution in the Policy Debate.* Washington, The World Bank.

Weder B., 2001. *Model, Myth, or Miracle? Reassessing the Role of Governments in the East Asian Experience.* Tokyo, UN University Press.

von Weizsäcker E., Lovins A. B., Lovins L. H., 1997. *Factor Four. Doubling Wealth—Halving Resource Use.* London, Earthscan Publications.

Wellisz S., 1996. Georgia: A Brief Survey of Macroeconomic Problems and Policies. *Studies & Analyses, Working Papers,* No. 87. Warsaw, CASE.

Wellisz S., 1997. Inflation and Stabilization in Poland, 1990–1995. In *Macroeconomic Stabilization in Transition Economies.* Ed. by M. I. Blejer, M. Škreb. Cambridge, Cambridge University Press.

Welt C., 2004. Georgia: Consolidating the Revolution. *Russia ans Eurasia Program.* Center for Strategic and International Studies. 2004, April 6, http:// www.csis.org/ ruseura/pubs/Agenda/040406_welt.pdf.

Williamson O. E., 1985. *The Economic Institutions of Capitalism. Firms, Markets, Relational Contracting.* New York, The Free Press.

Winckler G. (mod.), 1992. *Central and Eastern Europe: Roads of Growth.* Papers Presented at a Seminar Held in Baden, Austria, April 15–18, 1991. Washington, IMF.

Wolf Ch., Jr., 1994. *Markets or Governments. Choosing between Imperfect Alternatives.* Cambridge, The MIT Press.

Wolfenson J. D., 1999. *A Proposal for a Comprehensive Development Framework (A Discussion Draft).* Washington, The World Bank.

Woodruff D. M., 1999a. It's Value That's Virtual: Bartles, Rubles, and the Place of Gazprom in the Russian Economy. *Post-Soviet Affairs,* Vol. 15, No. 2.

Woodruff D. M., 1999b. *Money Unmade: Barter and the Fate of Russian Capitalism.* Ithaca, Cornell University Press.

Yarbrough B. V., Yarbrough R. M., 1997. *The World Economy: Trade and Finance.* Fort Worth, The Dryden Press.

Yevstigneeva L., Yevstigneev R., 1999. Where Do Reforms Lead To? (Reflections on a J. Stiglitz Essay). *Voposy ekonomiki,* No. 9. (In Russian).

Zevin L., 2001. IMF and Russia: Eight Years of Difficult Dialogue. *Mirovaja ekonomika i mezdunarodnye otnosenija,* No. 4. (In Russian).

Zhukov S., 1997. Kazakhstan, Kyrgyzstan, Uzbekistan in Social/Economic Structures of the Modern World. *Mirovaya ekonomika i mezhdunarodnye otnoshenija,* No. 3. (In Russian).

Zhukov S., 2000. Adapting to Globalization. In *Central Asia and the New Global Economy.* Ed. by B. Rumer. Armonk, M. E. Sharpe.

Zhvania Z., 2004. After the Rose Revolution: Building Georgia's Future. *CSIS Statesmen's Forum.* Center for Strategic and International Studies. 2004, April 26, http://www.csis.org/ ruseura/040426_zhvania_report.pdf.

Zukowski R., 1996. Transformation Crisis in Post-Socialist Countries: Patterns and Causes. *International Journal of Social Economics,* Vol. 23, No. 10/11.

Index

978-0-595-34915-9
0-595-34915-3